T0338562

ONTOLOGICAL INFORMATION

Information in the Physical World

World Scientific Series in Information Studies
(ISSN: 1793-7876)

Series Editor: Mark Burgin *(University of California, Los Angeles, USA)*

International Advisory Board:

Søren Brier *(Copenhagen Business School, Copenhagen, Denmark)*
Tony Bryant *(Leeds Metropolitan University, Leeds, United Kingdom)*
Gordana Dodig-Crnkovic *(Mälardalen University, Eskilstuna, Sweden)*
Wolfgang Hofkirchner *(The Institute for a Global Sustainable Information Society, Vienna)*
William R King *(University of Pittsburgh, Pittsburgh, USA)*

Published:

Vol. 13   *Ontological Information: Information in the Physical World*
by Roman Krzanowski

Vol. 12   *Trilogy of Numbers and Arithmetic*
Book 1: History of Numbers and Arithmetic: An Information
Perspective
by Mark Burgin

Vol. 11   *Theoretical Information Studies: Information in the World*
edited by Mark Burgin & Gordana Dodig-Crnkovic

Vol. 10   *Philosophy and Methodology of Information: The Study of*
Information in the Transdisciplinary Perspective
edited by Gordana Dodig-Crnkovic & Mark Burgin

Vol. 9   *Information Studies and the Quest for Transdisciplinarity*
Unity through Diversity
edited by Mark Burgin & Wolfgang Hofkirchner

Vol. 8   *The Future Information Society: Social and Technological Problems*
edited by Wolfgang Hofkirchner & Mark Burgin

Vol. 7   *Information Theory Models of Instabilities in Critical Systems*
by Rodrick Wallace

Vol. 6   *Information and Complexity*
edited by Mark Burgin & Cristian S Calude

More information on this series can also be found at https://www.worldscientific.com/series/wssis

World Scientific Series in Information Studies — **Vol. 13**

ONTOLOGICAL INFORMATION

Information in the Physical World

Roman Krzanowski

 **World Scientific**

NEW JERSEY · LONDON · SINGAPORE · BEIJING · SHANGHAI · HONG KONG · TAIPEI · CHENNAI · TOKYO

Published by

World Scientific Publishing Co. Pte. Ltd.

5 Toh Tuck Link, Singapore 596224

USA office: 27 Warren Street, Suite 401-402, Hackensack, NJ 07601

UK office: 57 Shelton Street, Covent Garden, London WC2H 9HE

Library of Congress Cataloging-in-Publication Data

Names: Krzanowski, Roman, author.
Title: Ontological information : information in the physical world /
    Roman Krzanowski, The Pontifical University of John Paul II, Poland.
Description: Hackensack, New Jersey : World Scientific, [2022] |
    Series: World Scientific series in information studies, 1793-7876 ; vol. 13 |
    Includes bibliographical references and index.
Identifiers: LCCN 2021058933 | ISBN 9789811248818 (hardcover) |
    ISBN 9789811248825 (ebook for institutions) | ISBN 9789811248832 (ebook for individuals)
Subjects: LCSH: Information theory. | Ontology. | Knowledge, Theory of.
Classification: LCC Q360 .K78 2022 | DDC 003/.54--dc23/eng20220208
LC record available at https://lccn.loc.gov/2021058933

British Library Cataloguing-in-Publication Data
A catalogue record for this book is available from the British Library.

For any available supplementary material, please visit
https://www.worldscientific.com/worldscibooks/10.1142/12601#t=suppl

Desk Editors: Balamurugan Rajendran/Rok Ting Tan

Typeset by Stallion Press
Email: enquiries@stallionpress.com

Printed in Singapore

About the Author

 **Roman M. Krzanowski** has received graduate degrees in engineering, philosophy, and information science from universities in Poland, UK, Canada, and the USA. He has a Ph.D. degree from UoL, London, UK and a D.Phil. degree from The Pontifical University of John Paul II (UPJPII), Krakow, Poland. He is currently an Assistant Professor at The Pontifical University of John Paul II. He is an expert in networking technology (holding 30+ patents and has co-authored several publications of international standards), spatial information systems, information processing, and philosophy of computing and information. He has published books in information science (*Spatial Evolutionary Modeling* with J. Raper, OUP, 2001), network technology (*Metro Ethernet Services for LTE Backhaul*, 2014 (Artech House Mobile Communications Library)), and Tae Kwon Do (*Studying with Grand Master: The Art of Tae Kwon Do*, 2014). He has presented papers at several conferences in USA, Canada, and Europe. His interests in philosophy include the philosophy of information and informatics, ontology and metaphysics of computation science, philosophical foundations of AI, ethics, and ethical problems created

in information society. He has also published papers on robotic ethics, phronesis in autonomous robotics, and Ethical testing of autonomous robots. His ORCHID ID is 0000-0002-8753-0957. The details of his work are at https://www.researchgate.net/profile/Roman_Krzanowski.

Acknowledgments

The book is a team effort. Specifically, I wanted to thank Prof. Paweł Polak for his unwavering support and guidance, Prof. Mark Burgin for his encouragement and insightful comments, Dr. Jacob Krzanowski and Dr. Eliza Krzanowska for their support, and anonymous reviewers from MDPI publishers. Without their help, this book, and the ideas constituting the bulk of this book, would not see the light of the day.

Contents

About the Author   v

Acknowledgments   vii

1. Introduction—What is This Book About?   1

   1.1 Puzzle of Information   2

   1.2 Varieties of Information   2

   1.3 Ontological Information   6

   1.4 Methodological Comments 13

       1.4.1 How do we refer to information in this
work? 14

       1.4.2 A few technical terms 15

       1.4.3 A word of caution 18

2. Visions of Ontological Information—Conjectures   21

   2.1 Conjectures 22

   2.2 Conjectures—What Did We Learn? 37

   2.3 A Biographical Note 42

3. Visions of Ontological Information—Studies   45

   3.1 Studies 46

       3.1.1 Between the mind, nature, and language . . . 47

       3.1.2 Form, structure, and information 53

       3.1.3 Between the physical and the abstract 58

       3.1.4 Information in and about things 62

3.1.5   The universe is information   64
3.1.6   Information is the mathematics of the
        heavens   70
3.1.7   The universe computes   73
3.1.8   Information is in everything   77
3.1.9   From music to information   80
3.1.10 Evolution, us, and information   82
3.2   Studies—What Did We Learn?   86
3.3   A Biographical Note   93

4. Ontological Information: Synthesis   97

4.1   Synthesis of Findings   99
4.2   Properties: How Many and Which Ones? 100
      4.2.1   The proposed three properties 101
      4.2.2   Two or one property? 119

**5. Ontology and Epistemology:
    Two Perspectives on Information   123**

5.1   The Dilemma of Information 123
5.2   Epistemic Information 126
      5.2.1   In search of the locus of epistemic
              information 134
5.3   Ontological Information as a Bearer of Epistemic
      Information 148

**6. Applications and Interpretations of
    Ontological Information   153**

6.1   Ontological Information and Quantified Models
      of Information 155
6.2   Ontological Information and Data 168
6.3   Ontological Information and Infons 175
6.4   Ontological Information and Natural Information . . . 178
6.5   Ontological Information: Abstract or Concrete? 181
      6.5.1   Dilemma of existence 181
6.6   Minimal Information Structural Realism 191

6.7   Ontological Information and Popper's
Three Worlds 198

6.8   Ontological Information and General Theory
of Information 204

    6.8.1   Elements of the general theory of
information 204

    6.8.2   The global world structure and information
dichotomy 206

    6.8.3   GTI and ontological information 208

6.9   Ontological Perspective on Information: A Proposal . 208

    6.9.1   Introduction 209

    6.9.2   Ontology: Basic assumptions 211

    6.9.3   Ontology and information 214

    6.9.4   Final observations 217

7. Final Comments—What Next?   **219**

7.1   What Is This Work About? 219

7.2   What was This Study Able to Establish? 220

7.3   Selected Criticisms of Ontological Information 224

7.4   Work to be Done and Future Research 229

Bibliography   **233**

Index   261

Chapter 1

Introduction—What is This Book About?

The primary aim of this study is to establish a minimal set of properties for ontological information in the light of the current research. It assumes that ontological information does exist, so it does not debate the matter. It also postulates that ontological information is an objective (mind-independent) physical phenomenon in the sense explained in the work. It can be perceived as the structure, organization, or form of natural objects and artifacts, but it has no inherent meaning or value, at least without a cognitive agent who can derive such value. Compared to most of the current (at the time of writing) concepts of information that have been formulated in communication theory, computing, information sciences, cognitive sciences, AI, biology, popular works on information, and library sciences, as well as in different strands of pancomputationalism, natural computing, and digital physics, the concept of ontological information represents information on a more fundamental level. Furthermore, this research studies "ontological information" rather than the "ontology of information". It therefore investigates the properties of one concept of information, namely, ontological information, rather than exploring the ontologies of different concepts of information or the ontology for a generic concept of information, if such a concept were to even exist. We consider the concept of ontological information as a metaphysical concept here, meaning that we study what the object is as a constituent of physical reality. It is therefore not an investigation of virtual ontologies, the ontologies of some domain, or some ontology of computer constructs. In addition, it is not a study of pure ontology or some form thereof. What ontological information is has already been briefly explained, so this study instead attempts to establish its properties. But, why do we choose to undertake such a study? After all, we do not know what information is. Well, the existing conceptualizations of information, such as Shannon and Hartley's celebrated formula, are not the answer here, as we will see later. We therefore need something else, because any attempt to understand the nature of information is important for one obvious reason: If we claim that everything that exists is made of information, we need to know what we are referring to.

1.1 Puzzle of Information

This book is about the nature of information. It touches on many core issues of philosophy of the mind, ontology, and epistemology, and draws in several domain-specific concepts from physics, mathematics, thermodynamics, computer science, and biology. The terms used in this book, such as the mind, a conscious agent, meaning, and knowledge, are used with very precise meanings because they can be easily misinterpreted.[1] A proper understanding of these terms can be gained from the referenced literature.

But, more specifically, this book is about the concept of information as a physical phenomenon (by being physical, we mean being an integral part of physical objects and being disclosed in physical phenomena). Rather than jumping directly to the main topic, providing some larger context on the nature of information may help one appreciate better the position of this book in relation to the ongoing discussions about information.

1.2 Varieties of Information

We begin with a trivial observation, one that is likely the only claim about information that almost everyone agrees with: We lack a universal concept of information that satisfies everyone. We have had some very good proposals, such as Shannon's Theory of Communication (TOC) and Floridi's (2010) General Definition of Information (GDI). They all have certain flaws, however. Quantifications such as those of Shannon-Weaver-Hartley (Shannon 1948, Shannon

---

[1]In this study, meaning is interpreted here as related to cognitive functions of some conscious agent. The more generalized interpretation of meaning, i.e., meaning as a response of a (any) system to an external stimuli, is not used here.

and Weaver 1964, Hartley 1928), Fisher (Friden 1998), Kolmogorov (1965), and Chaitin (2004), among others, are mathematical formulas denoted as information measures, but they are designed for specific purposes under specific assumptions. These metrics fulfill their specific purposes exceedingly well, so they are very useful. Nevertheless, the pragmatic (and domain-specific) or operational (technical) successes of an idea do not elevate its metaphysical status. Indeed, we may say that pragmatically efficient concepts are often metaphysically neutral.[2] Thus, these quantified concepts of information are not of general import, even if they are "interpreted" as such. So, what about the other plentiful conceptualizations of information? Floridi's GDI, while very valuable for its contribution to our understanding of the nature of information, is by definition a concept of semantic information, exclusively. However, on looking closely at the definition, the GDI assumes the existence of a quasi-physical foundation of information, which is denoted as the *infon*. The rather ambiguous explanation of this foundational *infon* leaves the whole concept of the GDI rather unfounded. Other less comprehensive classifications and definitions of information have not produced common classification criteria or common differentiating/classification factors, nor have they proposed generally accepted conceptualizations. They are either too divergent or too narrow, and they are often contradictory. On looking at these classifications and definitions, one may realize that the scope of the concepts associated with "information" is so wide that it makes this idea almost meaningless and empty. Some selected classifications of information are summarized in Table 1.1.[3]

---

[2]We may even say that Shannon's work on the theory of communication (TOC) has led to certain distortions regarding the concept of information, and we are still mostly living in his shadow. To be fair, the subsequent misinterpretations and distortions of the TOC were committed by his followers (against Shannon's better advice), so they were out of Shannon's hands. See Shannon's warning (Shannon 1956) or Pierce (1970).

[3]These are, of course, not all the classifications of information, because such a list would be extremely long. For example, John Collier (1989) classified theories of information into mathematical theories of information, communication theories, algorithmic or computational theories, physical information theories, and measurement theories. Giovanni Sommaruga (1998) proposed three

Table 1.1. Selected classifications of information.

Study	Classes, groupings, or differentiating features
Wersig and Neveling (1975)	Information as: • structure, independent of any human perceiving it; • knowledge built on the basis of perception of the structure of the world; • a "message" or the meaning of the message; • the effect of communication; and • the process of communication.
Buckland (1991)	Information as: • information-as-process; • information-as-knowledge; and • information-as-thing.
Loose (1998)	Information as: • the meaning and use of a message, as well as knowledge; • a fundamental characteristic of physical systems and structures (or it is a structure); • related to data transmission in communication systems; and • an output of the process.
Floridi (2010)	Information as a multi-dimensional concept: • analogue, digital or binary; • primary, secondary, meta-, operational, and derivative;
Lenski (2010)	Information as: • a difference that makes the difference; • the values of characteristics in the processes' output, capable of transforming structure; or • that which modifies a knowledge structure.
Nafria (2010)	Information as: • ontological—epistemic; • semiotic (syntactic, semantic, and pragmatic); and • discipline-based.
Adriaans (2019)	Information as: • quantitative (using mathematical formalism, such as Shannon's entropy, Kolmogorov, Fisher, Klir); and • qualitative (state of an agent).

The conclusion is rather self-evident and unilluminating (as it is rather obvious): Information is a polysemantic concept with many, often contradictory, definitions. Indeed, most people who write about information confess to having the same impression.[4]

To simplify things, we posit that the concept of information can be viewed from two perspectives, namely, epistemic and ontological.[5] In the epistemic view, information is associated with meaning, semantics, and knowledge, while in the ontological view, it is understood as independently existing objects. Information is most often perceived as epistemic information, yet a closer look at epistemic information reveals that this concept does not account for ontological information, which is a concept that is well established in physics, mathematics, cosmology, and computer science.

This proposed "bifocal" view is imperfect, however. There are likely cases where it is difficult to cleanly allocate information into one of these two categories. Nevertheless, with this proposed perspective, we can generally classify most concepts of information into one of these two classes and gain a revealing perspective on the concept of information.

The detailed discussion of epistemic information we postpone to the later part of the book. We will focus now on ontological information, how it has been conceptualized, and what properties have been attributed to it.

---

classes of concepts of information: ordinary language concepts, information theoretical concepts, and formal theoretical concepts. Peter Adriaans and Johan van Benthem (2008), meanwhile, proposed three major concepts of information: Information-A including knowledge and logic, information-B including probabilistic and information-theoretical formulations, and Information-C covering algorithmic and code-compression conceptualizations. Information B and C are quantifiable. Other classifications of information can also be found, but listing them all would be nonsensical, because what really matters is the weakness they share.

[4]This conclusion is shared by many researchers investigating the nature of information. See, for example, Wersig and Neveling (1975), Janich (2006), Floridi (2013), Nafria (2010), and Adriaans (2019).

[5]See the lecture of John Searle (2015c) for an explanation of objective/subjective ontological and epistemic division of concepts.

1.3 Ontological Information

Ontological information is a physical phenomenon. By being physical, we mean being an integral part of physical objects and being disclosed in physical phenomena. This information is epistemically neutral.[6] Its existence and properties do not depend upon a communication process or a cognitive process. This information is perceived as a structure, organization, or form of natural and artificial (artifacts) objects.[7] This information is therefore mind-independent, without any inherent meaning, and ontologically and epistemically objective (the meaning of this term will be explained in the subsequent sections). We will denote such information with the predicate "ontological" as in "ontological information", as well as by the symbol I_O and the indexed term "information$_O$".

Ontological information, or information as a physical phenomenon (understood as above), is a fairly recent concept by philosophical standards. Most of the literature referred to in this study has been published in the last 70 years or so, although we may speculate that concepts similar to ontological information have long existed in the vague and foggy, quasi-theological intuitions of Tao or Dao (Chan 2018), *Logos* (in the sense intended by Heraclitus),[8] the ancient cosmological theories of Plato's *Forms*, Aristotelian *eidos*, and Democritus' atomic theory of the universe and matter (Rovelli 2016), and it is only recently that the modern concept of ontological information has become gradually recognized in its own right in the physical sciences.

We define ontological information as being objective[9] and mind-independent. The terms "objective" and "mind-independent" may

---

[6]A concept is "epistemically neutral" when it does not have intrinsic epistemic import, or in other words, it does not mean anything by itself. The meaning is discussed in more detail in subsequent chapters.

[7]The synonymity of the terms "structure", "form", "organization", and "information" should not be accepted *a priori* despite the fact that these terms are often used synonymously.

[8]Heraclitus used the word Logos to denote *a principle of order and knowledge* (Audi 1999). Logos can take several meanings depending on the historical period or the philosophical school it is used within (e.g., Audi 1999, Bollack 2016).

[9]We need to be very careful with the claim of "objectivity" here. Objectivity of information means independence of existence from any cognitive system. This

seem synonymous, but this is not true for all aspects. "Objective" denotes the ontological status of something, as opposed to the "subjective", which depends on something other than itself for its existence, such as a human agent. "Mind-independent", meanwhile, denotes the property of being independent of the mind, as opposed to "mind-dependent" phenomena such as pain, joy, and love. However, being "mind-independent" does not necessarily imply objective existence, even if that is often the case.[10]

In this work, we assume that ontological information, or $information_O$, exists much like physical phenomena exist (i.e., mind-independent, measurable, and quantifiable), but its physicality should be interpreted as shaping or forming physical phenomena. In the research literature from the last 70 years or so,[11] $information_O$ has been recognized as a physical phenomenon in different domains under different names to refer to information that is detectable, observable, measurable, and quantifiable. In other words, $information_O$ has been attributed properties that make it more than an empty concept.[12] In this study, we therefore neither try to prove the existence of $information_O$ nor analyze how its existence has been justified. We simply focus on investigating its properties instead.

It seems that a contemporary, comprehensive, and complete description or conceptualization of the world, or indeed the universe, is impossible without some notion of form, organization, or

---

is not in the sense of "another name for objectivity is the public" as claimed by P. F. Strawson quoted by Ziman (1991, ft. 10). Such an interpretation of objectivity would bring us too close to Popper's Three Words (see Chapter 6).

[10]The interpretations of "objective" and "subjective" in this context are provided in later sections, although the ideas of ontological and epistemic objectivity and subjectivity have been discussed by Searle (2013a, 2013b, 2015a, 2015b).

[11]A selection of authors from this relatively short time span ensures that the meanings of the terms used in these writings have a significant chance of being similar, if not the same, so there is no need to "translate the meaning". This problem arises when comparing terms separated over time, context, or culture, such as when comparing ancient Greek writings on hylemorphism with contemporary works on matter and structure.

[12]A non-empty concept is one that has (i) a material, physical existence and (ii) a clear definition (Chischolm 2011). In this study, we focus on the first meaning. This interpretation is consistent with definitions of the existence/reality of physical phenomena in scientific realism (e.g., Worrall 1982, Chakravartty 2017).

structure.[13] We call this form-giving constituent ontological information.[14] A reductive description of the world in purely mechanical terms for the groups of elements is incomplete, so some form must be added to it. This means that the elements making up the world, whatever they may be, must have some organization or form to have become something. On the other hand, the existence of form by itself (i.e., pure form, abstract form) is difficult to conceptualize if you are not an idealist. Indeed, only Plato and some modern Platonists grant existence to "pure" forms.[15] This means that form must belong to something physical, and these two things, namely, the form and the material being formed, together constitute what exists. We see this idea of the form and what fills it recurring several times in modern research,[16] although under different names, such as modern hylemorphism (e.g., Turek 1978), paninformatism (e.g., Dodig Crnkovic

---

[13]Von Baeyer quotes synonyms for form: arrangement, configuration, order, organization, pattern, structure, and relationship. The term "relationships among the parts of the physical system" seemed to him the most general term that could cover "applications in mathematics, physics, chemistry, biology and neuroscience" (Baeyer von 2005, p. 22).

[14]Some denote this information as *the primary ontological unit of the universe* (Hayot and Pao 2018, p. 9).

[15]Modern Platonists claim ... *that there exist such things as abstract objects— where an abstract object is an object that does not exist in space or time and which is therefore entirely non-physical and non-mental. Platonism in this sense is a contemporary view* (Balaguer 2016). The topic is much larger and relates to some fundamental disputes in philosophy between the nominalism and realism of abstract concepts, as well as touching upon the essence of what is information and how we should understand it. See the comments from Paul Davies later and the discussion on the nature of information in Chapter 6.

[16]William Jaworski argues that the hylemorphic structure is the best (and perhaps only) way to explain the persistence of individuals who change their matter over time. Hylemorphism claims that some individuals, paradigmatically living things, are composed of physical materials with a form or structure that is responsible for them existing and persisting as the kinds of things they are. One objection to hylemorphism is that it is an account of the physical materials that comprise something is sufficient to account for everything it is and everything it does. William Jaworski, however, argues that this objection fails insofar as hylemorphic structure is the best, and perhaps only, way to explain the persistence of individuals who change their matter over time (Jaworski 2018). The same claim was made almost 40 years later by Krzysztof Turek in his 1978 article on the

2012), or the matter–energy–information complex (e.g., Mynarski 1981, Polkinghorne 2000, Hidalgo 2015). We will not speculate at this point about which of the above labels, among the other possible ones, is the right one to use, because the implicit presuppositions in such a labeling may color our understating of I_O.

However, not everyone agrees with the view that physical reality is some combination of matter and form, whatever that may be. In a crude approximation, structural realism, in its ontological variety, assumes that whatever exists is just "structures or structures of structures", nothing else. What occupies these structures or what these structures are comprised of is either unknown or beyond our cognitive ability. Thus, there is nothing to know other than structures, whatever they are.[17] This position seems a little too extreme, however, so it is not discussed further here.

This work has three reasons: First, despite the abundance of publications on the topic of information, we are still unsure about what information fundamentally is. Second, despite the many publications discussing the concept of ontological information (or the concepts similar to it),[18] we are still unsure what properties can be, or should be, attributed to it. Last but not least, nobody has explored what implications adopting such a concept of information will have for our understanding of the nature of information, the concept of computing, the concept of pancomputationalism, the concept

---

concept of information and its relation to the restricted form of hylemorphism (Turek 1978).

[17] For a quick overview of structural realism see, for example, Ladyman (2019) or Frigg and Votsis (2011).

[18] There are studies in physics (e.g., Carl von Weizsäcker 1971, Frank Wilczek 2015, Sean Carroll 2017, Carlo Rovelli 2016, Paul Davies 2019), cybernetics (e.g., Kowalczyk 1974), computing (e.g., Stefan Mynarski 1981, Gordana Dodig Crnkovic 2012), biology (e.g., Erwin Schrödinger 2004, Thomas Nagel 2012, Ricardo Sole and Santiago Elena 2019), cosmology (e.g., Michał Heller 1987, 2014, Tom Stonier 1990, John Polkinghorne 2000, Carlo Rovelli 2016, Paul Davies 2019), and philosophy of science (e.g., Krzysztof Turek 1978, John Collier 1989, Keith Devlin 1991, Jacek Jadacki and Anna Brożek 2005, Martin Schroeder 2005, 2014, 2017a, 2017b) that discuss the concept of ontological information, and they will be analyzed in detail.

of communication, information sciences, and the philosophy of information, epistemology, and cosmology. This study aims to at least partially fill these gaps.

We first need to explain the predicate "ontological" in the context of the term "ontological information". A claim may be subjective or objective and such claims may concern types of knowledge (epistemic claims) or the underlying mode of existence (ontological claims). Claims of knowledge about objects that exist independently of us—such as molecules, rivers, mountains, and so on—are epistemically and ontologically objective. Indeed, all epistemic and ontological claims about physical phenomena are of this sort. In contrast, claims of knowledge about the things whose existence depends upon us (i.e., *they exist only when experienced by a subject*) are epistemically and ontologically subjective. Such claims concern our knowledge of notions like feelings, pain, inspiration, and so on.[19] There can also be epistemically subjective claims about ontologically objective objects, such as noting the beauty of the landscape, where the landscape (the object of knowledge) exists independently of us, while its "beauty" is a subjective experience. Claims about consciousness, however, are, according to Searle, epistemically objective but ontologically subjective (see also Chalmers 2014).[20]

---

[19]See John Searle's (2015a, min.1:40) lecture at Google Academy for his detailed explanation of objective/subjective ontological and epistemic claims. The objective/subjective examples were borrowed from Searle's lecture on the Philosophy of Mind (Searle 2013a). See also Searle (2015b).

[20]One question where philosophers do not converge upon a single answer concerns the existence of abstract concepts such as mathematical objects or universals. See the discussion on the abstractness of mathematical objects, such as from Linnebo (2017, 2018). According to him, abstract objects lack spatiotemporal identity and are causally inefficacious (see also Rosen 2020). In this work, we assume that abstract objects do not exist in the same manner as concrete things, but this discussion will be extended in Chapters 6 and 7. The idea that the mind is not a separate thing (contrary to Descartes's view) is surprisingly not new. At the same time when Descartes theories about the mind–body problem were published, Newton claimed something very modern: He wrote that *the distinction between the ideas of thinking and extended substances cannot be so "lawful and perfect" as Descartes claims, so that both can pertain to the same created substance, that is, that bodies can think or that thinking substances can be extended.* This quotation is from Guicciardini (2018, p. 134), who was referring to Newton's

The ontological objectivity of information means that information does not depend upon the mind (any mind) for its existence. In other words, it does not require the involvement or even presence of a cognitive agent to bring about its existence. Information therefore exists objectively in the sense explained above, so it is ontologically objective (in the sense above), leading to the term "ontological information". Ontological information (information existing objectively) is also epistemically objective, because as an object of knowledge, it exists independently of the mind. Information that depends upon the mind for its existence—such as pain, beauty, and other abstract concepts—is both ontologically and epistemically subjective at the same time. Meanwhile, information that depends upon the mind for its existence but refers to an object that is ontologically objective (i.e., a concrete object) is ontologically subjective but epistemically objective. In general, for any information that depends upon the mind (i.e., *something that is experienced by the subject*) but refers to an object that may exist subjectively or objectively, we will call it epistemic (i.e., mind-dependent) information or information$_E$ for short. However, we will now postpone further discussion of information$_E$ and its relation to information$_O$ until Chapter 6.

The notion of information as ontologically objective and fundamentally free of value or meaning may be, and has been, contested, because it significantly changes the way we view the nature of information. Indeed, understanding the concept of ontological information may require a so-called "gestalt switch" (Chalmers 1994, p. 96),[21] which is not an easy thing to do for everyone, because a paradigm shift is always painful.[22] However, those who would deny the existence of ontological information would need to explain away all the

work *De Gravitatione*. Of course, Newton's motivations for this claim were far from modern.

[21] This comment should not be seen as an endorsement of Kuhn's view on science (Kuhn 1962).

[22] Note: Despite the claims of objectivity for scientific theories, which is certainly a target, the adoption of a specific theory is largely a matter of social acceptance. Commenting on Newton's theory of Universal Gravitation, Guicciardini notes, *It is often the case that the attitudes, mindsets and cultural fashions of a social group play a role that is difficult to demonstrate precisely because they act tacitly as presuppositions that determine what is to be accepted and what rejected*

facts presented in this study, as well as resolve the concrete–abstract dichotomy signaled by Davies, for example. Ontological information cannot be simply wished away, as some have already tried.[23]

We lack a fundamental understanding of the concept of information. We even lack a single, generally accepted definition of information, as we indicated earlier. For some of the more inquisitive minds, this situation is unsettling. Ratzan (2004) observes that our claims that we can "use" information would sound hollow if we do not know what information. In other words, how can we "use" information if we are unsure what it is? Hintikka (2007) goes even further stating that if we use information technology in almost all walks of life and we are information machines ourselves[24] (at least we think we are), we better know what this "stuff" we call information is. It therefore falls upon us, the philosophers, to do something about this situation, because the general public is unconcerned by these nuances as it is not concerned with anything less concrete.

(Guicciardini 2018, p. 154). The resistance to ontological information may share these origins.

[23]Personal communication during the public seminar, November 2019.

[24]This claim (i.e., that we are information-processing machines of sorts) has several versions. The most simplistic and obviously false one is that we are Turing machines (e.g., Penrose 1989, Searle 1998). Statements of the rather obvious fact that we, and indeed all living organisms, are information-processing systems (i.e., a system in the sense of *a set of connected things or devices that operate together* (System 2019)) are often found in research publications. One of the first researchers to claim this was Polish psychiatrist Antoni Kepiński. He formulated the concept of information–energy metabolism as a model for a human organism (Maciuszek 1996). On this topic, also consult Rudnianski (1981), Kaplan (1989), Maturana (1970), Maturana and Valera (1980), Bajić and Wee (2005), and Smith *et al.* (2009). You may also find some early intuitions defining information/knowledge as "food for the soul (thought)" in Plato's Protagoras: 313c5-314b5. Nowadays, nobody believes such claims are metaphors or exaggerations—they are statements of fact. There is even a neologism coined for this occasion, namely, *inforg*, where *Inforgs are informationally embodied organisms, entities made up of information that exist in the info sphere. These informationally embodied organisms are also called natural agents* ("What is inforg?" 2019). The term's origins can be traced to Luciano Floridi (2013).

If we do not know what information is, how can we make far-ranging claims about living in the information age, existing in an information-based society, being immersed in information, and acting as information-processing machines? Do we even know what we are claiming? Without precise terminology, any discussion is pointless, because we would never reach stable conclusions for any topic. When researchers talk about information in biology, physics, statistics, cosmology, communication, social sciences, and so on, they may talk about the same thing or maybe somewhat similar things, or maybe they are all talking past each other. How would we know? We simply need precision!

We may also mention a few other potential benefits to this study. The notion of ontological information may reshape our understanding of information, or at least put it in a different light. The notion of ontological information may also suggest a solution to the physical–abstract dichotomy that persists in almost every discussion on the nature of information. Furthermore, it may also justify modern claims about the prominent role of information in nature, because ontological information is, after all, an intrinsic part of nature.

Of course, every new endeavor to define information has begun with high hopes, so this study, like any philosophical enquiry, must be taken with a degree of caution and viewed as a contribution to the discussion rather than the final word on the matter, which is good thing to remember when reading this or any other philosophical work.

1.4 Methodological Comments

The analysis method used in this study resembles that used in the analysis of the classical works of the Pre-Socratics, Plato, and Aristotle. The method comprises a detailed reading of the original text, the identification of relevant fragments, and their extensive analysis and interpretation. The method has been used in the past quite extensively, such as by Thomas Aquinas in his famous commentaries on Aristotle. It has also been used by modern scholars of philosophy with the best of results. An exposition of classical works through this method reveals their depth and gravity in an unparalleled way. These detailed treatises are the paragon of philosophy and represent philosophy at its best. While not dreaming of equaling these works, we adopted their method in the hope that as it has been applied successfully in the past to elucidate complex ideas like *phronesis*, it may also succeed in revealing the nature of information (Reeve 1995, 2000).[25]

1.4.1 *How do we refer to information in this work?*

The key term in this study is "information", and if this is not qualified by a predicate, subscript, or other qualifier, it is a place holder, a generic term that does not signify any specific understanding of information by itself. Indeed, this term can be loaded with any sort of meaning associated with this concept. We therefore take the generic meaning of the term "information" as it is defined in its Wikipedia entry ("Information" 2018). While the quality of Wikipedia entries is not regarded as being on par with those of more established lexicons and dictionaries from research institutions such as The University of Oxford (OED), The University of Cambridge (Cambridge English Dictionary), and The University of Leeds (Collins), we may safely claim that Wikipedia entries better reflect the common or popular usage of terms. The unqualified term "information" may be used in a variety of contexts without further clarification about what it exactly means, such as in generic statements like "This study is about information", "Large quantities of information are stored", "We are living in the information age", "We are drowning in information", or "Information technology controls the world".

When we need to be more specific, we use additional qualifiers to specify the kind of information we mean, such as predicates,

---

[25]This is how the method was described by John Cooper when reviewing C.D.C. Reeve's translation of Aristotle's Metaphysics. When commenting on Reeve's book in the last page of the volume (Reeve 2000), he wrote, *it is a completely fresh, independently motivated philosophical reading of lots and lots of Aristotelian texts, assembled in order to buttress an ongoing interpretive project, and quoted in full and then analyzed step by step in the surrounding discussion. I am sure that any reader will find the book a spirited and instructive effort to deal intelligibly with these often quite daunting materials* (Reeve, *op. cit*).

descriptions, contexts, subscripts, or specific names. For example, in some of the reviewed work (e.g., von Weizsäcker), the author begins the analysis by asking something along the lines of "What is information?", implying that it is a generic concept yet to be defined. In these and similar examples, the term "information" needs further clarification, or such sentences will seem rather empty when not referring to any specific concept. When a different, more specific meaning is being attributed to the term, it will be indicated by a subscript or qualifier. For example, information$_E$ denotes epistemic information, while information$_O$ denotes ontological information. In addition, information$_D$ may be used to refer to the term's common meaning as set down in mainstream English dictionaries. What is more, we may also refer to abstract information as information$_A$, which is synonymous with information$_E$, and to concrete or physical information as information$_C$ instead of information$_O$. Information predicated as "semantic information" refers to information that is interpreted for semantic value, while biological information denotes information interpreted within the context of biological systems. Likewise, quantum information denotes information conceptualized in the context of quantum mechanics. The term "information" may also be qualified by an author's name to reflect his or her work, such as Shannon's information, although this is technically incorrect because Shannon did not explicitly define the term "information" but rather its measure. Likewise, Turek's information denotes the concept of information as defined by Turek, while Stonier's information reflects the concept of information set out by Stonier, and so on.

1.4.2 *A few technical terms*

We need to explain two key terms, namely, "physical phenomenon" and "mind-independent". We quite often refer to information as a physical phenomenon, but the term "physical" may have many interpretations, and some of these may put this work in the wrong light. So, what do we mean by the term "physical" in this study? The appropriate meaning of "physical" for this study is about *relating to things you can see or touch, or relating to the laws of nature: the physical world, or all physical objects that occupy space* ("Physical" 2018a). Thus, the term "physical" includes both living and non-living things, although this does not imply physicalism or physical reductionism. The term may also mean *having material existence: perceptible especially through the senses and subject to the laws of nature* ("Physical" 2018b). The antonyms for the term "physical" are immaterial, non-material, and non-physical, while its synonyms include *material, physical, objective mean of or belonging to actuality. Material implies formation out of tangible matter; used in contrast with spiritual or ideal it may connote the mundane, crass, or grasping; physical applies to what is perceived directly by the senses and may contrast with mental, spiritual, or imaginary; objective may stress material or independent existence apart from a subject perceiving it* ("Physical" 2018b).

A narrower meaning of "physical" often used in the philosophy of science (Stoljar 2017) is *of or relating to natural science, of or relating to physics, or characterized or produced by the forces and operations of physics* ("Physical" 2018b). Such an interpretation would, or may, imply physical reductionism, but simply put, physical reductionism would mean that everything can be reduced to a few basic physical laws and phenomena,[26] and this is certainly not the meaning being

---

[26]We need to explain some of the complexities for the term "physical reductionism". Taking apart the term "physical reductionism", we have a reductionism denoting the proposition that one concept can be expressed completely by another, with "physical" denoting the physical nature of whatever this predicate is. Put together, "physical reductionism" denotes the notion that everything can be described in terms of physical phenomena or seen as physical phenomena. If information, as we claim here, is of a physical nature, then reducing everything to energy–matter–information—as is often suggested in the studies of authors like Heller (1987, 2014), Mynarski (1981), and Turek (1978)—would be a physical reductionism of sorts. Yet, this would not endanger the concept of information$_O$, because we assume that information is physical and exists as a phenomenon in its own right (i.e., it would be a non-eliminative reductionism). This reduction would eliminate esoteric concepts of information as immaterial thoughts but not information as physical entity. However, an extreme, or eliminative, physical reductionism would claim that everything is reducible to some basic physical laws and phenomena, and nothing else exists. This would apparently eliminate information$_O$ as a physical phenomenon in its own right, but under closer scrutiny,

implied or intended in this study. To make things less confusing, we may often use the term "mind-independent" or "objective", rather than physical. Indeed, the adjective "objective" has a specific meaning in this work, as explained earlier.

The term "mind-independent" also has some interpretation issues, however. Taken at face value, it would imply a form of dualism where the mind stands in opposition to the physical world, as if it is something apart from the physical world. We do, however, assume that the mind is the non-reducible part of the physical world (in the sense of the first meaning of physical); this assumption is not so popular, but it can be argued for (see Searle's 2015a, 2015b) in lectures on the theory of the mind. Searle denotes his claim about the nature of the mind as biological naturalism. In this study, the term "mind-independent" means that the existence of information, or its definition, is not contingent on the existence of a mind, whether artificial or natural.[27]

We also occasionally refer to information as a "phenomenon" while also using this term when referring to notions like "the information-processing phenomenon as computing". A phenomenon is not understood here in the Kantian sense, like in the *phenomena–noumena* division. Instead, a phenomenon denotes objects of senses or something we may comprehend by senses that exist in nature

---

this may not be the case. The claim that at the root of everything are some basic physical laws is a rather empty claim, because the question then arises as to what these laws are. They do not have carriers aside from their mathematical expressions, which may account for some Platonic forms existing in the Platonic realm. As we will see, several studies suggest that physical laws are expressions of information or information itself. Thus, from this view, eliminative physical reductionism, as we call it, would not lead to the elimination of informationο but rather to paninformatism, an idea that not many studies would support. For more information on reductionism, see Ney (2019) and Van Riel and Van (2019).

[27]It should be noted that Newton did not accept Descartes' dualism, and he had quite a modern view. He wrote that *the distinction between the ideas of thinking substances and extended substances cannot be so lawful and perfect as Descartes claims so that bodies can pertain to the same created substance, that is, that bodies can think or that thinking substances can be extended* as reported by Guicciardini (2018, p. 134). However, we should add that Newton's argument was based on theological grounds, which was not the case for Searle.

("Phenomenon" 2018). Natural phenomena include things like *weather, fog, thunder, tornadoes; biological processes, decomposition, germination; physical processes, wave propagation, erosion; tidal flow, and natural disasters such as electromagnetic pulses, volcanic eruptions, and earthquake and many others* ("List of natural phenomena" 2018). In other words, anything that occurs in nature is a phenomenon, so we can refer to chemical reactions as chemical phenomena. We may also refer to biological processes as biological phenomena. In the same way, we can refer to ontological information as a natural phenomenon, because it exists in nature.

Last but not least, when we talk about Platonic form, we write "Form" with a capital "F". The meaning of the term "form" with a lower case "f" is left rather open to fit with the context that the term is used within. What is more, all quotes from non-English texts have been translated by the author.

1.4.3 *A word of caution*

The study does not purport to develop a new theory of information, a fresh concept of the universe, or a revolutionary theory of matter, energy, and substance, nor does it propose a new abstract computing machine. The objective of this study is merely to show that based on our current understanding of certain natural phenomena, we have good reason to claim that the conceptualization of information that we commonly hold (i.e., as a semantic or epistemic concept) has certain incongruities, so it is insufficient for completely describing the phenomenon of information. It therefore follows that a different view of information is needed.

This work also does not aspire to develop a new branch of physics or a new theory of everything. The boldest claim we venture to make is that this study aims to demonstrate that information can be conceptualized as a physical, concrete entity rather than as an abstract notion related to knowledge communication, or meaning. This study endeavors to justify such a view and show that it fits well with other concepts of information.

In addition, this study does not propose a formal definition of information, so readers should not expect to find such a definition here. Instead, this study investigates the properties of ontological information, ones that can be deduced from insights, scientific studies, intuitions, and previous research. Thus, this study formulates a list of properties that are, or can be, attributed to the concept of ontological information, along with a justification for the selection of these properties.

It also needs to be highlighted that this is a study of "ontological information" not an "ontology of information". An ontology of information would investigate the ontological properties of various ontologies, with each ontology corresponding to a specific concept of information. We would also have to accept some ontological position or ontological system to define these "ontologies" of information. Such studies would deviate from what is intended here.

This study investigates the properties of one concept of information, namely, ontological information, rather than the ontologies of different concepts of information or some formal ontology for a generic concept of information, if such a thing even exists.[28] The word "ontological" in ontological information can be understood along the lines of how it was explained earlier in this chapter. Moreover, this study does not investigate pure ontology, virtual ontologies, the ontologies of some domain, or the ontology of computer constructs.[29] We need to be explicit about this.

Last but not least, a word of caution: As we have said, the concept of ontological information is a metaphysical concept. Metaphysics here is understood as investigating questions about the general nature of reality. We may also say that metaphysics is the study of the fabric of reality, of concepts such as space, time, causation,

---

[28]See the discussion on the nature of ontology in the works of Ingarden (1964), Jacquette (2002), Effingham (2003), Smith (2003), Floridi (2013), Perzanowski (2015), and Bilat (2018), for example.
[29]We refer here to works like those of Noy and McGuinness (2018) and Guarino (1998), although this is just a small sample from the vast sea of publications on the topic of the use of ontological concepts in computer science.

existence, and, to reflect our own case, information. For reasons already explained, the focus on metaphysics also implies that this study is primarily concerned with the metaphysical aspects of the studied concept rather than with mathematics, computing, communication, biology, cosmology, or physics.

In some way, physics itself defines the division between its subject matter and the meta-discourse claiming "physical science may be defines as systematization of knowledge obtained by measurements". This leaves the study of nature somewhat truncated or limited, as some claim,[30] i.e., only quantifiable concepts are admitted in physical research.[31] Thus, assuming a purely physical perspective, this study would have to be limited to quantifiable interpretations of information which would put us back into Shannon's or Kolmogorov's conceptualizations, i.e., it would be missing the essence of this study.

---

[30] This definition of physics was attributed to A. S. Eddington by Ziman (1991, ft. 30, p. 28).

[31] Limiting perspective of quantifiable concepts is indicated, e.g., by Ziman (1991, ft. 31, p. 28).

Chapter 2

Visions of Ontological Information—Conjectures

The word "conjecture" here refers to the studies of the pre-Socratic philosophers, when a philosopher's world view was often reconstructed from dispersed fragments, quotations, and partial sentences rather than complete works. In this chapter, we examine some brief studies that have discussed the concept of information as an objective, physical phenomenon. Quite often, these studies may just be a paragraph or even a single sentence in length and include little supportive discussion. They therefore qualify as conjectures (in the sense explained above) rather than arguments. Regardless of the length of these fragments, however, they still provide valid, unique insights into the studied concept of information. Our use of these short pronouncements may be regarded as being analogous to the reconstruction attempts of pre-Socratic philosophy, which was founded on dispersed fragments and third-party quotations, but only up to a point, of course. The sources used here are not entirely comparable to the pre-Socratic sources, but they still need to be combed through for relevant observations. All the scholars referred to in this chapter have indicated that some form of organization exists in nature, one that is ontologically objective, all pervading, and fundamental. They rarely denote a special term for this, however, and generally refer to it as just information with some specific properties or certain utilitarian or explanatory functions or powers. Despite this, the concepts of information that they describe bear a remarkable similarity to what we call ontological information in this study. A note of explanation is warranted here, however: The physical theories of Wilczek, Barrow, Rovelli, Seife, and Davies are provided here without commentary, because interpreting them is beyond the scope of this study. This means that rather than focus on the physical theory itself and its description of reality, the study is more concerned with the role of information in describing that reality, as elucidated by the theory. In these cases, information is not an integral part of the theory but rather something that emerges either as a consequence of the theory or in support of it.

2.1 Conjectures

The observations in this chapter derive from the works of Edmund Kowalczyk, Keith Devlin, Frank Wilczek, John Barrow, Sean Carroll, Ricardo Sole and Santiago Elena, Carlo Rovelli, Charles Seife, John Polkinghorne, and Paul Davies. Kowalczyk intuits that there are physical and abstract dimensions of information, but he does not propose a coherent resolution to this dichotomy. He tries to create a concept of information based on assumptions from cybernetics, concepts of physics like entropy, Shannon's theory of communication, and the concepts of meaning and consciousness in human agents. His concept of information therefore seems rather incoherent. Keith Devlin, meanwhile, claims that information may be regarded as a fundamental element of the universe, much like how we regard energy and matter. Frank Wilczek also speculates that information is a fundamental aspect of the world, and he hints that the concept of information, in the way he describes it, might facilitate the development of a fundamental unification theorem in physics, although this suggestion is then abandoned by Wilczek without further elaboration. John Barrow, like Wilczek, connects information with the basic properties of the universe, with this connection being forged through the link between entropy and the concept of information as a measure of, or in relation to, arrangements of the constituent elements that form large cosmic structures. It seems that Barrow's intuitions are correct, yet his explanation of entropy and information is not worked out in detail. Sean Carroll, like previous authors, perceives the term "information" as being somehow related to the fundamental properties of the universe. Ricardo Sole and Santiago Elena, meanwhile, claim that the concept of information plays a critical role in explaining the evolution of viruses, which is something that cannot be explained by any other concept. For Rovelli, information is used as a concept in fundamental areas of physics. For Seife, though, information is again a basic property of the universe, with it being physical in nature (rather than abstract) and subject to physical laws. Next, Polkinghorne sees information as a third constituent of nature in a complex triad of matter, energy, and information. Finally, Davies envisages two types of information, namely, abstract and concrete, but he is puzzled by the dichotomy this implies, because abstract information exists outside of space and time (as all abstract things do), but the second type of information is physical and exists in nature.

In the context of cybernetics, Edward Kowalczyk (1970) developed the theory of information in the early seventies of the 20th century. Kowalczyk faced the same problem as Paul Davies did almost 50 years later, namely, how to reconcile the obvious physical character of information with its abstract, semantic dimension.[1] Kowalczyk's view of information reflects his interests in cybernetics in its "regional version", which fuses information processing, computing, and system control theory.[2] He claims that information the third basic element of nature, besides matter and energy (Kowalczyk

---

[1]Davies states in his 2019 book that *the challenge to science is to figure out how to couple abstract information* (Davies 2019, p. 35). See the later section on Paul Davies' work.

[2]*Cybernetics is control theory as it is applied to complex systems* (Cybernetics 2019). The modern origins of cybernetics are traced to Norbert Wiener's book *Cybernetics* (1948). Kowalczyk uses the definition of cybernetics as adopted in the non-Western countries of the so-called Eastern Bock, where the science of control (cybernetics) also included *all sorts of information processing*. In this view, computer science and the theory of information and communication were parts of cybernetics. It seems that with time cybernetics, or rather the ideas based on cybernetics, merged into everything dissolving this uncouth Western—non-Western split (Brockman 2019, p. xxi).

op. cit., p. 12). Furthermore, Kowalczyk states that information is quantifiable, because technical applications of information require information to be quantified. He also attributes to information semantic aspects and causal powers in controlling flow of energy and matter in artifacts and natural systems. In this cybernetics-inspired view, information is carried by specific physical signals, and sequences of these signals form a message. Information emerges in the communication (or signal exchange) process between the signal's source and the receiving system (artificial or biological, per Kowalczyk's comment). Any given message contains information if it triggers a change of state for the receiving system, and this interpretation was clearly inspired by cybernetics. Thus, a message may or may not have information, so information is not an intrinsic property of a signal message but rather exists "in the eye of the beholder"—which is a receiving system. This perspective on information conflicts with the previous claim that information is one of the three fundamental elements of reality, because it suggests that a significant portion of the macro-scale reality is observer-dependent. Kowalczyk seems to be aware that his concept of information is incomplete, but this is intuited in Kowalczyk's work rather than recognized and explained.

Kowalczyk derives the concept of information from the theory of coupling (ToC).[3] The ToC[4] is an epistemic theory, so it is concerned with what we know and how we know it. It claims that there is a "coupling" between the objectively existing reality and our consciousness. This coupling is a causal relationship between signals from the environment, which are perceived as messages, and the object immersed in it, particularly a human subject. The coupling occurs when the receiving system responds to the message by changing its state. There is also coupling in inorganic systems, according to Kowalczyk, such

---

[3]In Polish, the original term used to describe the ToC was "odbicie", which would be translated into something like mirroring or reflection. However, these terms do not correctly render the definition associated with the ToC by Kowalczyk. The translation of "theory of coupling" rather than the verbatim translation "theory of reflection" more accurately reflects the definition of the ToC.

[4]Kowalczyk's ToC has nothing to do with Shannon's theory of communication often referred to as the ToC.

as chemical, mechanical, and physical systems. However, these couplings are not information processes because such systems lack "system's memory". Kowalczyk claims that information is an aspect, or an element, of animate objects, technology, and society, and it is used for a purposeful action, namely, control and regulation. He brands this view of information as philosophical and differentiates this definition from the quantifiable concept of information related to the organization, properties, and relations of material objects. However, this "quantifiable information" is not an intrinsic property of the states of matter but rather our knowledge of them or the degree of our lack of precise knowledge about these states in probabilistic quantifications. Now, how can we summarize Kowalczyk's concept of information? Kowalczyk intuits the physical and abstract dimensions of information, but he does not propose a coherent resolution for this dichotomy. He tries to create a concept of information based on assumptions from cybernetics, concepts of physics, and Shannon's theory of communication that encompasses communication and concepts of meaning and consciousness in human agents, but these things taken together are hard to reconcile in one coherent package, as many writers have later observed and experienced (e.g., Davies, von Weizsäcker, and even Floridi in his General Definition of Information (GDI)). Moreover, cybernetics does not seem to be the right perspective within which to define a fundamental element of the universe, which is what Kowalczyk's information is supposed to be. The reasons behind Kowalczyk's concept of information may be better understood if one is more aware of role attributed to cybernetics in non-Western countries (see Cybernetics 2019).

Keith Devlin (1991) claims that information may be regarded as a fundamental element of the universe, much like how we see energy and matter. He observes that information can be manipulated, measured, and is related to entropy (thermodynamic). He also, like Kowalczyk, sees information as the third fundamental element of nature. In Devlin's study, the term "information" must be interpreted within the context of the study itself and should not be connected with other theories of information. Devlin is very cautious about what he claims. For example, he says that his concept of information is merely a suggestion for a theory. Yet, he sees the need for the ontological-like information that exists in nature rather than in the mind. Why is this? It appears that for Devlin, this "information" has great utilitarian value. Devlin sees information as a concrete entity that can be used and manipulated. Devlin's information is therefore a basic element of the universe, together with matter and energy, where "universe" here refers to physical reality. For Devlin, the term "physical" means ontological or "what is". One accepted version of scientific realism claims that *what can be manipulated, exists* (Hacking 1982, pp. 71–87). Devlin's information can be manipulated, so it is real, and it exists in the same sense as other physical phenomena that can be manipulated, such as electrons and photons. Devlin does not give us a definition for information but instead offers a description. Information may avoid a precise definition if it is a basic element of the natural world on par with energy and matter, as Devlin suggests. As such, basic concepts cannot be defined by other concepts, simply because they cannot be reduced to anything else. Other things may be reducible to them, but they are not reducible to other things, because this is what being basic (conceptually) means. The conceptual "buck" stops right there, because fundamental objects can only be described. Devlin's information may be interconvertible with matter and energy, but he does not explain what this "interconvertibility" would entail.[5] Devlin also claims that that information is some kind of intrinsic metric of natural order, although what this "intrinsic measure" may be is again not explained. Devlin suggests that information is related to entropy and possibly its inverse. Again, there is no explanation for what this means, but we may hazard that more entropy means less information and less entropy means more information. This claim seems to be either a reflection of Shannon's communication theory and his information entropy or some play on the commonly associated meaning of entropy as disorder, as opposed to information as order. However, we cannot push this interpretation

---

[5]We can only guess that "interconvertibility" may mean something like $E = mc^2 = I$, where I is information and the rest is the well-known mass–energy equivalence. But, there is nothing in physics that would confirm this formula.

too far if we are to avoid attributing to the author something that he was unwilling, or unable, to say.

Wilczek (2015) implies that information is a fundamental aspect of the world, and the concept of information, at least in the meaning he describes, may facilitate the development of a fundamental unification theorem in physics. Wilczek claims that his ideas about information and its function in physical theories are in the early stages of development but have great explanatory potential. Wilczek's information, as he sees it, plays an explanatory role in the well-recognized phenomenon of thermodynamic entropy, and through entropy, information is related to basic physical concepts of matter and energy (Wilczek's claim). Thus, information in Wilczek's view is not an abstract notion that depends upon the presence of the mind. It is a realization of the state of a physical system and a physical property of nature. Being embedded in the state of a physical system, information is connected to the fundamental laws and phenomena of the universe, much like entropy is. Wilczek may have the Second Law of thermodynamics in mind here.[6] Entropy may therefore play an explanatory role in *the unification of our description of matter and information,* but this is conjecture, an intuition on Wilczek's side and nothing more (i.e., it is not supported by any argument).

John Barrow, like Wilczek, connects information with the basic properties of the universe. This connection is achieved through the link between entropy and the concept of information in relation to the arrangements of constituents forming large cosmic structures. Barrow claims that entropy is a measure of disorder that can be related *to the more general and fruitful notions of 'information'.* While this point

---

[6]The second law states that there exists a useful state variable called entropy S. The change in entropy delta S is equal to the heat transfer delta Q divided by the temperature T (i.e., delta S = delta Q/T). For a given physical process, the combined entropy of the system and the environment remains a constant if the process can be reversed. If we denote the initial and final states of the system by "i" and "f", Sf = Si (reversible process). The second law states that if the physical process is irreversible, the combined entropy of the system and the environment must increase. The final entropy must be greater than the initial entropy for an irreversible process: Sf > Si (irreversible process) (Benson 2015).

is interesting, it is not novel, because most researchers suggest some kind of equivalence (whether conceptual or numeric) between entropy (the state of a physical system) and information, but such comparisons are very nebulous. Barrow claims that there are similarities between entropy and information, but information is a much more portent concept. He suggests that information may measure a basic property of the universe, namely, the maximum information content in a volume of space. For Barrow, information and entropy express "disorder".[7] We may argue whether entropy is really disorder or simply the magnitude or size of a state space of a system, but Barrow immediately provides the proper conceptualization of entropy as *the number of different ways in which its most elementary constituents can be rearranged,* which clearly denotes the magnitude/size of the system state space. With this formulation of entropy, entropy then becomes a concept closer to that of the degrees of freedom in a system or even the probability of a given sign occurring in a message, at least with an extended interpretation of the probability space from the physical state space to the message source state space. The differences, however, are significant between the state of a system as a whole and the occurrence (or the probability thereof) of a single message. This can be viewed as the key difference between information entropy (as defined by Shannon) and thermodynamic entropy. (See later chapters for a discussion of the quantification of information.)

From a description of the real (physical) phenomena, Barrow moves on to the realm of quantification, claiming that information expresses the number of binary digits that *specify in every detail the internal configuration of the constituents of the black hole.* This is effectively the Solomonov–Kolmogov–Chaitin complexity measure

---

[7]John Wheeler discusses the idea of the entropy of a black hole as a measure of the surface area of the horizon of the black hole and entropy as a measure of lost information, attributing this relation to Bekenstein (Wheeler 1989, pp. 312–313). He even states that *giving us its (physical entities) as bits [1/0 domain or yes/no indications as he puts it], the quantum presents us with physics as information* (*ibid.*, p. 313). His treatment of information is done in the light of information theory, which is effectively a reinterpretation of Shannon's Theory of Communication.

rephrased. This measure, expressed in a digital string of zeros and ones, like any other measure, is an interpretation or symbolization of a physical phenomenon rather than its explanation. In other words, we assign a certain function or number/symbol to a certain physical feature of nature. The Solomonov–Kolmogov–Chaitin complexity measure, in Barrow's discussion, is not a measure of a message but rather one of the states of organization for a large-scale cosmic phenomenon. Barrow's measure is therefore a measure of certain property of a natural object, namely, a measure of the maximum information content for a volume of space, so it quantifies how much information (conceived as a binary sequence) can be contained in that volume of space. Barrow proposes that "information" expresses certain fundamental properties of the universe, and no other concept can do this as well. For Barrow, information exists in nature and can be measured, so it is related to the organization of natural phenomena. This measure seems to express certain natural/physical properties, such as the maximum information content of a volume of space, at the fundamental level, so it determines other properties of a volume of space. Thus, information for Barrow has the characteristics that we would normally require from a physical phenomenon: quantifiability (i.e., a numeric representation), a physical or concrete realization, and explanatory power for certain physical phenomena. (See the discussion of scientific realism in work by Worrall (1982), Chakravartty (2017), and Liston (2019).) Nevertheless, quantifying a phenomenon does not explain its nature, as we discussed earlier in the case of quantum mechanics.

Sean Carroll, like the above authors, perceives the term "information" in relation to the fundamental properties of the universe. For Carroll, "information" has operational import: It facilitates the explanation and characterization of "physical realities". Carroll sees "information" as a multivalent concept, but in this multitude, he distinguishes two major kinds of information: information as knowledge, such as that contained within books, and information as the state of a physical system. He refers to the former as higher-level information, meaning that this higher-level information must have some fundamental, perhaps physical, base or lower level. He also ties his second kind of information to physical laws. Carroll introduces the concept of information as *the knowledge you actually have about a state of affairs*. This perception of information contrasts with the physical interpretation as *the state of the system*. What Carroll offers here is an interesting suggestion: The concept of information in nature is not necessarily related to Aristotelian *eidos* but rather to the Laplacian view of nature, so we eliminate the Aristotelian "enigmatic" nature of things (*eidos*) and purpose (*telos*, where things have *telos* because of *eidos*).[8] We are then left with just concepts of the structures or patterns that form nature (the Laplacian view of nature). The term Carroll uses to denote this information, namely, "microscopic information", is a little misleading, but we need to consider that "microscopic" does not relate to the size but rather to the level of specification. Thus, "microscopic information" is *the complete specification of the state of the system*, implying that it is complete on all levels of organization. This is another way to say that the "microscopic information" is the state of the system or its structure/organization of parts. Carroll also proposes that the law of conservation of information is as fundamental in the universe as the law of conservation of momentum. What such a law would mean, however, is not clear. For Carroll, the concept of information is a fundamental idea behind the shift from the Aristotelian world view to the Laplacian one (i.e., the shift from nature as essences to nature as organization), with organization being the *essence*, form, or *eidos* in this view. The concept of information was not around at the time of Laplace, so he could not use it. We have it now, however, and the concept of information illuminates the nature of the Aristotelian–Laplacian shift. Now, nature is a pattern, and information is patterns of organization. In this view, the terms *eidos*, *telos*, and "Form" or "form"[9] are too nebulous, so they may be substituted with a more concrete idea of information as a pattern or organization in nature.[10]

---

[8]This was the Aristotelian explanation of gravity.

[9]The difference between "Form" and "form" was explained in Chapter 1.

[10]This perspective is somewhat reflected in the modern structural realism, but for reasons not related to Laplacian metaphysics.

Such a change would also attribute quantifiability to information, because while one cannot quantify *eidos*, one can certainly quantify structure under some abstractions.

Ricardo Sole and Santiago Elena (2020) claim that the concept of information plays a critical role in explaining viral evolution (i.e., the evolution of viruses), which cannot be explained by any other concept. They write that the ability to evolve for viral populations is defined by the amount of information (the genome length) that is considered stable. If random mutations destroy the amount of this stable information, the error catastrophe occurs and evolution cannot take place. While the *error catastrophe problem* can be explained with some form of description, like with the mutation rate, the use of the concept of information provides a frugal description that is lacking in other explanations. In other words, the term "information" has an explanatory power that other concepts lack. The information that Ricardo Sole and Santiago Elena are referring to is the structure of the genome (i.e., *the amount of information (in terms of genome length, i.e., v)*). In explaining this information, there is no reference to meaning or communication. This information is purely the length (the numbers of genes) of the viral RNA or DNA. In this case, the concept of information explains why certain biological (natural) processes do or do not occur. Indeed, there is a certain property of a biological system that relates to information, much like with molecular weight or molecular composition. These processes therefore depend upon information or the organization of nature. To put this differently, these natural systems (viruses) have to have a certain measurable property for evolution to take place, and this property is best denoted as information. What is more, this information is a precondition on the molecular level for Darwinian evolution to take place. The existence of molecular mechanisms alone is not in itself sufficient for evolution to occur; for evolution to occur, these biological structures must have certain characteristics that can be best described as information. We need to add that Sole and Elena's conclusions about the role of information in evolution relate to the evolution of viruses. Any generalization to the evolution of more complex organisms would need to be confirmed.

For Rovelli, information as a concept is used in fundamental areas of physics (e.g., QM, thermodynamics). Furthermore, he writes that the concept of information may be useful in providing fundamental understanding of the world. This is, as he explains, because information is a measure of "communication" between physical systems. Referring to the idea of Democritus where atoms combine to form structures (i.e., an atom can be compared to the letters of the alphabet), he writes that physical systems communicate with each other in the sense that the arrangement of atoms is correlated. Rovelli's comment on Democritus' idea is quite interesting in that it substitutes the concept of the nature of things as *eidos/Form* with the mechanistic concept of a structure that determines all the properties of nature. We also saw this in Carroll's reference (as discussed earlier) to the Laplacian view of nature. Could we therefore hazard to claim that the concept of ontological information is closer to the mechanistic view of Democritus than the elusive *Form* or *eidos*? Maybe these two concepts are two sides of the same coin? Furthermore, Rovelli posits that *the entire structure of quantum mechanics can be read and understood in terms of information.* He formulates two principles, which in his view would *express the entire formal structure of QM* in terms of information. These principles are as follows: (1) The relevant information in any physical system is finite and (2) you can always obtain new information on a physical system. This "relevant information" is information about the state of a system that allows us to predict future states. He also claims that information (about the state of a system) is finite because measuring of a state of a system can only present a final number of alternative states. This is an important observation, because it stipulates that the amount of information in the universe at any given time is not infinite, as would be suggested by the classical mechanics of continuous space and time. The fact *that only a finite number of possibilities exists* is a reflection or result of the granularity of quantum mechanics.[11] Rovelli attributes physical presence to information. This information

---

[11] *According to recent developments in the quest to devise a so-called theory of everything, space is not an infinitely divisible continuum. It is not smooth but*

expresses correlation between states of the systems. The *correlation between states of systems* is another name for the organization of matter, and it is the term used in this study to refer to information. Rovelli postulates that information is a critical concept in basic physical sciences and biology. Information is the organization of nature or its elementary particles and *the structures formed by combinations of these atoms*. The *organization of nature* is obviously something that exists independently outside of the mind, and he also says this about information in a physical system: *We are dealing with physical facts, not mental notions*. From the perspective of this study, this is an important observation, because abstract things are things of the mind, such as thoughts or epistemic information, at least as we define it. The "structures of atoms", meanwhile, are physical things, so they represent ontological information. These structures "give" shape to nature, or to put it differently, nature can be seen as structures, which in some sense are information, or at least they express it.

For Charles Seife, information is a basic property of the universe, with it having a physical (rather than abstract) nature and being subject to physical laws. Seife posits that conceptualizations of information based on the interpretations of Shannon's information entropy do not really reflect what information is. Seife also states that physical processes (i.e., *the most fundamental rules in physics*) are de facto information processes (i.e., processes in which information is manipulated). In Seife's writing, we therefore have an indirect reference (i.e., he talks about it without naming it) to the concept of pancomputationalism, where every natural process is a form of information processing and therefore computation as it is generally understood. Seife goes even further, however, because he claims that physics itself may be fundamentally about information (*the most fundamental rules in physics are, deep down, actually laws about information*). This is obviously conjecture, yet pancomputationalism in its many different forms has been proposed several times, so maybe we are not so far from actually recognizing this idea as having some merit (e.g.,

---

granular, and the Planck length gives the size of its smallest possible grains (Johnson 1999). The implications for the concept of information are significant.

Zuse 1970, von Weizsäcker 1971, Floridi 2004, Dodig Crnkovic 2011, Piccinini 2017).

For his part, John Polkinghorne brings the concept of information into the matter–energy complex as an idea for solving the mind–body dualism problem. For Polkinghorne, "information" is a necessary element for fully describing nature alongside matter and energy. The "information" he talks about is not a thought or some other product of the mind, which we would usually classify as an abstract entity,[12] but rather a real thing. For Polkinghorne, "information" has a physical presence, and it is concrete. He denotes his proposal of the information, matter, and energy triad as "holistic order". Thus, on the one hand, we have the Aristotelian hylemorphism of substance and *eidos*, while on the other hand, we have Polkinghorne's "holisticism" of matter–energy–information. This is certainly a daring analogy considering that the word "holistic" does not get good press, with it often being associated with New-Age pseudo-mysticism. The over-interpretation of the term "holistic" may take Polkinghorne into never-never land ("A world of fantasy we enter in our dreams" 2019), which is perhaps why Polkinghorne qualifies his view by saying, *a glimmer (no more) of.* In discussing Polkinghorne's views, we may remind ourselves that Heraclitian views, despite the volumes of press attention, are not justified as being more accurate than those of Polkinghorne's. Polkinghorne suggests in his writings that if information is a property of the mind (i.e., the mind processes information, or the mind is information, or the mind is composed of information), because of how it combines with matter and energy to create physical reality, the problem of dualism is explained/settled, at least in his view. This view would imply that the mind is an integral part of the matter–energy complex.[13] Of course, being a theologian, Polkinghorne may have allowed himself to be more relaxed in suggesting a hypothesis on the far frontiers of science or on the boundary between theology and science. However, the view that the mind is a

---

[12]See the discussion about abstract vs. concrete information in Chapter 7.

[13]Polkinghorne continued his discussion of the role and function of information in nature in his later book (Polkinghorne and Beale 2009).

part of the natural world but still not reducible to it (having no ontological presence) is not too far removed from the biological naturalism
of Searle, a researcher who does not have theological inclinations by
any measure.[14]

Paul Davies, meanwhile, conceptualizes information as an essen-
tial/constituent element of all living things, with it having a real
physical and causal nature. Davies writes that while the concept
of information originated in the context of human agency as an
abstract concept, information has physical presence. The problem
is how to couple the abstract concept of information *to the concrete
world of physical objects*. Davies observes how the concept of information evolved from the abstract notion associated with the functioning of the mind (e.g., thoughts, ideas) to one that relates to the
origins of life with causal powers in the physical realm. Davies points
out that information became preferred by *many scientists now* to
explain natural processes *in the world, not least in biology*. Davies
gives us an interesting insight into this idea of information. The term
"information" originated in relation to a person (vide *informare*),[15]
so it is in origin an anthropomorphic-centered concept (i.e., the idea
of information derives from the realm of human discourse). Along
with the development of natural sciences, however, the concept of
information has moved into nature's realm. We thus became able
to relate this concept of information to the ideas that were originally conceived to describe the properties of nature, such as form or
eidos, organization, and order. We could then detect not just strong
similarities but almost equivalence between human-centered information and some properties of nature. This shift in our perception
of information implies that limiting information to its epistemic version is a strong anthropomorphization of information and nature, at
least if we consider information to be a constituent of it. As in many
other concepts and ideas that came before (e.g., "Anthropomorphism

---

[14]See also Boehm (1980) and Chalmers (1994).

[15]Early 14c., "to train or instruct in some specific subject", from Old French
informer, enformer "instruct, teach" (13c.) and directly from Latin informare "to
shape, give form to, delineate", figuratively "train, instruct, educate", from in—
"into" (from PIE root *en "in") + formare "to form, shape", from forma "form"
(Informare 2019).

in science" 1968), to understand what information (or in our case, ontological information) is, we need to remove ourselves from the picture (i.e., de-anthropomorphize it). After all, on the 24-hour clock of the universe's history, we came to this place less than 2 minutes ago, at 11:58:43 ("History of The Earth in 24 hours" 2019). We arrived at a fully furnished house as guests. Note, however, that the Anthropocene is a recent event with a rather dubious provenance (e.g., Edwards 2015, Waters *et al.* 2016). Davies indicates the perennial problem that we have with the concept of information, namely, *how to couple abstract information to the concrete world of physical objects.* Von Weizsäcker (see the next section), Kowalczyk, and others also ran into this dilemma and failed to resolve it. Information as knowledge, ideas, or thoughts is an abstract concept (this is our information$_E$), but information as a physical phenomenon is real and physical. Indeed, how can one thing (i.e., information) be abstract and physical at the same time? Or, is it just one of these things? This is a problem for the philosophy of information and also maybe metaphysics, and at this point, definitions that attempt to be "comprehensive" by trying to account for abstract and physical aspects under one term generally fall apart (see, for example, Floridi's (2013) GDI concept or Carl von Weizsäcker's (1971) information). One solution suggested by this study is to deal with two different concepts and not question this. Indeed, unless we make the content of the mind and consciousness an integral part of physical reality, we will always stumble at this point. Just as a reminder, the term "physical" in this context does not mean something is reducible to the fundamental laws of physics but rather exists in reality as part of the world of concrete, measurable, detectable objects. The possible *glimmer of solution*, taken from Polkinghorne's statement, to the concrete–abstract problem for information is presented in later chapters.

While it may seem that the authors' expressed views do not necessarily converge onto some coherent whole, we can claim that all these scholars perceive information as having a concrete, physical existence. Moreover, these authors attribute to the concept of information properties such as causality in the physical world, quantifiability, a close relationship with the structure of matter or the universe, and usability. They also indicate that the concept of information is the only concept that can explain certain phenomena, including the forming of black holes and the natural evolution of viruses (and by extension, Darwinian evolution). The presented conceptualizations of information differ radically from the conceptualization of information that is employed when describing information from the perspective of semantics. Thus, these studies clearly, at the very least, indicate that there is more to information than semantics, which is an assumption of this study.

2.2 Conjectures—What Did We Learn?

The concepts of information emerging from the works of Edmund Kowalczyk, Keith Devlin, Frank Wilczek, John Barrow, Sean Carroll, Richard Sole and Santiago Elena, Carlo Rovelli, Charles Seife, John Polkinghorne, and Paul Davies are summarized in eight observations: (1) Information as a natural phenomenon, without meaning, is not related to knowledge but to the properties of the universe (i.e., nature), and this has obviously found a place in the research literature. (2) In several studies, we see the tension between the abstract (mental) concept of information and information as a concrete, physical thing. (3) In any discussion about information as a natural phenomenon, entropy (thermodynamics) plays a prominent role. (4) The term information is usually not clearly defined. (5) Despite the diverse descriptions, there are several commonalities in terms of information existing in nature. (6) Information in nature is closely related to organization in nature (i.e., its structure). (7) Information in nature can be quantified. (8) Information in nature is often conceptualized as part of a matter–energy–information complex.

Observation (1) states that information is a natural phenomenon, without meaning and unrelated to knowledge, but connected with the properties of the universe (i.e., nature), and this figures prominently in the research. The authors describing this concept of information take care not to make too many specific claims, but it seems to be the exact properties of this information they are cautious about rather than its existence. Indeed, they all agree that this information is "out there" in nature as a part of it. In the sense that these authors use the term "information" (i.e., as a natural phenomenon), it has explanatory value in fundamental physics (e.g., a unification of physical laws, the maximum information content of a volume, a specification for the state of a physical system, a fundamental explanation in QM, and the fundamental laws of physics).

Observation (2) points out that there is a perceived tension between the abstract (mental) concept of information and information as a concrete, physical thing. Davies who identified this tension forgets, however, to add that one thing cannot be both abstract and concrete at the same time and in the same way. (This problem is discussed further in Chapter 7.) This dichotomy is so critical that Davies even claims that this abstract–concrete split is one of the greatest challenges that science and philosophy face. We may say that the view of information as an abstract thing (i.e., as knowledge or related to the mind's operations) is more rooted in tradition, so it is more widely accepted. Information as an element of the natural realm, meanwhile, is more a case of a forgotten idea. The original concept of information as an ordering/organization in nature has existed in some form since the early days of human thought (e.g., Tao, *eidos*, Form, *morphe*). In this tradition, information is bound with what exists, and no information is in a nonexistent state, so information implies existence and existence implies information.[16]

---

[16]We may claim that facts require information in the sense that information is ontologically fundamental. Thus, negative facts, being unrepresented by specific information, are purely abstract concepts. As Barker and Jago state, *Negative facts get a bad press. One reason for this is that it is not clear what negative facts are. We provide a theory of negative facts in which they are no stranger than positive atomic facts. We show that none of the usual arguments hold water against this account. Negative facts exist in the usual sense of existence and conform to an acceptable Eleatic principle. Furthermore, there are good reasons to want them around, including their roles in causation, chance-making and truth-making, and in constituting holes and edges* (Barker and Jago 2011). In the sense of information, negative facts are an abstract construct rather than a concrete entity. Thus, they would not exist in the same way as positive facts (see also the discussion of Rosenberg, 1972). Can the concept of information add anything to the discussion about negative facts and the Eleatic principle?

Schrödinger's view is that existence, at least in terms of life, depends on information (Schrödinger 1944). The modern tradition of seeing information as something apart from nature, as something existing in the mind, probably has Kantian and Cartesian roots, but it has certainly been cemented in the age of information processing with the abstraction of information emerging in digital formats. This split between abstract and concrete information is seen throughout the presented studies. We will conclude that in the case of abstract and concrete information, we are dealing with two ontologically different concepts, implying that this tension (abstract vs concrete) is apparent.

Observation (3) claims that in any discussion about information as a natural phenomenon, entropy (thermodynamics) usually plays a prominent role. Putting aside mathematical formulations and interpretations, it seems that the concept of information entropy—due to Shannon's Theory of Communication and the term "entropy of information", which he coined—is seen as being almost synonymous with organization (or disorganization) and order (or its inverse) in nature. As such, the concept of information entropy plays a role in linking ideas of information to the concepts of fundamental physics, chemistry, biology (see the theories of life, viral theories, or genetics), and metaphysics. This information in nature exists without the presence of the mind, communication, or a message from someone to another. It is just a feature of nature. Thus, it may be that information entropy has become a concept that has allowed us to find or discover similarities across these diverse conceptual domains of metaphysics, computing, physics, cosmology, and biology despite the different meanings that entropy has in each of these domains. Moreover, we cannot forget Schrödinger's work on entropy and the origins of life (Schrödinger 2004). The capacity of nature to create local complexes with a high level of information content, which in Schrödinger's language is called negentropy or negative entropy, works against the Second Law of Thermodynamics,[17] but it is at the origin of life according to him.

---

[17]This is Schrödinger's so-called paradox, which seems to be nonexistent for open systems (i.e., a biosphere is an open system).

Schrödinger's book was originally published in 1944,[18] and it does not mention the term "information". On reading the book now, however, one gets the impression that this concept was somehow forgotten by the author. (Tom Stonier made this connection easily, but only 30 years later.) This may have partially been the case, but it seems that the actual reason for this "omission" was the fact that the link between entropy and information had not been recognized, or rather popularized, yet. In Schrödinger's work, entropy plays the role of the concept of information in that it is a function of, or an indicator of, the degree of organization for a physical system.

Observation (4) states that the term "information" is usually not clearly defined in the sense that we do not get a formal definition in the form of "information is..." or "by information, we understand this and that...". In most of the reviewed studies so far, the term "information" is explained only through an extended description, sometimes over several paragraphs. It is often not attempted, on the part of the authors, to denote the information that they are talking about with a single term, such as "natural information", "objective information", "physical information", or some other concise phrase. The lack of a clear definition is unsurprising, given that information may have several, often contradictory, meanings. One would therefore assume that when writing about information, to avoid confusion, the authors would say something like this: "The concept of information I am talking about is ... and it is denoted as..." Instead, we need to perceive this explanation implicitly and mine out its meaning from the text. Such interpretations are always prone to misinterpretation, however, because we may incorrectly guess an author's intentions. Thus, the studies cited in the discussion have been denoted as "intuitions" rather than "definitions". Such a positioning of these studies relieves both the authors and us of some pressure, because intuitions do not have to be completely accurate.

Observation (5) claims that several commonalities exist among the descriptions of information in the reviewed studies despite the

---

[18]Since 1944 (the original publication date), Schrödinger's book *What is Life?* has been published in at least 24 editions in English alone.

apparent lack of convergence from their authors. While different characteristics are attributed to the concept of information, studies show strong similarities in their descriptions of information. In almost all of these studies, information is explicitly positioned as a property of physical systems, and it is closely connected to the organization of the physical world, so information is physical or has a physical presence. The point to observe here concerns how all these authors talk about information in terms of an organization of nature or physical systems, and this organization exists regardless of the presence or not of any cognitive system. This "information" is natural, physical, and mind-independent, and it is devoid of meaning.

Observation (6) claims that information in nature is closely related to the organization of nature, its structure, or form. Information, in its different names (e.g., structure, order, form), is synonymous with organization in most of the reviewed studies.

Observation (7) claims that information in nature can be quantified, meaning that information is a measurable property of nature, just like mass and energy are. As information can be quantified, it can be isolated as an entity with its own characteristics. Moreover, as it can be quantified, this also means that it can be used for some operational gain.

Observation (8) claims that information in nature is often conceptualized within a matter–energy–information complex. Matter, energy, and information are what physical reality is at the fundamental level. The precise manner in which this unification is accomplished is a matter of speculation, however. This unification of form and matter has a long tradition in notions like *eidos*, Form, hylemorphism, and *morphe*, both in the ancient Greek and modern versions of such concepts. The unification of information and matter is expressed in many ways by the different authors. We do not get any new sort of hylemorphism or other new theory from these writers. They only point to the close relation between the fundamental physical concepts of energy, matter, and information, but the nature of this relation remains unknown.

We now move from the intuitions to the more detailed studies of information and analyze which properties the authors of these studies attribute to it.

2.3 A Biographical Note

Below are short biographical notes on the authors cited in this chapter.

Edmund Kowalczyk was professor of cybernetics at Warsaw Polytechnic in the 1960s and 1970s. He specialized in the theory of communication, cybernetics, and the theory of information (Kowalczyk 1974).

Keith Devlin is the Director of the Stanford Mathematics Outreach Project in the Graduate School of Education. His research interests include the theory of information, models of reasoning, applications of mathematical techniques in the study of communication, and mathematical cognition (Keith Devlin at Stanford University 2019).

Frank Wilczek is considered one of the world's most eminent theoretical physicists. He is known, among other things, for the discovery of asymptotic freedom, the development of quantum chromodynamics, the invention of axions, and the discovery and exploitation of new forms of quantum statistics (anyons). Professor Wilczek's interests include "pure" particle physics, the behavior of matter at ultrahigh temperature and/or density, the application of insights from particle physics to cosmology, and the quantum theory of black holes (Wilczek 2018).

John D. Barrow is a cosmologist, theoretical physicist, and mathematician. He is a professor of mathematical science at the University of Cambridge and Director of the Millennium Mathematics Project. He is the author of several books including *Pi in the Sky*, *The Origin of the Universe* (Science Masters Series), *The Artful Universe*, *The Constants of Nature: From Alpha to Omega—the Numbers That Encode the Deepest Secrets of the Universe*, and *The Book of Universes* (Barrow 2019).

Sean Michael Carroll is a theoretical physicist specializing in quantum mechanics, gravity, and cosmology. He is a research professor in the Department of Physics at the California Institute of Technology. He has been a contributor to the physics blog Cosmic Variance, and has published in scientific journals such as *Nature* as well as other publications, including *The New York Times, Sky & Telescope,* and *New Scientist* (Carroll 2019).

Ricardo Sole is an "ICREA research professor" (the Catalan Institute for research and Advanced Studies) currently working at the Universitat Pompeu Fabra, where he is the head of the COMPLEX SYSTEMS LAB. He has degrees in both Physics and Biology from the University of Barcelona and received a Ph.D. in Physics from the Polytechnic University of Catalonia (Sole 2019).

Santiago Elena holds a Ph.D. in Molecular and Evolutionary Genetics from Universitat de València. His scientific interests are focused on the evolutionary biology of microbes. More concretely, he has focused on the mechanisms that generate and maintain the genetic variability of RNA viruses (Elena 2019).

Carlo Rovelli is an Italian theoretical physicist and writer who has worked in Italy, the United States, and since 2000, in France. His work is mainly in the field of quantum gravity, where he is among the founders of the loop quantum gravity theory. He is the director of the quantum gravity group of the Centre de Physique Théorique (CPT) at the Aix-Marseille University (Rovelli 2019).

Charles Seife is the author of several books, including *Proofiness and Zero*, which won the PEN/Martha Albrand Award for first non-fiction and was a *New York Times* notable book. He has written for a wide variety of publications, including *The New York Times, Wired, New Scientist, Science, Scientific American*, and *The Economist* (Seife 2019).

John Polkinghorne is most notably known for his groundbreaking work in bringing science and theology together. He is a British mathematical physicist and Anglican priest. He was selected as a fellow of the Royal Society based on his mathematical models used to calculate the paths of quantum particles. He was the recipient of the 2002 Templeton Prize (Polkinghorne 2019).

Paul Davies is a theoretical physicist, cosmologist, astrobiologist, and best-selling science author. His research interests have focused mainly on quantum gravity, early universe cosmology, the theory of quantum black holes, and the nature of time. He has also made important contributions to the field of astrobiology (Davies 2019).

Chapter 3

Visions of Ontological
Information—Studies

In this section, we analyze how concepts that resemble our notion of ontological information have been presented in the existing research literature. This includes the research of a cosmologist (Michał Heller 1987, 2014), physicists (Carl von Weizsäcker 1970, Krzysztof Turek 1978, Tom Stonier 1990), philosophers (John Collier 1989, Thomas Nagel 2012), computer scientists with philosophical leanings (Mynarski 1981, Jadacki 2005), a philosopher and concert pianist (Anna Brożek 2005), a computer scientist and philosopher (Gordana Dodig Crnkovic 2012), and a computer expert in Big Data (Cesary Hidalgo 2015). Von Weizsäcker's information is a mixture of concrete and abstract concepts, but what is important is his admission that information itself cannot be just a thought—it must be something in nature. He fails, however, to explain exactly what he means by this. Summarizing Turek's work, we may conclude that in the world of things (i.e., the universe), shapes are due to the factor of form, while individuation is due to prime matter. Form is realized in a physical medium as structure in the sense explained earlier, and this structure is information, so all the products of nature contain information as a structuring element. This element is epistemically neutral, meaning that it exists not because we or someone else perceive it, but simply because that's how nature is. Mynarski, meanwhile, bases his idea of information in cybernetics as being conceived not just as the science of systems but as a general paradigm of nature. Thus, for Mynarski, information is as much a part of nature as energy and matter are, but Mynarski's information still in some way depends upon a system to recognize it as information. Collier, meanwhile, recognizes two kinds of information, namely, information with meaning and information without meaning, where the latter is an intrinsic property of nature. According to Stonier, there are two types of information: (a) physical information that exists independently without meaning, and this forms the fabric of the universe, and (b) information with meaning, which is interpreted as information for someone or something. Heller, meanwhile, identifies information with the "hidden" structures of the universe. Next, Dodig Crnkovic sees one form of information, namely, physical information, as being expressed in natural structures. According to her, the constant changes in these structures are a form of natural computation. Hidalgo, meanwhile, claims that information is the form of natural objects and artifacts, so according to him, everything around us contains information. Next, Jadacki and Brożek claim that information is the physical structure of natural phenomena that exist independently of our presence. According to Nagel, though, structure is a feature of nature that has been driving the evolution of organisms and the mind. This natural information is, in his view, primarily the causal order for information that is created by the mind. In all the above studies, information is recognized as being some sort of organizational factor in nature, one that is objective, all pervading, and fundamental, because without this, the concept of nature (and consequently nature itself) would not be possible. The authors rarely coin a special term for it, however, and simply refer to it as information with some specific properties or information that has certain utilitarian functions or operational significance.

3.1 Studies

Diverse perspectives from scholars in different fields (e.g., cosmologists, philosophers, physicists, and computer scientists) are important for this study. Keeping a narrow focus on one or two disciplines, such as mathematics or computing, or limiting views to just one or two authors would lead to this study presenting conclusions that were narrowly conceived, idiosyncratic, specialized, and domain specific. Such conclusions would not have universal import for our metaphysical understanding. Thus, a wider range of perspectives will help mitigate this potential criticism, although it is still of course not inconceivable.

In each of the passages presented, the term "information" should be understood precisely as each specific author intended it to be. In the subsequent analysis, concepts of information, form, structure, and other key concepts will be attributed to a particular author if and when required for the sake of clarity.

Note: What follows is not a detailed picture of the metaphysics of information being presented by each specific writer. Many aspects that these authors discussed have been omitted, with only those fragments that pertain to this study's topic being presented. However, these selections were made under the understanding that they could be presented outside the context of the larger work while preserving the author's intended meaning.

3.1.1 *Between the mind, nature, and language*

Carl von Weizsäcker (1971), in his work *Die Einheit der Natur*,[1] explores several facets of the concept of information. He seeks the *objective character of information*, with *objective* meaning something that is *independent of a human subject* or *independent of the physical carrier* (e.g., a sheet of paper or a telegram). In short, *objective* means that something that is common across physical carriers exists independently of them. He claims that information reduced to language, which is the most common meaning associated with information, is insufficient to explain what information is. Instead, von Weizsäcker understands "language" as a general means of communication between human agents rather than the written or spoken form of any particular language.

Von Weizsäcker claims that information is not a thought (i.e., a product of consciousness or the mind), nor is it a material object (i.e., it is not concrete). What is more, information is not a telegram or a collection of letters (i.e., ink blots on paper). He says information is not a message that can be understood. In other words, it is not a message conveying particular facts.

Further, von Weizsäcker claims that information is fundamental to nature, and it has no meaning or intentionality like consciousness does. He says that information is some third "thing" that is independent of consciousness and matter (i.e., the physical world). Von Weizsäcker therefore fashions a puzzle here: If information is not physical (i.e., it is independent of matter) and not related to consciousness (i.e., is independent of the mind), then what is it?

---

[1]Note that the page numbers refer to the Polish edition of Carl von Weizsäcker's 1971 book *Die Einheit der Natur*, Munchen: Verlag, Berlin. Polish edition, 1978, PIW, Warszawa.

He does not tell us. He later claims that information must have meaning, but meaning is always associated with some sort of intellect—whether human, animal, or artificial—and a conscious agent.[2] So, if information is not material, and if it is separated from the consciousness as the source of meaning, yet it has meaning, where is this meaning located? What is it? It seems that von Weizsäcker faces the same dilemma that was indicated by Paul Davies, namely, that of abstract versus concrete information.

He observes that information has the characteristics of Platonist *Form* or Aristotelian *eidos*, but these notions must be rendered in a modern conceptual framework to be properly understood. Many researchers, as indeed von Weizsäcker does, point to similarities in the ancient concepts of *Form* and *eidos* as early intuitions about information acting as a forming factor in nature, but they stress that these ancient terms must be reinterpreted within the context of our current knowledge of nature. In other words, they cannot just be adopted "as is" for our metaphysical debate. The open question is therefore what should we adopt from the old concepts and what should we leave out? Thus, von Weizsäcker's statement that information is like *Platonic form, or Aristotelian eidos, interpreted within the XX century idiom* is not entirely clear or satisfying.

Von Weizsäcker returns to the (original) Latin meaning of information, where *informare* means to form or give form. Information, in this context, possesses causal power in that it is responsible for the shape/form of objects (i.e., information gives shape). However, the terms "shape" and "form" do not correspond to an object's external three-dimensional geometric configuration but rather to its *eidos* (i.e., what that object is). This distinction is not entirely obvious,

---

[2]What is meaning, how it arises, and whether a conscious biological agent is needed to be present for meaning to be created are questions without a good answer. Here, we make the certain assumption that nature by itself is meaningless, with meaning being created by, and for, an agent interacting with nature. Such an agent must have a certain level of complexity in its cognitive system to create meaning. Precisely what level of complexity is needed here is discussed in Chapter 6.

because the *eidos* of something is related to its geometric shape, yet they are not the same. What is more, *eidos* itself has several other interpretations beyond geometry. Unfortunately, von Weizsäcker is not clear about what he precisely means by *eidos*. He posits that information cannot be understood in isolation from matter–energy, and it should be connected with matter–consciousness. How exactly this complex of matter, consciousness, and information should be brought about, as well as what it is in relation to modern physics and contemporary concepts of matter and energy, is not explained. For von Weizsäcker, the matter–consciousness–information complex is an obscure concept, so it remains for the reader. It seems that consciousness would need to be transcendental like Descartes' *res cogitans* rather than something empirical. As von Weizsäcker observes, the terms "matter–consciousness" and "transcendental" in this context are rather obtuse in that they do not explain much. However, even if it is somewhat confused, this claim would suggest that information does not depend on the mind for existence. Later on, however, there are passages in which von Weizsäcker seems to claim the opposite.

Von Weizsäcker assumes an intuitive understanding of the terms "form", "shape", and "structure" and does not try to provide any formal definitions. Thus, we accept these intuitions at face value and deduce their meaning from the context. Indeed, the terms need to be taken literally without implying any deeper theory or connection to some metaphysical or physical theory, simply because this is not intimated by the author. We need to keep this in mind and not assume that that von Weizsäcker seeks to revive Platonic ontology and Aristotelian hylomorphism in their original forms, because he has already cautioned against these interpretations. Indeed, he made it clear that such ancient concepts need to be reinterpreted in a new language, although he did not indicate what this new language may be. This note of caution from von Weizsäcker is not really such a revelation, however, because no sane person would take the Ancient Greeks so literally.

So, what else can we learn about information from von Weizsäcker? Information is comprehended by the senses, but it is not the specific physical form that one perceives, such as the particular shape of a letter of the alphabet. Information is something different, and it comes from the immediate sensual form of an object or phenomenon. Moreover, information is intentional in the sense that a thought is an intentional act. For von Weizsäcker, this means that every thought has meaning. In the modern interpretation of thought, thoughts are intentional and directed toward some object, which is somewhat equivalent to having meaning (Searle 1983). Thus, for von Weizsäcker, information depends upon consciousness, yet it is separated from it. This claim seems rather strange.

Von Weizsäcker posits that information is an abstraction of the form/shape of thought. Information is carried in a shape/form that can be sensed (e.g., sound waves and electric impulses), yet it is not the medium itself (i.e., not the sound waves or electrical impulses). Information is what these objects or phenomena convey, in some way, and it is common among the different physical carriers. However, if information is common among different physical carriers, what is it? Where is it? Von Weizsäcker's claim only makes sense if we assume that information is something extra-physical and (von Weizsäcker ends his discussion on this note) subsists in the mind in some form, or that information has an independent existence like in Popper's third world. Any of the three options brings significant metaphysical and ontological consequences. One may argue that it is a shadow of Descartes' dualism (the mind–body separation), which is quite a common problem in the study of information, because literal Cartesian dualism is difficult to maintain in the light of the modern philosophy of cognition and neuroscience (e.g., Robinson 2017).

Von Weizsäcker argues against the concept of information as an objective, meaningless element of nature. This discussion introduces certain incoherence, because information cannot be *form* or *eidos*, even in von Weizsäcker's reduced version of these notions, and at the same time mind-dependent, as he claims in previous fragments. Von Weizsäcker clearly identifies information with an (en) coding (an intentional representation of thought) and certain intentional processes (e.g., creating *a series of electrical impulses in computers*). He does not consider the form/shape of natural phenomena or objects that do not convey thought as information. He also admits that the division between information-carrying form (i.e., a linguistic form carrying information as some sort of language) and a form that is not information (i.e., not a linguistic form) is fluid but nevertheless required and real. The term "fluid" in von Weizsäcker text means relative.

We may ask what this is relative to and how? What would it mean to have two entities with a fluid boundary between them? How could we say that one is this and another is that? All these questions arise from von Weizsäcker's ambiguity about information. Von Weizsäcker's concept of language is based on a series of intentional signs/forms but abstracted from their particular realizations. This may indicate some kind of proto-language, but it is not a language that anyone may speak. Is it therefore the language of thought? Or, is it thought itself? Von Weizsäcker is unclear here. For von Weizsäcker, language, of sorts, seems to be critical in conceptualizing information. This is generally always the case when the concept of information is relative to cognitive agents. Von Weizsäcker seems to express the concern that the conductor Kent Nagano put in the following statement: *Without language there is nothing; without language there is no thinking, no consciousness, no human existence* (Nagano 2019, p. 36). We agree with the claim that language is fundamental to humanity and human culture, but Nagano's statement needs revising: Nagano's "nothing" is not "nothing" as in "no existence" (i.e., an ontological nothing) but rather the absence of the thought and consciousness that typifies human existence. Nagano therefore forgets about nature, as did von Weizsäcker. While this omission is not surprising for an orchestra conductor (Nagano), it is for a professional physicist like von Weizsäcker. Music will not exist if we are not here, but nature will.

Von Weizsäcker claims that for a shape/form to be information, there must be a communicator (i.e., a sender) and at least a potential receiver. Language here is understood as the means of communication. Von Weizsäcker clearly refers to the Shannon–Weaver–Hartley

Theory of Communication (ToC) and the model of communication (i.e., sender, channel, message, and receiver) in general (e.g., Cherry 1978, Pierce 1961). This is why for von Weizsäcker there is no "genetic information" in DNA, because you cannot identify a human or other subject as the sender or receiver of such a "genetic language". Of course, this view comes from the early seventies of the 20th century. These days, we have no problem in assigning an informational interpretation to DNA. For examples of this, see the works of Yockey (1999, 2005), Barbieri (2016), Cartwright *et al.* (2016), Gonzales *et al.* (2016), Koonin (2016), Roederer (2016), Walker *et al.* (2016), Wills (2016), and Davies (2019).

Von Weizsäcker's view of information in the context of the communication process is clearly a literal interpretation of Shannon's communication model (or indeed any generic communication model) (Cherry, *op. cit.*). Von Weizsäcker tries to reinterpret this model by adding the dimension of meaning, but as we know, the Shannon–Weaver–Hartley information concept explicitly focuses on structure (i.e., the statistical structure of a language) to the exclusion of meaning.

Von Weizsäcker adopts a very narrow understanding of communication as an exchange (of information) between human agents. He does not consider machine-to-machine (M2M)[3] communication or communication between artificial agents or biological forms. It is therefore a purely anthropomorphic perspective, and such a perspective will clearly result in anthropomorphic information. Maybe this is a sign of the times when von Weizsäcker was writing his book (1970), when information technology was in its early stages. Von Weizsäcker's perspective, which was rather common in the 1970s, obviously evolved, as we can see when reading research from later decades. Von Weizsäcker is unable to disassociate the

---

[3] *Machine-to-Machine (M2M) communication is a form of data* ("White Paper on M2M" 2019). In fact, M2M covers many variants of communication, including Man-to-Machine and Machine-to-Man (communication between a human-operated device and a machine). See, for example, Pandey (2016), Pawan *et al.* (2016, pp. 83–105), Zanini (2017), and Galetić *et al.* (2019).

notion of information from language and its narrow definition as a human communication tool. Yet, in the following sentences, he cannot resist the attraction of the idea of meaning-free information.

Von Weizsäcker considers the concept of information to be similar to ontological information in this study, so it is information existing objectively without meaning and *without reference to language or communication.* He even identifies it with measurable structures. However, he states that he cannot accept the concept of meaningless information. He claims one needs a language to bestow the concept of information on physical structure. Thus, for him, a structure is an enumerable, measurable, perceivable element or aspect of nature, and if it is measurable, it must be in some sense "visible" or available for sensual introspection. However, he also sees (as expressed in the earlier claims) structure as *eidos* (i.e., the essence of a thing), and *eidos* is not perceived by the senses but rather intuited or rationalized (i.e., we need *eidos* to have objects). So, how can a structure be *eidos* and yet be measurable? Would this imply that a measurable structure is just an expression/representation of *eidos*? It seems that information is either a sensible structure or it is *eidos*—it cannot be both, because how can the external shape be the cause of itself? In other words, how can it have the causal power of *informare* (i.e., shape-giving) if it is conceived as a perceivable structure? All structures are notoriously difficult to define at the fundamental level, which is why modern structural realism often skirts the question of what a structure is and tries to get away with some domain-specific definitions. By locking himself in a definition of structure as an enumerable, sensory object, von Weizsäcker loses an opportunity to free himself from anthropomorphism and the assumption that measurement is a quintessentially human domain.

3.1.2 *Form, structure, and information*

Krzysztof Turek (1978), for his part, introduces the notion of information as a physical phenomenon without meaning. In addition, Turek's information is not related to any communication system or process but rather expressed in the internal/hidden structure (or form) of things. These terms will be explained in detail, because Turek provides specific, narrow definitions that differ from the meanings usually associated with them.[4]

Turek's interpretation of the meaning of the Latin word *informare* goes beyond the usual readings of this term, such as by Carl von Weizsäcker. Turek points out that this Latin word suggests that (a) information is a causal factor in shaping things (objects) (i.e., *giving form, shape* and *creating form*) and that (b) the shape, in this case, is the internal form of the thing.

Turek explains that the meaning of the internal shape of an object, which is attributed to information, can be found in the concept of what he calls *hylemorphism*, a sort of form–matter composite. Indeed, the word "composite" may be a better choice than hylemorphism for denoting Turek's proposed concept, because Turek's form–matter composite has a very narrow interpretation when compared to Aristotelian hylemorphism.[5] As such, it does not carry all the baggage that comes with Aristotelian metaphysics. It should therefore be interpreted strictly according to Turek's explanation rather than Aristotle's.

So, what is form and what is matter in Turek's form–matter composite? Form for Turek is an element that shapes formless matter. It imposes upon matter its external contours or shape, as well as its internal configuration. Turek restates the position of realism, where reality exists independently of us and our conceptual schemes, linguistic practices, perceptions, and beliefs, while our thoughts accurately reflect the external world.[6] Without this, the whole discussion

---

[4]Turek's writings, which are in Polish, have been translated by the author.

[5]Aristotelian hylemorphism clearly has several acute problems that exclude it as a potential model for information, at least when following the original too closely.

[6]This claim is obviously a shorthanded complex epistemic claim that we have, within the limits of our sensory and cognitive systems, contact with the world as it is rather than its image, reflection, or other facsimile. Our senses and our minds have evolved to relay to us the state of what is out there, so we can survive (e.g., Searle 1998). In Searle's terms, we have a direct experience of outside reality, not mediated by any other construct (we do not see "the world by means of seeing something else first" (Searle 2015c). By introducing any intermediate objects, we run into unsolvable problems.

would be meaningless, and we could not talk about the world out-side of us as having any independent properties. As we will see, this position creates some tensions in Turek's philosophy, because later in his writings, he suggests some kind of mind–matter separation, implying the dual nature of reality (i.e., mind and matter).

The role of form and matter in the form–matter composite, in Turek's work, is illustrated through the example of a collection of identical billiard balls. We have a collection of individual objects with the same form, external shape, and internal constitution (i.e., a billiard ball). We implicitly assume that these balls are made out of the same "matter" and have exactly the same shape. Matter, how-ever, imposes individuality on each ball, making them unique. This individualization includes occupying an exclusive location in space, because no two balls can be in the same place at the same time. The form (i.e., a billiard ball) shapes matter into individual instances of the same genus. There is no priority between form and matter, and they cannot exist separately. In the example, the balls may seem like identical objects because of their shared form, but they are individual objects due to matter.[7]

Turek relates the concept of form to the concept of structure. An abstract structure is a system with a given number of collections (or sets),[8] as well as relations between elements of those collections. An abstract structure can be exemplified by a DNA polymer, which is a highly organized complex of interconnected units of molecules that form complexes at multiple levels of organization, from the atomic to the molecular level. This is in fact a structure of structures, a struc-ture whose elements are other structures.[9] The concept of a structure

---

[7]It is an open question as to whether a location in space is a sufficient criterion for individuation. See, for example, Ladyman (2015).

[8]Strictly speaking, it would be a mistake to equate collections with sets, because sets come with certain implied properties, while collections do not have such restrictions.

[9]This example comes close to the following interpretation of the Aristotelian form–matter composite: *In one understanding of matter, it is the counterpart of form—the stuff that gets informed—so that whenever there is a form, there must also be some matter that serves as its subject. In this conception, there will often be hierarchies of matter, with the most basic stuff, prime matter, at the bottom,*

is contained within the concept of a form, meaning that every structure is a form, but not every form is necessarily a structure. Turek explains that the concepts of form, structure, and information are closely related, but they are not the same, as we can see in Turek's definition of information as *a certain subset of sets of forms reducible to structure.*

Turek defines three types of forms. Forms may or may not contain structures, and the differentiation between forms containing structures and forms that are reducible to structures defines the boundary between reductionist and non-reductionist theories. By claiming that every form is reducible to structure, we assume that every structure can be represented in a formal language (i.e., described by some symbolic system), so we ultimately claim that everything is reducible to the language of logic and mathematics. In other words, we assert that the logico-mathematical representation is complete with respect to the universe. Forms without structures, meanwhile, are mental in nature. We can only describe them as simple, non-definable concepts taken to the limits. This claim obviously incurs some kind of mind–body dualism. While Turek can certainly posit the dual nature of reality, this puts him on a collision course with most of the contemporary philosophies of the mind and cognitive theories that claim that a purely physical description of nature is complete. While Turek's claim of dualism makes his proposal difficult to accept as a whole, it does not invalidate his concept of information. As we have seen already, and we will continue to see in other work, the act of balancing two aspects of information (i.e., abstract and concrete) pervades the philosophy of information (e.g., von Weizsäcker 1971, Floridi 2013, Davies 2016).

Turek defines information using the concepts of substance and form. In Turek's view, substance is not necessarily the Aristotelian substance but rather an individual complex of form and matter.

---

and various form–matter composites at higher levels, which may themselves be conceived of as the matter for some further form. Wood, for example, is a form–matter composite that can itself serve as the matter for a bed (Pasnau 2015). This commonsense interpretation of hylemorphism comes from medieval times, but it was controversial even then.

Turek's substance can therefore be anything that can be differentiated as a form–matter composite, so it includes artifacts and natural objects. Example substances offered by Turek include spoken or written language, a magnetic tape, a computer punch card, a chromosome, a man, a computer, and a natural object. All these entities are concrete and belong to some genus. Turek writes, *if a certain substance S1 is formed by the finite structure I or its fragment, and the structure S2 can be formed by a structure I, I is called information* (Turek 1978, p. 4). In other words, a substance S1 is constituted/formed by the finite structure I (i.e., it has a finite number of elements), so if a substance S2 can also be potentially formed by structure I, we refer to structure I as "information". Thus, information is one of three enumerated types of form that can be either imposed on matter (prime matter) or found in substance (form–matter composite). The former is of type (a) (see above), while the latter is of type (b). Information can also be both realized and potential. In the case where the form has a structure (i.e., type (a) and maybe type (b)), information may be represented by logical and mathematical formalisms. Information must be, or is, what is potentially realizable or what has been realized in substance, as it is understood above. Structures that are infinite and conceptual (i.e., mental concepts) or structures that express categories or genera are not information in the sense set down by Turek. The nature of such abstract structures differs from the nature of structures as it is understood in this study. There is no further explanation in Turek's work about what these abstract structures could be, although some similarities with Davies' real–abstract dilemma for information come to mind.

Interpretations of information, like those in Shannon's ToC or information in an epistemic or linguistic context, derive from the concept of form in type (a). The substance here is understood as a complex/unification/fusion/oneness of matter and form. Information in this view is a species of structure. In Turek's view, there are abstract structures that resemble functions (i.e., relations/mappings between sets) and embodied/physical structures that are objects of scientific research. These embodied structures are formed by the elements of reality, namely, objects and relations. This definition of structure should not be taken as an ultimate definition but instead limited to just what Turek understands as a structure.

Thus, summarizing Turek's work, we may say that in the world of things (i.e., the universe), shapes are due to form and individuation is due to prime matter. Form realized in a physical medium is structure in the sense explained above, and this structure is information, so all elements of nature contain information as a structuring element. This is an epistemically neutral element of nature. This means that this element exists not because we perceive it, or because someone else perceives it, but because nature is this way. When reading Turek's work, the terms "information", "form", and "structure" must be interpreted as Turek's idioms. Alternative interpretations will distort the argument, so they should not be used with the principle of charity in mind,[10] because this would lead to bad philosophy.

3.1.3 *Between the physical and the abstract*

Stefan Mynarski (1981), in *Elements of system theory and cybernetics*, states that the term "information" without any qualifiers can denote quite dissimilar concepts, both real and abstract. He says that two kinds of information can be differentiated, information related to a physical object (i.e., anything physical) and information without a physical reference. In the former case, we have what he calls "real information", while in the latter case, we have "abstract information". Mynarski describes "abstract information" as being related to events or phenomena that do not exist as physical entities, so such information is created by the mind. We may say that it is a thought, assuming that thoughts are the content of the mind.

---

[10]The principle of charity, as it is used in this context, is not the principle governing the Red Cross, for example, although this may accidentally be the case. Instead, *The principle of charity governs the interpretation of the beliefs and utterances of others. It urges charitable interpretation, meaning interpretation that maximizes the truth or rationality of what others think and say* (Feldman 1998). See also Woodhouse (1994).

Abstract information, as a creation of the mind, bears a strong resemblance to epistemic information as it is defined in this work, although with the restriction that epistemic information is information about any phenomenon, whether it exists or not and not necessarily in the past or future. (These restrictions are imposed by Mynarski.) We are unsure how Mynarski interprets the verb "exist" in his work, but it cannot carry the same meaning for "real" (physical) and "abstract" information. A charitable reading of the text suggests that Mynarski is aware of the nuances for the existence of real and abstract entities, because he differentiates them into the physical and the abstract. However, he does not qualify the verb "exist". We focus here on "real information", information that exists in physical things or is connected with physical phenomena.

Mynarski begins with a claim that information, or real information, is fundamental, although this term is not clearly explained by Mynarski. His concept of information is related to the organization of a system, to its structure. The degree of "structural complexity" is inversely related to the system's undefinability. In other words, the more structure/organization a system possesses, the less that remains unknown about the system (i.e., it can be more precisely defined). Mynarski denotes this information as "structural information". This is a measure of a system's organization and consequently its undefinability or definability, depending on which way one views it. Mynarski does not explain what kind of a measure information is, such as probabilistic, deterministic, and something else. We may only guess from the later chapters of the book that Mynarski attempts to connect his concept of "real information as a measure" or his "structural information" with the concepts for measuring the amount of information that were defined by Shannon and Hartley. Alternatively, maybe we could interpret the "measurability of information" as simply being quantifiable.[11] However, every system, even a completely

---

[11]The term "measure" may have philosophical and mathematical interpretations. Finkelstein defines it as *a symbol assigned empirically, objectively to attributes of objects and events of the real world in such a way as to represent them, or to describe them* (Finkelstein 2005). In a stricter sense, a measure is a function that assigns a non-negative number to a subset of a set X under certain properties.

unorganized one, can be quantified (see, for example, Chaitin's measure of algorithmic complexity). Thus, the term "definability", if it means "quantifiability", requires some explanation, but one is not offered by Mynarski.

Furthermore, Mynarski discusses how real information (i.e., information in physical things) relates to fundamental concepts of physics. He states that information is the third constitutive element of nature, with the first two being matter and energy. Structural/real information defines the *positioning/configuration* of elements in the organization of matter–energy systems. While the matter–energy balance is constant, the structure is not, so it changes, and this change of structure is equivalent to a change in information.

Mynarski states that any physical system may be conceptualized along the three dimensions of matter, energy, and information. Matter provides mass, substance, and phase. Energy is the ability of matter to change,[12] while information is the degree of organization, or to put it differently, it is the capacity of a system to yield to rational description.[13] Thus, physical things in Mynarski's metaphysics have three components/dimensions, each being equally important. In the modern view, the distinction between matter, energy, and information would be blended into matter–energy and information, suggesting that physical things are energy–matter phenomena that are shaped by information. Such an interpretation conforms, at least at face value, to the original ancient meaning of information as *informare* or giving shape. The concepts of matter and energy in

---

The Shannon–Hartley measure of information is defined under the axioms of the Kolmogorov Probability Theory and is therefore a probability measure (Hájek 2012).

[12]This definition of energy is rather simplistic, so it needs to be taken not as a strict definition but rather as a simplification of it. However, the inaccuracy of this definition does not affect the understanding of information.

[13]We may ask whether an irrational description is possible. Would this mean it is incoherent? It seems that any description must already have some rationality in it. Thus, the term rationality must be further qualified to avoid ambiguity, but such an explanation is not offered by Mynarski.

Mynarski's work are not explained further, so it appears that he does not use them in the strict physical sense, because this would require further elaboration, but rather in the popular interpretations of the terms. (Mynarski was not a physicist.) Furthermore, Mynarski states that we may also look at the concepts of matter, energy, and information in three dimensions: matter–energy, matter–information, and energy–information. The first dimension defines the thermodynamic properties of the system and energy changes. The second dimension defines the properties that are dependent on the organization of the system's components, while the third dimension defines the capacity of the system to transfer/exchange/change information or communicate it. Only in these pair-wise combinations do these three dimensions provide a complete description of the properties of a physical system. Of course, this is just Mynarski's view and not a theory of physics.

Mynarski claims that information (i.e., real information) is the most important of these three dimensions, because it introduces coherence, structure, and order into reality, although the three elements of physical reality—matter, energy, and information—are mutually dependent. Mynarski concludes that these three elements are the foundations of reality or even, as he states, existence. One may argue, however, about the precise meaning of the claim that *energy cannot exist without matter*. One may ponder what Mynarski means here, seeing as how matter and energy are quantifiably equivalent in modern physics. Mynarski's suggested relationship between information and energy (i.e., that information cannot exist without energy) has also been indicated by other researchers, such as Landauer (1996) and Ladyman *et al.* (2007), even if the nature of such a coexistence is not entirely clear or without controversy. These dependencies have been explored further through Landauer's (1996) principle and the research on Maxwell's demon. See, for example, Landauer (1996), Bennett (2003), Lutz (2012), Ladyman *et al.* (2007), Moore (2012), and Hong *et al.* (2016).

The claim about information and energy does not concern some causal relation between energy and information. It only stipulates the existence of some sort of dependency between energy and information.[14] The connection between matter, energy, and information, in Mynarski's study, is an intuitive observation rather than an empirically confirmed fact, because he does not propose any adequate physical theory or experimental observations in support of this thesis. (Note that Landauer published his findings more than a decade later.) Thus, it is safer to regard these intuitions as merely plausible conjecture, at least in the context of Mynarski's study. However, such connections have resurfaced in several works in the form of the entropy of physical systems and information as its quantification, as well as in Landauer's ideas about the physical nature of information. Thus, Mynarski's intuitions, while not grounded in a solid physical study, may not be completely off the mark.[15]

3.1.4 *Information in and about things*

John Collier (Collier 1990) introduces two concepts of information: information-in-things (IiT), which is intrinsic information or information$_{INT}$ and denotes the structure/information embedded in physical things, and cognitive information (CT) or information$_{CT}$, which denotes information gleaned by a cognitive agent. Collier states that information$_{INT}$ is non-intentional (i.e., not about something),[16] but it is a (partial) cause of CT. (Alternatively, maybe we should describe it as a primary source?) There is no direct relation (i.e.,

---

[14]One may wonder about this relation in the light of a claim by Majewski (2020) that "Miracles are information overtaking energy". But, this claim was made by an artist, not a scientist so it must be seen as a piece of poetry.

[15]It often happens in science that intuitions predate the mathematical or formal expressions of phenomena. This was the case with Newton's theory of universal gravitation. It was first conceptualized as an intuition by Hooke, although Newton never acknowledged his debt to him. Two views of "gravitational forces" existed in Newton's times: Descartes' theory of vortices and Hooke's concept of gravitation as attraction between masses. Initially, Newton preferred Descartes' solution, but Hooke's intuition ultimately won (Guicciardini 2018). It may therefore be a similar story with Mynarski's view of information.

[16]*Intentionality is that feature of the mind by which mental states are directed at, or are about, or refer to, or aim at, states of affairs in the world* (Searle 1998, p. 64).

a one-to-one mapping) between information$_{INT}$ and information$_{CT}$. The emergence or creation of CT is a complex process that is not completely understood. This process involves the combination of sensory information, background information, and other factors. (Note that this creates the problem of how the cognitive agent creates the meaning.) The emergence or creation of CT is not discussed further in this study. Collier attributes causal powers to information$_{INT}$, but only in relation to information$_{CT}$ rather than with respect to nature. Collier argues that nature has a structure or organization, so we may say that natural objects are structural. However, he is not clear whether these structures are information itself or the results of information. Maybe the effect of information on things should be understood in the same sense as energy, which is not seen not as energy itself but rather through changes in the physical state of objects?

Collier justifies his claim of a causal factor existing behind information$_{CT}$ by stipulating that information$_{CT}$ (i.e., information "assimilated" by a cognitive agent) must correlate with the outside world to be reasonably predictable and regular. Collier states that the notion of information is not related to cognitive gains, because it is more general than the notion associated with cognition. In other words, information$_{CT}$ is a subspecies of information$_{INT}$. Furthermore, Collier observes that external objects (i.e., nature) must have a property that is a source of information for cognitive agents. This property is communicable, and it is foundational for CT. For Collier, information$_{CT}$ denotes information that is derived from an interpretation of information$_{INT}$ by the cognitive agent. Information$_{CT}$ therefore corresponds to our concept of epistemic information in this work.

Collier posits that the (primary)[17] source of CT is the external world (i.e., information$_{INT}$). Information$_{CT}$ is therefore constructed from outside stimuli by a cognitive system/agent, so this agent creates epistemic or semantic information. Thus, information$_{CT}$ must

---

[17]The term "primary source" means that cognitive information is "blended" with the content of the mind and mind-specific processes, which are components that may, in principle, differ between individuals.

have causal sources in the physical constituency of the world, otherwise information$_{CT}$ would represent phantasms, illusions, or mirages. By creating information$_{CT}$, the mind imposes meaning upon the otherwise epistemically neutral information$_{INT}$.

But, how is meaning derived from epistemically neutral stimuli by a cognitive system? One answer would be to say that no meaning is conveyed in the neural stimuli. Another answer would claim that information$_{INT}$ must be somehow isomorphic to information$_{CT}$, because these two information modes are highly correlated, although the latter one is "augmented" by meaning.[18] The precise notion of what he means by "isomorphic" here is not explained by Collier. Indeed, the creation of meaning is a problem for the theory of meaning, so it falls outside the scope of this study. The problem of meaning and the question of its *loci* (i.e., where it is seated) are part of an ongoing discussion between externalists and internalists.[19] However, it seems that Collier's claim that the substrate of information$_{CT}$ is physical, and that this substrate exists in physical things regardless of the presence of any cognitive system, is impervious to these discussions on the creation of meaning.

3.1.5 *The universe is information*

Tom Stonier (1990) conceptualizes information as the third fundamental element of nature, with matter and energy being the first two. Stonier claims that information, together with matter and energy, is a part of the universe. However, information is not immediately visible, or at least observable, in the same way that matter and energy are. Stonier adopts the term "internal structure" to express the role of information in nature, using this term to state that while the visible

---

[18]The meaning assigned to sensory stimuli is agent-dependent. For a trained ear, a noise in the forest can represent the calling of an elk, but to an untrained ear, it is just a noise. Ambiguous imagery like the rabbit–duck illusion is a good example of how the mind imposes meaning on otherwise meaningless optical stimuli (Myers 2003).

[19]This is part of a larger discussion about where meaning is located, such as whether it is external or internal to the cognitive system.

shapes/forms of objects and phenomena reflect the existence of information, they are not what information really is. That is why when we talk about information, we usually do not consider the external three-dimensional structure of things (i.e., the visible shape). Information is therefore not the shape of the letters printed on a telegram or the notes in a musical score but rather something behind them. Stonier says that information is *more subtle* than what is obvious to the senses. Stonier takes the *text-book case* of a falling tree in the forest to demonstrate how the anthropocentric perspective on nature limits our understanding of natural phenomena, including information. In this case, the word "Anthropomorphic" refers to seeing information as being dependent upon the (re)actions of a human agent. The lesson to take from the example of the falling tree is that if we limit our concept of information to the human perspective, we forget its real "nature". In other words, we forget that we left something out from the phenomena, namely, its physical nature.

Further, Stonier points out that as energy, which is the fundamental element of reality, has different forms of appearance or realization, so does information. Thus, anthropomorphic information is just one realization of information, a mode under which it appears to us. This is a significant claim, because it goes against all the epistemic definitions of information that prevail in the current discourse, namely, that information is something that has some meaning to a human observer (or, more generally, any cognitive agent). Information has different physical realizations and different physical carriers. Thus, one cannot assume that information is the external shape of the physical carrier. These "external forms" differ depending on the carrier media. Stonier posits that the diversity of carriers used in the communication of information demonstrates that information has physical realization, so it is a property of nature (or the universe) in the sense that everything that exists contains information. We just have problems recognizing information as a property of nature, preferring instead to focus exclusively on our own perspective

So, what is information for Stonier? He proposes several definitions. What is more, he says information is a part of the universe, so this is "physical information". There is also the information of an interpreter (i.e., cognitive agent interpreting physical information) or interpreted information. The difference between physical and interpreted information lies in the meaning added to the physical information. Physical information has no meaning and exists independently/objectively with an independent reality. Information equated with meaning therefore exists for some agent, and it is *physical information interpreted*, as Stonier states that meaning is not information but rather an aspect of information.

Thus, according to Stonier, we have two types of information: (a) physical information existing independently without meaning and (b) information with meaning, at least for someone or, in other words, interpreted information. For Stonier, it is generally a human agent or other living system that does the interpretation, although again we do not have a fine differentiation here for what forms of living systems (e.g., animals, plants, and bacteria) perform interpretation and thus add meaning to physical information. It seems that these more subtle divisions came to light later around the transition from the 20th to the 21st century, because artificial agents, tree lovers, and animal activists were not yet common at the time. Stonier's division of information clearly separates ontological and epistemic information, as also proposed in this current work. Stonier goes further by declaring that this information does not need to be perceived, it has no meaning, and is necessary to understand the universe.

Stonier defines meaning as the relationship between physical information and mental representation. Of course, limiting meaning to "mental interpretations" inevitably excludes artificial and natural agents as interpreters of information. "Meaning", as it is understood in this study, does not have such limitations, so it is more general than Stonier's concept of meaning. To characterize this relationship, Stonier uses the term "gradient". This would suggest meaning having different quantifiable (as they can be ordered by a gradient) realizations for different agents, not just from agent to agent of the same species but across species. Such an interpretation would confirm our current understanding of meaning in that it is very subjective. Stonier uses the predicates "real", "latent", and "potential" to enumerate the different modes in which information can be conceived. Stonier emphasizes that these terms denote the same thing, however, so they are not different types of information. They are just different modes in which that information can be perceived. In other words, "information" is the same under all these denotations, but they show different aspects of information that may be mistaken for information itself.[20]

Moreover, Stonier observes that there is an opportunity to define a different concept of information if we are careful about the details of the conceptual context. This statement points to the reason behind different perceptions of the nature of information, many of which are often in conflict. The difference stems from the confusion between what exists and what is transferred, interpreted, or processed. It seems there is also a philosophical problem here: We resist attributing some physical, intrinsic capacities or role, even a causal role, to information, but this position brings us closer, as some would think, to Aristotle's *morphe* and *hylemorphism*, which have generally been judged as not being philosophically viable (at least in the original form). However, this may not hold true anymore,[21] at least for some aspects of this concept. As we saw with the works of Turek and Mynarski, Aristotle's *morphe* and *hylemorphism* may be impossible to defend, yet alone define, in their original formulation, but more restrictive modern interpretations may be formulated in a more acceptable way. Stonier formulates several interesting claims. The first is that chemical processes or physical processes (i.e., processes in inorganic matter) are, in general, information processes or processes manipulating information. The second claim is that the same can be said about organic processes (i.e., those which involve

---

[20]One cannot help but recall the parable of the blind men and the elephant (Shah 1974).

[21]See, for example, Marmodoro (2013), Austin (2017), or Rea (2014). Also, *Aristotle famously held that objects are comprised of matter and form. That is the central doctrine of hylomorphism (sometimes rendered as "hylemorphism"—hyle, matter; morphe, form), and the view has become a live topic of inquiry today. Contemporary proponents of the doctrine include Jeffrey Brower, Kit Fine, David Hershenov, Mark Johnston, Kathrin Koslicki, Anna Marmodoro, Michael Rea, and Patrick Toner, among others. In the wake of these contemporary hylomorphic theories, the doctrine has seen application to various topics within mainstream analytic metaphysics* (Bailey and Wilkins 2018).

organic matter), so there are no material differences between these two types (inorganic and organic) processes. The obvious conclusion is therefore that natural processes are information processes in the sense that they manipulate information that is encoded in a physical structure. This information is perceived as patterns or organization. Alternatively, we may say that every physical object has some structure that encodes information. For Stonier, these "patterns of organization" are not information but rather encodings or expressions of information. We evidently see here an idea that would later reemerge as pancomputationalism, which is still a difficult pill to swallow for some because it requires a redefinition of what computing is.

Stonier links information with organization, but information is more than just a static organization—it has causal powers to organize systems. Energy is seen as the capacity to perform work, although this is a greatly simplified description of energy, so is the description that information is the capacity to create and maintain order. Stonier states that order is the opposite of randomness, but it is not clear what Stonier means here. Even seemingly random phenomena exhibit structure and can be quantified (e.g., Chaitin's measure of complexity or even Shannon's and other related measures for random phenomena). Stonier's randomness must refer to the lack of any visible (i.e., recognizable) organization. Further, Stonier states that information and order are not the same, demonstrating that he is not equating information with order or structure. He uses here the analogy of light and shadow to convey that organization is a "manifestation" of information. In other words, it is the result of information interacting with matter and energy, much like how a shadow is a result of light interacting with an object rather than just the light itself. This critical claim about the interaction between matter, energy, and information is not explained further, however. We may only guess that Stonier's view is that information can be perceived as organization and structure, but it is not identical to these phenomena.

Stonier describes information as an abstract concept, but with the addition of physical realization. Information is therefore not a concept that can be reduced to physical phenomena, like a rainbow, for example. It is more like energy, although it is not clear in what way, so this is more of an intuition. Stonier brings up the comparison between energy and information many times. Energy, before it was defined in its own right, had been disguised in several concepts, such as mass, force, heat, radiation, and work. Only in the process of understanding the nature of heat, mass, and work did the concept of energy finally emerge. The case is similar for information, which has been obfuscated by several concepts, such as form, shape, organization, and *morphe*. Only later was a common, unifying concept of information developed. Further, Stonier observes that to quantify these different notions, a new concept was needed: information. Just as energy was abstracted from concepts like mass, force, heat, work, and other energy-related phenomena, information was abstracted from concepts like form, shape, organization, and *morphe*. Only in this form could we start quantifying it and assign a number to it. However, we need to be careful not to fall into the trap of believing that if we can measure something, we know it. Associating information with numbers—such as in the cases of Shannon and Hartley, Fisher, and Chaitin, as well as Burgin (2003, 2005), who, as we will see later, lists about 32 mathematical formulas for information—does not clarify the essence of information. On the contrary, we may say these quantifications have rather blindsided us, acting as a red herring of sorts.

We may also see some incongruence emerging in Stonier's description of information. He claims that information may be converted from one physical form to another, but this is only true if we assign meaning to information. In our view, what is common between different carriers is meaning rather than information, at least if information is conceived as structure. If we see information purely in terms of physical form, there is no connection between, for example, a music sheet with Chopin's nocturnes and a recording of the same music on a compact disc, because their physical structures are radically different. These physical carriers embody different structures, so they contain different information in the sense of organization. Their similarity, however, lies in the meaning assigned to these structures by a cognitive agent, so recognizing this similarity requires the presence of the mind. (To be more accurate, we would have to refer to the presence of some sort of information-processing system.) Thus, what links two or more different physical structures—such as a music sheet, a pattern of air pressure waves, patterns of light pulses in an optical cable, magnetic patterns on a tape, the groves on a vinyl record, or the pit patterns on a compact disc—is simply the potential for these structures to be interpreted in the same way. Nothing intrinsic in the structures themselves makes them similar. For example, there is no intrinsic similarity between waves of air pressure conveying a sound and a digital recording of 0s and 1s or a music score written on a sheet and the grooves on an LP. The transfer of structures and organization in physical objects therefore needs to be mediated by the meaning in someone's mind (see also Brozek and Jadacki discussion on music later in this section as well as Chapters 6 and 7 on this topic).

One may ponder what the best word for information is, such as form, structure, organization, pattern, order, and so on. Stonier's use of these terms is not consistent. He may think that these words are synonymous or that none of them alone is adequate to define information, so they should all be used together. However, it seems that "structure" is not the right word after all. It implies, or may imply, the existence of something concrete and tangible, a sort of scaffold. Information does not seem to be like that, though. Terms like structure, organization, and pattern refer more to expressions of information or some factor imposing order or organization. Thus, it seems that the most fitting term for information, at least in Stonier's sense of it, is "order" or "organization". This conveys the causal role (formative power) of information and its effects on matter–energy in a way that other terms do not (or so it seems).

3.1.6 *Information is the mathematics of the heavens*

For Michał Heller, his view of information has resulted from studies into the fundamental structures of the cosmos (i.e., the universe), related mathematical models, and the properties of nature (i.e., physical phenomena here on Earth). In a series of observations, Heller

(Heller 2009) outlines his vision of information in nature. Heller posits that the laws of nature may be interpreted as information, or at least as providing information, and that this is a complementary view to the scientific structuralism. What he means by "complementary" here is not clear, but it may be interpreted as stating that there is no structural–information dichotomy in his view of nature, meaning that structure and information are both characteristics of nature. Heller, when interpreting Shannon's ToC, claims that an increase in the information content of a structure is inversely proportional to the structure's degrees of freedom.[22] Heller observes that the laws of nature impose certain constraints on nature's structures, so in a way, they control what can and cannot be, so not everything is possible in physics. What is possible is therefore just the limited, although very large, number of combinations for the fundamental elements, being constrained by physical laws. The presence of quantum or discrete building blocks therefore makes the universe possible. This view is also reflected in the models of the universe found in combinatorial ontologies, ancient atomism, or the ontologies of Leibnitz and Laplace.

The laws of nature, for Heller, act like information (they are not information, but act as like ...) and they determine or constrain what is possible. The more constrained or complex (and at the same time, less likely to exist) structures are, the more information they contain, according to Shannon's law. So, do these structures code information or express information? Is Heller suggesting here that the laws of nature are information, or is he saying that they express information? This resembles the problem of the chicken and the egg, but we do not get an answer to this in Heller's writings.[23]

This interpretation of nature, information, structures, and natural laws is further discussed in Heller's article titled "Science and Imagination" (Heller 1995). Heller perceives structures and the laws

---

[22]The degrees of freedom are the number of independent variables (dimensions) that a system may be characterized or exist in.
[23]See the similar comments on the priority of laws of nature and nature's organization expressed by Laughlin (Laughlin 2006, pp. xi–xvi).

of nature as information. This information (as natural laws) is partially decoded and expressed in scientific laws. These scientific laws represent a fragment (or an aspect) of cosmic structures, and they are clearly much less complex than these natural structures really are. However, Heller does not explain in what sense the laws of nature are structures.

Further, Heller states that while the laws of nature and structures are not isomorphic, they act in concert with nature, implying a sort of interdependency. In other words, the laws of nature are the results of nature's properties to some degree, although to what degree we are unsure. The point of this remark is to convey that laws and natural structures are not the same but somewhat interdependent. Heller refers to this similarity between nature and abstract mathematical structures as "harmony". Harmony, as proposed by Heller, is an intriguing property of abstract models of the cosmos. According to Heller, the mathematical models of nature are highly simplified (when compared to the complexity of nature) and formalized, so they have a high level of abstraction. They are therefore not of the same "nature" as physical entities. So, how are they able to reflect some of nature's properties, often quite accurately? One may be tempted to see Platonic forms in these abstractions and nature as their realization. Such a view would certainly explain this strange harmony. This would be the position of modern or mathematical Platonism, which by the way has little to do with the ontology of Plato (e.g., Linnebo 2018).

Additional explanations of the concepts of nature, structure, information, and form can be found in Heller's paper titled "Evolution of the concept of mass" (Heller 1987, pp. 152–169). Heller posits that information can be thought of as a foundational element of nature instead of matter. In particular, modern physics models the universe through mathematical formulas, which are shapes/structures without content. In this view, is information expressed through "empty" mathematical structures, or are these structures information? Heller does not address this problem.

Further, Heller suggests that even if there is something beyond these "Platonic" structures, modern science is unable to detect it.

Such a statement approaches the position of epistemic structuralism (i.e., adopting the mathematical version of structuralism), which claims that the structures of nature are mathematical structures, and nothing else (i.e., ontology) can be known about them.

Also, Heller observes that this concept of information is not the same as the concept of information that arises from the Shannon's ToC. The ToC would perceive the structure as encoding something rather than as the "stuff of the universe". Thus, the concept of information in the ToC is inadequate for expressing anything beyond the concept of a number for information. In fact, Shannon's ToC does not define information, as some have come to mistakenly believe, but rather its measure. To put it more precisely, the function defined by Shannon is a measure of information, with the elementary unit of information being a digital bit (i.e., 0 or 1). Thus, Shannon's measure of information does not define information any more than the definition of a kilogram of mass defines what mass is (Kilogram 2021). It just quantifies a certain property of a physical phenomenon under certain assumptions. Such a reading of the ToC will be less prone to misinterpretation and possibly closer to Shannon's original intentions.

3.1.7 *The universe computes*

Gordana Dodig Crnkovic discusses the nature of information in the context of ontology (i.e., what exists) and computing. Dodig Crnkovic (2012) claims that information has an objective presence, so it is not an intentional object (i.e., an object of thought) but instead represents objective ontology (i.e., fundamental ontology). Dodig Crnkovic's ontology is not an ontology of computer objects—such as virtual ontology, an ontology of knowledge systems or computer games, or suchlike—but rather an ontology responding to the general question of "What is".

Dodig Crnkovic (2008, 2013a) conceptualizes nature as a complex of patterns (or structures) and natural processes, which are transformations of, or interactions among, these structures/patterns. By recognizing natural structures/patterns as information—and she denotes these natural uninterpreted (meaning not assimilated by a cognitive agent) patterns as "proto-information" or "potential information"—the whole of nature appears to be formed on, or by, information or, more accurately, proto-information. It follows that natural processes are computations in the sense that they process/transform or act on information ("proto-information") or structures that are information. Thus, from this perspective, computation is information processing, but not in the narrow sense of the UTM (and therefore the Church–Turing thesis), where information is a series of signs and computing involves UTM artifacts performing syntactic-informed operations on these signs. Instead, it occupies a more generalized sense where information is a structure/organization and computing involves general transformations of these structures. In other words, they are structural transformations rather than symbolic operations.

Dodig Crnkovic states that information is part of the fabric of the universe in the sense that information forms the structures/patterns that in turn form nature.[24] It is not clear whether information is a structure qua structure or exists in structures, as well as what these structures are. So, what structures does Dodig Crnkovic have in mind? Are these structures perceivable or are they the structures of mathematical models of nature or other deep structures of some sort? In the absence of clear definitions, we are left with the difficult task of supplying an interpretation ourselves, namely, that Dodig Crnkovic's natural structures are proto-information or potential information.

Dodig Crnkovic's further work (2012, 2013b) brings important clarifications. She states that proto-information is, or may become, information for a cognitive agent. Thus, proto-information is potentially information about the world when it is received and processed

---

[24]The term "fabric" is frequently used in discussions about structural realism. It was used in David Deutsch's book *Fabric of Reality* (Deutsch 1998) and Brian Greene's book *The Fabric of the Cosmos*(Greene 2004) in the sense of being the "foundational stuff" of physical reality. In both books, the term "fabric" refers to the basic aspects of nature or the physical world of time, space, quantum mechanics, and symmetry, to list just a few concepts associated with this term by Deutsch and Greene. We will retain this interpretation for this term.

by a cognitive agent. Further, she claims that proto-information is always embedded in a matter–energy entity. This means that there is no information without a physical embodiment (i.e., a physical carrier). This condition therefore excludes any non-physical concepts of information, such as a thought or other abstract Platonic-like form. For Dodig Crnkovic, information, as opposed to "knowledge of the world as information", is clearly physical, and it exists at the foundations of reality (i.e., the fabric of the universe) and at the foundations of information for a cognitive agent.

Dodig Crnkovic extends the concept of information beyond ontological and structural claims and makes information a part of the world view of pancomputationalism, natural computing, morphological computing, or info-computationalism.[25] Dodig Crnkovic (2009, 2011, 2013b) provides another perspective on information, namely, that information (organization) is as fundamental to nature as change is. The claim that nature is structural and constantly in flux is thus "translated" to the claim that structures that form/constitute nature are actually information that undergoes constant changes. This notion of "constant changes" may be seen as a Heraclitan flux or as it is in modern language computations. Computation, in this view, is the information/structure flux. We may therefore ask the following: Is this *information rhei* rather than *panta rhei*? This new perspective changes our current conceptualization of computing, which his mostly regarded as Turing's notion of computing extended (justifiably or not) by the Church–Turing thesis.[26] (Note of course that the Church–Turing thesis is conjecture rather than a physical or metaphysical law.) In the view proposed by Dodig Crnkovic, the Turing computational model is a subset of natural computation, not

---

[25]See, for example, Dodig Crnkovic (2009, 2011, 2012a) for a summary of claims and references.

[26] *The Church–Turing thesis (formerly commonly known simply as Church's thesis) says that any real-world computation can be translated into an equivalent computation involving a Turing machine. In Church's original formulation, the thesis says that real-world calculation can be done using lambda calculus, which is equivalent to using general recursive functions* (Church–Turing Thesis 2018).

the other way around, because the former does not represent a generalized concept of computation (Dodig Crnkovic 2011) as is often claimed (e.g., Piccinini 2015, 2017). Indeed, the Turing computation is at most a generalized concept for computation on symbolic (i.e., human-constructed) structures. Natural computations are therefore much richer than what the Turing computational model would permit. In this view (i.e., computation as information/structure flux), all processes in nature are computations on information. In other words, computation is understood as information processing, where changes and transformations are applied to structures that are information. The Church–Turing thesis was extended by Wolfram to cover this concept.[27]

Dodig Crnkovic redefines computing from Turing's symbol processing to information/structure change.[28] But, is Dodig Crnkovic's view of computing an intuition or is it a well-justified claim? We do not have a definite answer to this question, but we have several possible answers, just as we have several variants of pancomputationalism. The ideas of pancomputationalism, natural computing, morphological computing, and info-computationalism worlds are not without controversies, even if they sound plausible.[29] These claims are difficult to swallow because they change a certain established paradigm, an entrenched way of seeing things. Pancomputationalism and natural computing, in some versions, carry heavy metaphysical claims that are difficult to substantiate, although can we ever substantiate such deep metaphysical claims? When interpreting Dodig Crnkovic's words, one may, however, reject or dispute the concept of natural computing or pancomputationalism, but retain the concept of information as a structure of nature and the flux/changes in nature as

---

[27] *The Church–Turing thesis has been extended to a proposition about the processes in the natural world by Stephen Wolfram in his principle of computational equivalence, which also claims that there are only a small number of intermediate levels of computing power before a system is universal and that most natural systems are universal* (Church–Turing Thesis 2018).

[28] See, for example, the claims of soft computing in Nakajima *et al.* (2015).

[29] See, for example, the references in (Pancomputationalism 2019), Piglucci (2013), or Copeland (2017).

information changing, because the concept of pancomputationalism depends upon the latter claim, but the opposite is not true.

3.1.8 *Information is in everything*

Hidalgo (2015), in his book *Why Information Grows: The Evolution of Order, from Atoms to Economics*, sets out the framework for his view of information. He posits that *the world is made out of matter, energy and information* without explanation other than to state that everything in the world (i.e., matter and energy) in addition to occupying space–time has some form or shape, which is synonymous with information for Hidalgo. Thus, from this viewpoint, information is one of the three essential components of the universe in the energy–matter–information triad. This information is responsible for the organization/shape of matter–energy. The physical world (i.e., what exists objectively in reality) is characterized by order, the arrangements of things, structure, or the organization of matter–energy at all scales, from the sub-atomic to the cosmic. This idea is expanded further. Hidalgo observes that the universe is full of—or as he puts it, "pregnant with"—information. Visible structures are not information, although they do manifest in the presence of information. In other words, information should not be equated with the visible structure of something, and this thought has come up many times in this study. Information is order, an organization of things or objects. The order in things also characterizes man-made artifacts, from a pen to the Large Hadron Collider (LHC). Indeed, the type of order/organization defines what something is. This seems to echo, albeit rather distantly, the ancient concepts of form or *eidos*. Form and *eidos* are replaced by Hidalgo with information, making form or *eidos* less mysterious and quantifiable. Information as order or arrangement in things is intrinsic to making those things what they are, so for Hidalgo, the fundamental concept of information is the order or arrangement of things.

Hidalgo clearly states that information is separate from meaning. Although information can be interpreted as a message with meaning, it can also be regarded as a source of the message in the right circumstances. However, meaning is not a defining characteristic of information, because information with meaning (i.e., epistemic information in this work) only emerges when information encounters a cognitive agent, whether artificial or natural, because the agent creates meaning. Information as it is understood by Hidalgo as the organization of things is epistemically neutral, i.e., it has no intrinsic meaning.

We can derive meaning from some natural phenomena because information as order is always present everywhere. (Indeed, this universal capacity of the human mind has been understood and abused by diviners, shamans, and seers seeking to derive meaning from bones, tea leaves, sheep's entrails, and so on.) We can even see epistemic information where there is none, such as in TV shows, the popular press, or social media posts. From this position, the claims that information surrounds us and that we are information-processing systems can be easily comprehended. All man-made artifacts are also filled with information as order, such as cars, tables, radios, and so on. Indeed, because nature is full of information, everything in nature embodies order (although the origins may differ), and physical order is information.

Meaning is the interpretation of a quality, a sort of property, attributed to a physical phenomenon or an artifact by a cognitive agent. It is fundamentally different from the *physical order that carries the message*. Similar observations were made by Boltzmann, Shannon, and Schrödinger. What is left after separating meaning from physical phenomena is physical order. Boltzmann, Shannon, and Schrödinger, each in their own way, denoted this "physical order" as information. Such information is independent (i.e., it exists independently) of a human perspective, so it is not relative to the human agent perceiving it—it is objective in this sense. Information as physical order can be destroyed or created, but it is not equivalent to thermodynamic entropy, as some have claimed.

The concept of information as the physical order of a system—as was conceptualized by Boltzmann for gases, Shannon for communication messages (although only through analogy), and Schrödinger for DNA—can be generalized to any physical order of nature.

This order of nature is embodied in natural structures, and it expresses the order or organization of natural and man-made things. Hidalgo claims that no concept other than information could embody the existence of order, form, or observable structures (i.e., those that can be detected, quantified, abstracted, simulated, partially recreated, and described) at all levels of nature, from atoms to galaxies. (This is what "the scale-independence of information" means for him.) In Hidalgo's view, people, as cognitive agents, "read" this order and generate epistemic information.

Hidalgo attributes additional properties to information, making a series of statements about information and entropy. In Hidalgo's view, information is not in any way equivalent to entropy. Information embodies the concept of order, which is opposite to entropy. The similarity between information and entropy has unfortunately arisen from the Shannon–Hartley formula for the amount of information (information entropy) and the syntactic similarity of this formula to the Boltzmann (Gibbs's formulation of entropy) formula for the entropy of ideal gas. This syntactic similarity has led to one of the most frequently repeated misconceptions about the nature of information. Of course, as we discuss later, there is absolutely nothing wrong with using Shannon's formula as a measure of information and attributing to this measure the properties derived from this model. Shannon's formula provides a measure of information because we decided what it measures, and we denote this as information. However, the properties of Shannon's formula can hardly be attributed to the general concept of information.

Hidalgo postulates that physical processes are in fact computations, because in these processes, information as an organization of matter undergoes changes. In this view, computations bestow upon matter *an ability to compute*. This changes the concept of what computing is, from the symbolic algorithmic/procedural operations performed by a UTM to computing as a physical process operating on structures as information, much like we discussed in several previous cases. Again, this claim leads to some variant of pancomputationalism.

3.1.9 *From music to information*

In their paper titled "What does it mean to understand and what does it mean specifically to understand information", Jacek Jadacki and Anna Brożek (2005) postulate the existence of information as *a certain internal state of [the] object*. To formulate this concept of information, Jadacki and Brożek question what "kind" of information, in the common dictionary understanding of the term, may be associated with perceptions of music.[30] All forms of information that are comprehended by an agent can be denoted as *anthropomorphic information*. The concepts of such information are highly intuitive and imprecise, and in order to treat information as a scientific concept, its definition must be more specific. The authors begin by defining information in the anthropomorphic sense. Through a series of eliminations and reductions in the elements of this initial definition, they come to the conclusion that information exists independently of the mind, so it is essentially a state of things or a state in things that may potentially or not be an object of cognition. This obviously implies that information, in this sense, exists independently of whether someone is perceiving it or not.

Jadacki and Brożek define anthropomorphic information as having seven attributes—sender, receiver, meaning, veracity, actuality, comprehension, and novelty—and in general outlines, it is a communication model. In more detail, these are as follows:

- The *sender* and *receiver* denote the agents originating and receiving the information.
- The *meaning, veracity, actuality, comprehension,* and *novelty* are attributes of the sentence being transmitted and later comprehended by the *receiver*.
- The *sentence* is the carrier of the *anthropomorphic* information.

---

[30]The discussion about information by Jadacki and Brożek originated in some way from listening to Prelude in *E-minor* (op. 28) by Frederic Chopin. The ontological status of Chopin music has been explored in the discussions on Ockham's nominalism (Kolakowski 2008, p. 110). Ockham did not have resources to conceptualize music as epistemic information, placing it in the realm of nonexisting things. With all the modern philosophy at his disposal, Kolakowski clearly identified music as belonging to the real of ideas.

- In addition, the *meaning* and *veracity* attributes imply that the sentence reflects some true state of affairs, while the sentence must be understood by the receiver (*comprehension*) and be previously unknown to him or her (*novelty*).

The definition of information does not change if the sender is eliminated. The definition of information may therefore be even further reduced by eliminating the sentence, which is understood here as the carrier of information. This is what happens during a musical performance, where the audience listens to the same composition, but each listener may receive different information. The audience may learn about the performer, glean information about the structure of the musical piece, decide whether the performance was correct, have memories of some past events evoked, or receive information in some other way. A concept of information that would subsume all these possible types of "information" would need to exclude a sender and a sentence as the carrier of information. Thus, information obtained in this communication process depends upon the understanding of a message in communication, but it can be interpreted in many ways. It seems that information, however, is something common to the multitude of possible interpretations.

The proposed abstraction/reduction process leading to the generalized concept of information leaves out the *sender, receiver, meaning,* and *veracity*. Information defined only with these attributes has no specific meaning, and it can only be interpreted by a cognitive agent. Thus, such information may be understood as carrying the variety of anthropomorphic information that is associated with a musical performance. Information, as it is defined above, is a raw material for semantic interpretation, because it may have different meanings.

Jadacki and Brożek conclude that any object with some state (i.e., a physical state) has information that may potentially be recognized by a cognitive agent. The concept of information as semantic or *anthropomorphic* information can be generalized to cover all possible interpretations of it, and this generalized concept denotes the structure of physical phenomena that contain that structure. The structure of an object can be denoted as its state, but information as the state of an object exists whether it is being observed or not. Of course, it can potentially be received or decoded, but authors do not clarify the meaning of terms like *state of an object*, *be in a state*, or *contains a certain state*. However, these could be interpreted as referring to a "physical state" or "physical structure" through the analogy of the musical composition, which is the main subject of the discussion, being carried through the state of the physical media (i.e., the air).

One may certainly ask whether, for Jadacki and Brożek, a musical composition "is the physical state" of the carrier (e.g., sound waves, digital media, and music sheets) or something else. The answer to this question lies in the statement that "music is in the object" rather than that music is the object. This claim would indicate that music exists as something beyond the physical realm. However, we do not get any explanation about what this "beyond" could possibly be, and this comment seems more poetic than factual.

3.1.10 *Evolution, us, and information*

Thomas Nagel, in his book *Mind and Cosmos* (Nagel 2012), argues that the existence of information with ontological properties is rooted in the concept of evolution. If we assume the validity of evolution and evolutionary principles (i.e., organisms evolve under environmental pressure to maximize their odds of survival), as most do, the claim that the world order (the structure of nature) is our creation leads to a contradiction and denial of scientific realism and evolution.

Nagel argues that the rationality, intelligibility, or order pervading nature and perceived by us is not a human creation or invention, thus arguing against the Kantian philosophy of knowledge.[31] This order is a property of nature, and it long predates humans. This all-pervading order/rationality is the factor that enables all sciences to emerge

---

[31] This statement must be qualified. We can certainly "read" to some extend the organizational properties of nature. We may call it rationality of nature or its intelligibility. But, it does not equate with the statement that the Universe is rational (as humans are) or that we can understand the nature. At best, we can say that we can comprehend some of the aspects of nature, usually in the form of some mathematical formulas. But, it seems that the essence of nature will remain beyond the grasp of our cognitive powers (see, e.g., Chomsky 2012).

as sciences and allows us to investigate order in the world. Science assumes a priori that the world is ordered in some way; otherwise, the efforts of scientists would be doomed to fail before they began.[32]

Nagel observes that the world is intelligible, so it can be partially explained by the universal laws of physics.[33] The order in the natural world is a result of the laws of the physical universe, so these laws create order in Nagel's view. Physical laws explain why the universe is ordered, organized, and intelligible.[34] This view does not equate to physical reductionism, however, because some aspects of the universe are not reducible to the pure laws of physics, such as biology. We, and all living things, are products of evolution. The pervading order and "rationality" in nature is, in a way, a foundation for the reasoning behind the theory of evolution. Evolution could not take place in an absolutely random universe, because environmental pressure must be persistent and predictable to some extent for organisms to adapt to it. The rationality of nature is a foundation or a condition, *sine qua none*, of rational scientific methods. Scientific methods in turn "discover" rationality in nature, much like how we may refer to the discovery of America or other places and phenomena that already existed long before their discovery. However, the primacy (i.e., the order of appearance of rationality) belongs to nature, and we, with our rational minds, are its creations, so we are the order from the order.

Further, Nagel states that our perceptual functions are products of evolution: They give us a more or less accurate, or objective and

---

[32]We may argue whether nature is rational or is intelligible. These discussions pivot on the understanding on these terms. In this way, equally true is the statement that we do not understand the nature as we do not understand its very foundations, thus nature is not intelligible. One may also claim that perceived rationality of nature is human creation. And, this is what Nagel is arguing against (see also Barrow (1995) for the similar to Nagel argument about nature and evolution of human mind and Newton–Smith (1996) for the argument about rationality of nature).

[33]Here, Nagel guards himself with "the world ... explained partially..." against materialist monism or strong reductionism.

[34]Again, this is an exposition of Nagel's argument, not the discussion of the nature of physical laws and their ontological status (on the topic see, e.g., Feynman (1995)).

reliable, account of the world (auth. Otherwise, we would not be able to survive, never mind evolve). The information that we get from the world is from the world and about the world. Information from nature therefore shapes us and our knowledge, which is intimately bound with the universe, and binding us with the universe in the process. We are not separate minds looking at a spectacle—we are an intrinsically integrated part of the game. The causal objects (including rationality or the order/form of things) of our thoughts exist in nature. However, as reasonable beings, we can go beyond the practical truths of sensory perception. We can abstract, generalize, and synthesize, so we create integrals, differentials, moments, unicorns, centaurs, griffins, and other things that do not exist in nature. Translating this into our concepts of information, we say that nature has inherent order, and this order shaped us and our senses to perceive this order. Indeed, evolution cannot deceive its creations, because that would achieve nothing. We perceive this order because we have evolved to do this, but we also reshape the received information. This is how epistemic information, or knowledge about the world, "emerges". Our concepts and knowledge (i.e., information about the world that is called epistemic information in this study) reflect the world. They do not have to do this by definition, but we have evolved to reflect this order, so we are reflections of it. Otherwise, we would not be here. Even "here" would not be here.

Nagel also provides an argument for why he thinks an anti-realist is wrong and why evolution is a proof against this anti-realist. The argument goes like this: There is a world out there that is objective and is independent of our beliefs. Nagel repeats here the argument that our senses reflect the world out there and its structure or organization, just as they have evolved to do so. This in fact is the principle of evolution. Nagel observes that our perceptual, mental, and reasoning capacities are together representing the world out there for evolutionary reasons. (Of course, we do not talk about evolution as an intentional act or even as having *telos*.)

Nagel clearly evokes the original concept of information (as in *informare*) as shaping the mind or maybe the archaic and simplistic

Aristotelian idea of *a ring imprinting its shape in the wax.*[35] One should also not take this claim to be an endorsement of Hume's view of the mind. The mind plays an active role in interpreting the perceptual "feed", but as the mind is also a product of evolution, the interpretation it imposes on this feed generally reflects the world outside, at least if cognitive function has not been disrupted, such as by hallucinogens, to the extent that the whole perceptual feed can be barely comprehended, let alone related to the world.

We get another look at the causal powers of information. For several researchers mentioned in this study, information may have causal powers at the fundamental level forming the universe (i.e., ideas similar to Plato's forms and Aristotle's substantial forms). In Nagel's view, information lies at the root of evolution and its causality. For Nagel, if we believe in physical laws, we need to accept information as *something about the world that eventually gave rise to rational beings.* The question is then whether *informare* denotes the shaping of nature or the shaping of the mind or both? Alternatively, are the mind and nature of the same kind, in a way where the mind is not apart from nature but rather a part of it?

Nagel does not agree that materialist reduction (physics) explains everything in the world, including the mind and consciousness. The mind and consciousness are part of the physical world, however, so they ultimately have to be explained by it. Whether materialism offers a full explanation of the world, including the mind and consciousness, is beside the point here. What is important is that we, and all other animal life, are an integral part of the universe, and our minds are reflections of its underlying order, not anything else, at least under normal conditions.[36]

---

[35] Aristotle (2001), DA 424b1–b3, DM 450a31–2.

[36] One may argue about the term "normal" here, but it would detract from the goal of this study and be a rather bad example of philosophy. For example, knowing how philosophy goes, we could end up concluding that there are no "normal" conditions or that the term is too nebulous to be defined precisely, despite it being used quite successfully in everyday language.

3.2 Studies—What Did We Learn?

The concept of information that emerges from the writings of Heller, von Weizsäcker, Turek, Stonier, Collier, Nagel, Mynarski, Jadacki and Brożek, Dodig Crnkovic, and Hidalgo can be summarized in eleven claims: (1) The notion of information associated with knowledge does not exhaust the concept of information. (2) Information is a physical/natural phenomenon. (3) Information is a physical/natural phenomenon with no meaning. (4) The meaning of information is derived by the mind of a cognitive agent and not intrinsic to information as a physical/natural phenomenon. (5) The role of information in nature may be conceptualized within a matter–energy–information complex. (6) Information as a physical/natural phenomenon is fundamental to nature, so whatever exists physically contains information. (7) Information as a physical/natural phenomenon is expressed in the structure/form and organization of things. (8) Information as a physical/natural phenomenon is not, and cannot be reduced to, what we conceptualize as structures. (9) Information as a physical/natural phenomenon is responsible for the internal organization of nature's objects and artifacts. (10) Natural processes are information processes that we may denote as computing. (11) Quantifications of information provide measures of sensible structures that reflect the presence of this information but are not information itself.

(1) Information as knowledge does not completely cover the concept of information. Information, in most lexicons and dictionaries (e.g., "Information—Merriam-Webster" 2019, "Information—CED" 2019, "Information—OED" 2019, "Information—Collins ED" 2019, "Information—Macmillan" 2019), as well as in common parlance ("Information" 2018),[37] is most often associated with knowledge, the transfer of knowledge, communication, and the reception of knowledge, with these involving facts or news about something.

---

[37]We regard Wikipedia entries as representing the popular meaning of concepts rather than their scientific renditions. Thus, researching the use of the term "information" in the popular, non-scientific context seems appropriate for establishing the use of this term outside of the domains of philosophy and science.

This is how information is interpreted in the works of Bar-Hillel and Carnap (1953), Brooks (1980), Buckland (1991), Devlin (1991), Losee (1998), Sveiby (1998), Dretske (1999), Casagrande (1999), Burgin (2003), Lenski (2010), Floridi (2013), and Vernon (2014), to list but a few authors. However, information as knowledge, news, a fact about something, or a message does not exhaust the meaning associated with this concept. The reviewed studies show how information may be conceptualized as a purely natural phenomenon. Stefan Mynarski states that two kinds of information can be differentiated: information related to a physical object and information without a physical reference. In the former case, we have real information, while in the latter case, we have abstract information. "Abstract information" is a creation of the mind and related to events or phenomena that do not (or may not) exist as physical entities. Being a creation of the mind, abstract information bears a strong resemblance to epistemic information as it is defined in this study, albeit with the qualification that epistemic information can be "information" about any phenomenon, whether it exists or not. We are not sure how Mynarski interprets the verb "exist" in the cited fragments, but it cannot have the same meaning for "real" (physical, concrete) and "abstract" (a creation of the mind) information. A charitable reading of the text would suggest that Mynarski was aware of these nuances in the existence of real and abstract entities, as he differentiated them into physical and abstract. We focus on Mynarski's term "real information" for information existing in physical things or connected with physical phenomena. Collier admits that two meanings are usually associated with information, information as a physical thing and as related to the mind. He claims that information has causal powers. Collier justifies this claim about the existence of causal factor behind information by stipulating that information that is "assimilated" by a cognitive agent must correlate with the outside world to be reasonably predictable and regular. Collier also claims that the notion of information as not related to cognitive gains is more general than the one that is associated with cognition, or in other words, "cognitive" information is just a subcategory of a more general form of information. Stonier, likewise, states that information has different modes of existence.

We may have information in physical systems or information in people's heads; these types of information are different in nature. Energy, a fundamental element of reality, has different forms of appearance or realization, so it is information, and human information is just one form of this. This is a significant claim, because it goes against most of the definitions of information that currently prevail, where information is something that has some meaning to a human observer. Information has different physical realizations and carriers, so one cannot regard the external shape of a physical carrier as information. These external forms differ depending upon the carrying medium. In the same fragment, Stonier posits that the diversity of carriers used in the communication of information demonstrates that information has physical realization and that it is a property of nature, and we just have a problem realizing this, preferring instead to focus exclusively on our perspective and asking what value "it" has for us. For Nagel, the reason and order we perceive in nature are not a direct reflection of our minds, as postulated by Kant,[38] but of the organization existing independently in nature. Nagel argues for the existence of a rationality (i.e., intelligibility, order) pervading nature that is not a human creation or invention. (Note how Nagel argues against the Kantian philosophy of knowledge.)[39] The rationality, intelligibility, or order that pervades nature is therefore a property of nature, one that long predates humans. This all-pervading order/rationality is what enables all sciences to emerge. Finally, he suggests another reference to the causal power of information. For several researchers, information may have causal power at the fundamental level, at the forming of the universe. In Nagel's view, information lies at the root

---

[38]Greatly simplifying it, we could say that Kant's transcendental argument is the claim that while there must be an external source for our knowledge of the objects in nature, the mind imposes upon the senses its own interpretation (i.e., pure forms of perception), and this is what we perceive (McCormick 2019).

[39]We talk here about the Kantian thesis that the "thing-in-itself" (or in Kant's German, *Ding an sich*) is not knowable, and the mind imposes its structure on our perception of nature, so pure categories of understanding are found a priori (before experience) in the mind. Thus, we cannot deduct from observation that nature is structural or something else.

of evolution and its causality. Dodig Crnkovic expresses a similar idea, differentiating information into proto-information and information for a cognitive agent. Proto-information, or information embedded in nature, is, or may become, information for a cognitive agent, so proto-information is potential information about the world when received by an agent. Hidalgo clearly indicates that information is separate from meaning, although it can be interpreted and regarded as a message, but this is not the defining characteristic of information. Information with meaning emerges when information encounters a cognitive agent, whether artificial or natural. In other words, the agent creates meaning. The order of, or in, nature that is understood here as information is epistemically neutral, so it has no intrinsic meaning, but it may represent meaning for someone. Information-as-order or order-as-information is always and everywhere. That is why we humans can derive meaning from any natural phenomena, and this universal property of nature has been understood and abused by diviners, shamans, seers, and suchlike, as we have pointed out several times already. In this view, claims like "information is all around us" and "we are information-processing systems", which are often found in the popular press and popularized science books, can be explained and understood (apart from the recognized fact that we are de facto information-processing biological systems).

(2) Information is a physical/natural phenomenon. What does it mean when we claim that information is a physical phenomenon? It means that information is an aspect of physical reality, so it can be measured, quantified, and observed because it has a physical existence. Information is not some form of "spooky" fluid or, in the language of von Weizsäcker, some "transcendental" entity. It belongs clearly to the physical universe. Von Weizsäcker claims that information has physical expression and characteristics and belongs to the world of physical phenomena. Mynarski, meanwhile, claims that information is a part of physical systems. For Collier, information is a part of the physical world, the world of real objects. Likewise, Tom Stonier claims that information is a part physical reality. Heller, meanwhile, postulates that information is a part par excellence of physical reality, so it must be physical. For Dodig Crnkovic, information is ontologically fundamental; then, it must be a part of the real world and therefore physical. Hidalgo has little doubt that information has a physical presence. It is embedded in physical things. Yet, Hidalgo's work does not explain to us what information is. It only establishes the fact that the information is part of the physical world and that as a physical phenomenon, it can be studied through the methods of the physical sciences.

(3) Information as a natural/physical phenomenon has no meaning. This claim is somewhat related to the previous one in stating that information has no intrinsic meaning because information and meaning are two separate concepts. Meaning is attributed to information, because information as a natural/physical phenomenon is meaningless. Information just exists, much like the physical world is out there regardless of whether there is a cognitive agent to see it or not.

(4) Meaning in information is derived by the mind of a cognitive agent. Meaning is not an intrinsic aspect of information. This means that meaning (in information) is derived from, or added to, physical stimuli (i.e., physical information) by a cognitive agent,[40] implying that information is relative to that agent. How meaning is derived and what we mean by an agent are detailed in the following chapters. Of course, the fact that meaning is derived from, or added to, physical stimuli, which we denote as physical or ontological information, allows us to say that information carries meaning. Information in nature is positioned as having no meaning, but meaning is derived by cognitive faculties from information that exists, in some sense, in nature.

(5) The role of information in nature may be conceptualized as a matter–energy–information complex. Information as an element of nature is conceptualized as a complex in a form resembling

---

[40]The strong similarity between epistemic and ontological information and the perception of color are difficult to escape unnoticed. Color is how we perceive different electromagnetic wavelengths, which are of course colorless. Meaning is, in a sense, how we perceive an epistemically neutral physical stimulus.

that of Aristotelian hylemorphism (i.e., a matter–form compound). Different authors conceptualize this matter–energy–information complex in different ways, but regardless of the specific details, all the cited authors agree that information is responsible for the structure, organization, and shape of things, and this is clearly an acceptance of the compositional nature of existing entities.

(6) Whatever physically exists contains information. This claim is made without any Aristotelian/Platonic connection (i.e., Form, *eidos, morphe*), so it may be judged as "cleaner" or more palpable for philosophers who prefer to avoid the ancient theories. If information exists, it must be a part of all physical things, so we assume that when we talk about things, we talk about them having a definite shape or form. This view is expressed by Stonier, Heller, Dodig Crnkovic, and Hidalgo.

(7) Information is expressed in structures/form and the organization of things. All the cited researchers associate information with some kind of structure, form, or organization, but structure/form/organization and information are not exactly the same (i.e., they are not synonymous).

(8) Information is not structure. Information is most often associated with structure, as we concluded above. We have in mind the visible form of an object, and we also see it in quantifications of information where functions assign some number to visible structures. However, information is not the structure that we are quantifying or even the one we can see. This observation about the nature of information is one that most of the studies agree upon. We should, and this is one of the conclusions of this study, stop associating information with the concept of a structure without clarifying it further. For example, what kind of structure do we have in mind? What kind of association are we talking about, and how does this structure relate to information?

(9) Information is responsible for the internal organization of nature's objects and artifacts. Information is perceived as the cause of the shape of objects and their internal organization. This role is rarely substantiated or compared to the Aristotelian four causes, however, and it is usually rooted in the meaning of the Latin verb *informare*. Attributing a causal role to information would require substantial and rather speculative analysis. We therefore acknowledge the causal role of information as indicated by many writers, but we do not explore this topic beyond directly citing what these authors claim. That said, the causality of information would be rooted in its physicality if we accept that information is a physical phenomenon. This view can be also found in writings of, for example, Turek and Heller. Thus, from this perspective, the structures of nature are functions of the laws of nature (i.e., information).

(10) Natural processes are information processes that we may regard as computing. Natural processes are information processes that we may regard as a form of computing: This claim would require changing our definition of computing from Turing computation. This is a rather canonical definition of computing, and not everyone would agree to replace it. This view is posited by Hidalgo (who sees physical processes as a sort of computing or information processing). Dodig Crnkovic postulates that any information processing is computing, because computing is in essence information processing. Computing, or information processing, always involves changes in the structures of some physical system, and in the canonical case, this system is a computer. Thus, we may generalize that any changes in physical structures are changes in information, so they are computations. Symbolic computation (the canonical view of computation) is therefore a narrowly understood form of computation or an imposed interpretation for a certain class of physical processes.[41]

(11) Measures of information provide quantifications of sensible structures that reflect information but are not information itself. Quantified models or measures of information (a) quantify tangible structures that are not information itself. Thus, we may say that they measure just (b) the expressions or effects of

---

[41]Computation or computing has several definitions. Thus, the definition used here (symbolic computation) is not the only one used (see, e.g., Denning and Martell 2015, DasGupta 2016). A different model of computation has been proposed in earlier works of Dodig Crnkovic and Stonier.

information. While claim (a) is rather obvious, claim (b) has also been made several times in the preceding analysis. Thus, we may conclude that measures of information provide quantifications of sensible structures that reflect information but are not information itself. Few authors posit this explicitly, however. Heller writes that the mathematical model of information provided by Shannon–Weaver–Hartley is a reduction of the concept of information to a specific mathematical function and associated axiomatic structures, as any mathematization is.[42] Von Weizsäcker, meanwhile, states that quantification changes the character of information. Associating information with a syntax (language) takes away its objective character, because syntax is a human-imposed interpretation of nature. For his part, Stonier states that imposing the concept of bits on information, which is what Chaitin and Shannon–Weaver–Hartley proposed, reduces the concept of information to exactly that (i.e., bits or symbols). This reduction may make information "quantifiable" but only in a narrow sense (i.e., in the sense of counting bits).

3.3 A Biographical Note

Below are short biographical notes on cited authors.

Carl Friedrich von Weizsäcker was a German physicist and philosopher. Weizsäcker made important theoretical discoveries regarding energy production in stars from nuclear fusion processes. He also did influential theoretical work on planetary formation in the early Solar System (von Weizsäcker 2019).

Krzysztof Turek was a physicist and a philosopher of science and an adjunct professor at the University of Science and Technology, Cracow, Poland. He obtained his doctorate in philosophy at the Pontifical University of John Paul II, Cracow, Poland (Turek 2019).

Stefan Mynarski was an expert in marketing and cybernetics working at the Cracow University of Economics. He developed the

---

[42] *Mathematisation is the act of interpreting or expressing something mathematically or the state of being considered or explained mathematically* (Mathematisation 2020) (see also Gellert and Jablonka 2008).

concept of information as an element of the physical world, one that is responsible for form and organization (Mynarski 2013).

John Collier received his Ph.D. in the Philosophy of Science from the University of Western Ontario in 1984. Currently, he is a professor in the philosophy program at the University of KwaZulu–Natal (Collier 2018).

Tom Stonier was a biologist, philosopher, information theorist, educator and pacifist. His scientific studies centered on information to provide a plausible explanation for the evolutionist concepts of Pierre Teilhard de Chardin. He drafted the principle of the transformation of a primordial energetic soup (big bang) toward a pure informational state (the de Chardin's Omega point) (Stonier 2019).

Michał Kazimierz Heller is a Polish professor of philosophy at the Pontifical University of John Paul II in Kraków, Poland, and an adjunct member of the Vatican Observatory staff. In 2008, Heller was awarded the Templeton Prize for his extensive philosophical and scientific probing of "big questions". Heller also founded the Copernicus Center for Interdisciplinary Studies in Cracow (Heller 2018).

Gordana Dodig Crnkovic is Professor of Computer Science at Mälardalen University and Associate Professor at Chalmers University of Technology. She holds Ph.D. degrees in Physics and Computer Science. Her current research is in Morphological computing and the connection between computation, information, and cognition via interacting agents on different levels of organization—from physics to biology and cognition (Dodig Crnkovic 2018).

Cesar Hidalgo is an MIT Associate Professor and the leader of the Macro Connections group at MIT. He has a degree in statistical physics and he is also an expert on Networks and Complex Systems (Hidalgo 2015).

Jacek Jadacki was professor of philosophy at Warsaw University (1974–2016) and specializes in semiotics and the history of Polish philosophy (Jadacki 2021).

Anna Brozek is professor of philosophy at Warsaw University who specializes in semiotics, the history of Polish philosophy, and logic. Anna Brożek is also a concert pianist (Brozek 2020).

Thomas Nagel is an American philosopher who was University Professor of Philosophy and Law Emeritus at New York University, where he taught from 1980 to 2016. His main areas of philosophical interest are philosophy of mind, political philosophy, and ethics (Nagel 2018).

Chapter 4

Ontological Information: Synthesis

All the authors mentioned in the preceding chapters regard information as something other than knowledge or a message. They all perceive it as some fundamental element of nature, one that is related to the structures and organization found in nature. Several authors also attribute causal power to information, so information is essentially responsible for the state of nature. However, the external structure of a phenomenon is never in itself identified directly with information but rather as a manifestation of that information, or maybe information is a deeply hidden structure. Indeed, some authors prefer to use the term organization rather than structure, because it is less loaded with meaning. Most of the researchers regard information as having no intrinsic meaning, with meaning being bestowed later by a receiving agent or other interpreter of information. Some authors return to the concept of hylemorphism and its variants to explain the information–matter–energy interaction, but such interpretations tend to lean only slightly on the Aristotelian concept, with it serving more as an inspiration than a point of reference. Several authors also refer to the Latin origins of the word "information" (i.e., *informare*) to reveal the original meaning of information. Meanwhile, only a few recent authors have extended the concept of meaning to biological systems and machine-to-machine (M2M) systems, thus avoiding anthropomorphizing information, but it remains to be seen whether such an extension is justified. Some authors perceive natural processes as information processes in both organic and inorganic entities. The overall image of information that emerges from the review is one where information is a foundational element of natural objects, artifacts, and natural phenomena. In other words, it is an intrinsic part of the universe. In addition, information does not need to have meaning to exist, because it is embedded in physical forms, and as such, it is closely associated with nature.

Conjectural or "intuitive" claims can be found in the works of Keith Devlin, Frank Wilczek, John Barrow, Sean Carroll, Richard Sole and Santiago Elena, Carlo Rovelli, Charles Seife, John Polkinghorne, and Paul Davies, and these can be summarized into eight points: (1) Information as a natural phenomenon, without meaning, is not related to knowledge but rather to the properties of the universe (i.e., nature), and this concept has clearly found its place in the research literature. (2) In several studies, we see the tension between the abstract (mental) concept of information and the concrete, physical representation of information. (3) In any discussion about information as a natural phenomenon, entropy (thermodynamics) tends to play a prominent role. (4) The term information is usually not clearly defined. (5) Despite the diverse descriptions, there are several commonalities in terms of information existing in nature. (6) Information in nature is closely related to organization in nature (i.e., its structure). (7) Information in nature can be quantified. (8) Information in nature is often conceptualized as part of a matter–energy–information complex.

The findings of the studies by von Weizsäcker, Turek, Mynarski, Heller, Collier, Stonier, Jadacki and Brożek, Dodig Crnkovic, and Hidalgo were combined into 11 claims about information: (1) The notion of information being associated with knowledge does not exhaustively explain the concept of information. (2) Information is a physical/natural phenomenon. (3) Information is a physical/natural phenomenon without meaning. (4) The meaning of information is derived by the mind of a cognitive agent, rather than being intrinsic to information as a physical/natural phenomenon. (5) The role of information in nature may be conceptualized within a matter–energy–information complex. (6) Information as a physical/natural phenomenon is fundamental to nature, so whatever exists physically must contain information. (7) Information as a physical/natural phenomenon is expressed through the structure/form and organization of things. (8) Information as a physical/natural phenomenon is not, and cannot be reduced to, what we conceptualize as structures. (9) Information as a physical/natural phenomenon is responsible for the internal organization of nature's objects and artifacts.

(10) Natural processes are information processes that we may denote as a form of computing. (11) Quantifications of information provide measures of sensible structures, and while these reflect the presence of information, they are not information itself.

In order to extract the most minimal and synthetic list of properties, we combined the above 11 characteristics of information from the preceding chapter into three statements:

- (EN) Information has no meaning, but meaning is derived from information by a cognitive agent.
- (PE) Information is a physical phenomenon.
- (FN) Information is responsible for the organization of the physical world.

These are supplemented by two corollaries:

- (C1) Information is quantifiable.
- (C2) Changes in the organization of physical objects can be denoted as a form of computation or information processing.

4.1 Synthesis of Findings

We now ask the following: What kind of information emerges from the previous studies? Is our claim for the existence of ontological information justified? Are the four intuited properties of ontological information (see Chapter 1) confirmed in the studies? Which properties can we ultimately assign to this information? How many are there: all four, just three, or do we need to add more? Could the concept of ontological information add any clarity to the already numerous and confused conceptualizations for information, or is this just another red herring? Should we, as is often suggested, just adopt Shannon's Theory of Communication (ToC) as the overall framework for discussing information in general? Alternatively, is the ToC just another take on the problem, something that is operationally useful (even very useful) but conceptually and metaphysically deficient? Finally, does ontological information (the concept of it) help us to resolve any of the conceptual difficulties of information, such as the concrete–abstract dichotomy that has been indicated by many authors?

The existing studies do not directly answer these questions, because their ideas about information do not share exactly the same set of features, and despite their many similarities, they are not quite aligned. Among their several commonalities, the studies agree that there is information as a natural phenomenon, so it is without meaning, unrelated to knowledge, independent of a cognitive agent for its existence, and unrelated to a communication process, but it is connected with the properties of the universe or may be one of these properties itself. Several authors indicate the tension between the concept of information as an abstract object of thought (i.e., the most common view of information) and information as a concrete, physical thing (i.e., information as it is understood in this study). And, the solution to this tension would also resolve the nature of information, as some writers claim. In many studies ranging from cosmology to the foundations of life, the concepts of information and entropy (thermodynamics) are very closely related, even to the extent that both are seen as almost equivalent in a numerical sense or even in a conceptual sense, but this claim is disputable. Moreover, every author confirms that information is closely related to the organization of nature, so information is a structure of sorts. Some authors also point to its causal efficacy. This claim should not surprise anyone, because causal efficacy will be a natural property of information if it is indeed a natural phenomenon. The information these studies describe can be quantified, and it is often conceptualized as part of a matter–energy–information complex. Some propose that this "complex" is a new kind of hylemorphism, while some talk about a similar concept but drop the Aristotelian reference. What the authors exactly state in support of these conjectures is detailed in the following sections.

4.2 Properties: How Many and Which Ones?

We now ask how many properties we should attribute to information from the features conceptualized in eight intuitions and eleven claims.

Initially, it was proposed that I_O has four properties: structural presentation (SR), ontological objectivity (OO), physical embodiment (PE), and epistemic neutrality (EN). Judging what will be a minimally sufficient set of properties is subjective out of necessity, but the process is not entirely unjustified. First, it is based on insights from the reviewed studies, and these studies should support the proposed set of features. Second, the smallest set has to account for what these studies conclude, preferably completely and exhaustively. We will then attempt to develop minimal yet sufficient set of properties. The following sections propose solutions to this challenge.

4.2.1 *The proposed three properties*

We propose reducing the characteristics of ontological information to just three features and two corollaries. These seem to correlate well, as we will show, with the claims and intuitions from the studies. Moreover, they subsume the four initial properties, somewhat confirming our intuitions about ontological information, which have guided this study. Seeing as there are only three properties rather than eleven like in the claims from the studies, eight like in the intuitions from the investigated fragments, or four like in our introduction, they are more minimal than the other options and therefore more conceptually efficient. The three proposed characteristics are as follows:

- (EN) Information has no meaning: Epistemic Neutrality.
- (PE) Information is physical phenomena: Physical Embodiment.[1]
- (FN) Information is responsible for the organization of the physical world: Formative Nature.

The two corollaries are as follows:

- (C1) Information is quantifiable.
- (C2) Changes in the organization of physical objects are denoted as computation or information processing.

---

[1] By being physical, we mean being an integral part of physical objects and being disclosed in physical phenomena.

Why we chose to separate the two corollaries (C1 and C2) from the first three properties will be explained later. Table 4.1 lists these properties, together with their characteristics, and correlates them with the claims from the detailed studies.

We do not consider the properties and characteristics attributed to an ontological information-like phenomenon in the works of Edmund Kowalczyk, Keith Devlin, Frank Wilczek, John Barrow, Sean Carroll, Richard Sole and Santiago Elena, Carlo Rovelli, Charles Seife, John Polkinghorne, and Paul Davies. They in fact coincide with the findings from the more detailed studies. Thus, they do not contribute much to the analysis.

Now, why do we combine claims (3) and (4) into the property of EN; claims (2), (5), and (6) into the property of PE; and claims (7), (8), and (9) into the formative nature (FN) property?

First, claims (3) "information as a natural/physical phenomenon has no meaning" and (4) "meaning in information is derived by the mind of a cognitive agent" both concern the meaning associated with information, with claim (3) declaring that information has no meaning and claim (4) stating that meaning is derived from information. Thus, they refer to the same characteristic of information, namely, that value is attributed to information as a natural phenomenon by an agent, because such information has no intrinsic meaning. The claims can therefore be subsumed under one heading: Information has no meaning.

Next, claims (2), (5), and (6) describe how information is encountered in the physical world: (2) "Information is a physical phenomenon"; (5) "information can be conceptualized in a matter–energy–information complex"; and (6) "information is fundamental to nature". The last claim (6) is effectively confirming the claim of the causal closure of the physical world.[2] If ontological information

---

[2]How do we understand the term "causal closure" in the case of ontological information? This is certainly not a strong causal closure (i.e., every event is reducible to pure physical phenomena at the fundamental level; this position assumes the upward only causation) (e.g., Kim 1993, Vincente 2006). Ontological information (organizational structures) emerges on several layers of physical reality, with the properties at each layer not reducible to the lowest layer (which is what strong

Table 4.1. The three properties and two corollaries of ontological information.

Claim	Property	Description
(3) Information as a natural/ physical phenomenon has no meaning.	Epistemic neutrality (EN)	Information has no meaning.
(4) Meaning in information is derived by the mind of a cognitive agent.		
(2) Information is a physical/natural phenomenon.	Physical embodiment (PE)	Information is a physical phenomenon.
(5) The role of information in nature may be conceptualized as a matter–energy–information complex.		
(6) Information is fundamental to nature, so whatever exists physically contains information.		
(7) Information is expressed in structures/form and the organization of things.	Formative nature (FN)	Information is responsible for the organization of the physical world.
(8) Information is not structure.		
(9) Information is responsible for the internal organization of nature's objects and artifacts.		
(10) Natural processes are information processes that we may denote as computing.	Corollary C2	Changes in the organization of physical objects are denoted as computation or information processing.
(11) Measures of information provide quantifications of sensible structures that reflect information but are not information itself.	Corollary C1	Information is quantifiable.

is a part of this world, it must be physical, thus reflecting claim (2). Claim (5) indirectly refers to the same property, as it positions information as part of a complex that constitutes the physical reality of objects, phenomena, and entities. All three claims position information as part of the physical world, so they can again be subsumed under a single heading: Information is a physical phenomenon.

Claims (7) and (8), taken together, express the notion that information is expressed in structure, but it is not structure in itself. Next, claim (9) as "information is responsible for the internal organization of nature's objects and artifacts" adds the concept of a causal role for ontological information. Thus, claims (7), (8), and (9) together describe the role of structures and organization in the conceptualization of information, so they can be grouped under a single heading: Information is responsible for the organization of the physical world.

Now, why are claims (10) and (11) singled out as corollaries? Claim (10) states that "natural processes are information processes that we may denote as computing", but this is an interpretation of ontological information, so it does not constitute an essential feature. Next, claim (11) refers to measures of information. Measures are functions assigned to things or phenomena, so they are of secondary import in terms of characterizing something's nature. In other words, they are devised for utilitarian purposes rather than metaphysical ones. Of course, they can be immensely useful, but their explanatory powers are limited. They are descriptions of nature within the confines of a certain symbolic language with specific syntax and semantics.

---

causal closure requires). In other words, the properties of a layer i are not explainable by the properties of the layers $i-1$, $i-2$, $i-k$, etc. (vide biological systems), with the properties of the layers $i-1$, $i-2$, $i-k$ impacting the properties of the layers below (i.e., the layer i impacts some properties of layers $i-1$, $i-2$, $i-k$, etc.). This requires downward causation, which does not lead to dualism (see Searle 1998, Nagel 2012). However, these complex systems are still physical, not some outwardly phenomena, and information is part of them. This is what is meant by "causal closure" in the case of ontological information.

Thus, we claim that ontological information is characterized by EN, PE, and FN. The property of EN means that information has no meaning, with this being derived by the capacities of a cognitive agent based on information. The property of PE means that information is a physical phenomenon, so it may be conceptualized in a matter–energy–information complex (one not directly implying Aristotelian hylemorphism), and it is fundamental to nature (i.e., whatever exists physically contains information). Finally, the property of FN means that information is responsible for the organization of the physical world, so information is expressed through structures/form and the organization of things, but information is not structure itself—it is merely responsible for the internal organization of natural objects and artifacts.

The properties EN, PE, and FN are well expressed in the published studies, as can be seen in the correlation of these properties with the eleven claims. Thus, with these three properties, no characteristic of ontological information from the reviewed studies is lost. The following section discusses how the properties EN, PE, and FN should be understood.

Note, as we have pointed out already, that we do not provide a correlation of these three properties with the eight intuitions for two reasons: First, such a comparison would extend the analysis substantially without moving our discussion forward. Second, we can clearly see that these eight intuitions are entirely subsumed by the eleven claims, so any correlation of the three properties with the eight intuitions would be somewhat redundant and not bring any new perspectives to the discussion.

EN: Information has no (intrinsic) meaning

This property states that ontological information has no meaning, which is defined as representing some value for a cognitive agent. From specific ontological information, an agent may derive something (some value) that has significance for that agent's existence or functioning. The same ontological information may result in a different meaning for different agents. Likewise, this information may have no

meaning at all to some agents. Jadacki and Brożek give an example
that exemplifies this point: An agent is primarily a conscious being
that creates meaning for itself, so the difference between the artificial
and biological systems' reception of environmental stimuli leading to
the creation of meaning is not very obvious. In this sense, is a robot
a conscious being if it senses light and interprets the image? These
questions are discussed further in Chapter 6. However, an agent can
in principle be any system, whether organic or artificial, if it senses
ontological information or the organization of natural phenomena.
Natural agents (i.e., biological systems) have been shaped by nature
to perceive nature's properties, including organizational properties,
but artificial agents are of our own making of course, so in a sense,
they also have biological origins. We are therefore creations of nature,
not separated from it. Nagel (2012) discusses this idea in detail. We
are built to interpret nature, not falsify it, and evolution assumes
this, because organisms that fail to correctly perceive the environment will likely not survive. This is also the general idea behind
how we build our artificial agents. However, Kant misinterpreted the
nature–mind dependency.[3] This is not an excuse for the failings of
his philosophy but rather an explanation.

---

[3]Kant assumed that the mind "creates" the reality that we perceive. Kant does
not propose (because the concept of evolution was obviously foreign to him) that
the mind evolved to represent reality as closely as was needed for a given entity
to survive. One may argue that evolution itself does not guarantee that the mind
must evolve to represent reality. But, things in nature generally take the simplest,
most energy-efficient form for the given task. So, why would the mind, in order
to represent reality, represent something else that would represent reality? Kant
also did not ask where the mind came from. The conceptual separation between
Kant's concept of the mind and its functions and the modern view can only be
fully realized after reading modern studies of the brain, the mind, and its role,
such as the work of Damasio (2003, 2018). The issue here is not some kind of
model of the mind—such as that of Dennett, Fodor, or someone else—but the
close, organic relation between the mind and nature. The mind is part of, or is,
nature, not something apart from it. The consequences of this are far reaching.
If we postulate that the mind is a computer of sorts, then does the mind being
part of nature imply that nature computes much like the mind does? Is the mind
not something apart from it? Would we still wonder what it is?

An agent may also create meaning from his/her own resources in the absence of a specific sender or a receiver (i.e., sending a message without a particular destination target, a broadcast message). This may have meaning for that agent but not necessarily anyone else. We hope that the Arecibo Message (2018) has been sent to someone other than ourselves. If there is no one to decode it, however, it is simply cosmic noise, something close to it, or maybe not even this (i.e., it is too weak and too focused). The fact that ontological information is meaningless means that data, which for some researchers are a primary source of epistemic information, are information that has already been interpreted. Consequently, every fact is laden with theory, and there is no theory-free data. We simply impose a certain format and language on nature's processes and then call them data, but we need to recall from Philosophy of Science 101 that there is no theory-free data (Chalmers 1994, Bird 2002).[4] As data are interpreted signals, much like meaning, data for one agent may not be data for another. This is the conceptual context where von Weizsäcker got lost when he said there is no information without language, so information for him must have meaning.

The same argument applies to "information" defined by probabilistic (Shannon–Weaver, Hartley, Fisher) and combinatorial measures (Solomonoff–Kolmogorov–Chaitin). The information defined by these formulas is ontological information that has been interpreted within the formal language of probability calculus or combinatorial algebra. Any interpretation of ontological information is an imposed interpretation (sic), so it is very difficult to talk about information by looking at its quantifications. When we talk about information expressed through some mathematical formula, we talk about the models we are imposing on the phenomenon. Once we remove ourselves from the context, however, we should clearly recognize that a tree falling in the forest creates a physical pattern of air pressure waves, whether we are there to hear it or not. There is no *Music of*

---

[4]In university curriculum parlance, the 101 number is usually assigned to an introductory course in a given discipline.

the Spheres or *Musica universalis* (Musica universalis 2019). However, there is Gustav Holst's *The Planets* in Popper's sense of three worlds. One cannot accept the concept of ontological information while holding on to the concept of information as meaning or knowledge.

The property of EN implies that I_O exists independently of any natural or artificial cognitive, cognitive system. Several researchers indicate that this is the case for information. Von Weizsäcker differentiates between information that is "understood in a form–matter composite" and information that includes past experience and past and current knowledge. He says that information in the first sense is form or *eidos* (i.e., a form–matter composite) in the sense that it is a source of knowledge. Thus, he differentiates between information as a physical thing and information as a cognitive product, with the first one being the raw material for the second, although von Weizsäcker later obfuscates this difference. Collier, meanwhile, states that IiT (information in things) is a cause and a source of cognitive information (CI), which must be correlated with the outside world. Thus, outside objects must have a property "that allows us to have information about them", so there must be "either pre-existing meaningful information or else it must be converted by cognition into meaningful information". Collier sees information CI as being created from IiT by cognitive systems, because CI is information with meaning, so meaning has been "added" to external information (IiT). Thomas Nagel states that our knowledge, which is denoted as epistemic information in this study, reflects the world. As this is done in a more or less reliable way, the world must be a source of stable information. This information is what we interpret as the "rationality" of the world, its order, or nature. Nagel calls it a "natural order" that expresses itself, or finds expression, in the universal laws of the physical realm. Nagel concludes that the existence of the independent, ordered world is the source of our knowledge and *if we believe in natural order, then something about the world that eventually gave rise to rational beings must explain this possibility*. Thus, in Nagel's research, we have two *locis* and types of information: information in the world perceived as its rationality and laws, independent of the mind, and information in the mind that reflects, rather than accurately copies, the rationality of the world. Dodig Crnkovic postulates the existence of proto-information (PrI), which is patterns or structures in, and of, nature. PrI is "interpreted by an agent", and it becomes information when "a cognitive agent interacts with aspects of the world". PrI should be interpreted as ontological information, while "information" in Dodig Crnkovic's parlance is created by a cognitive agent, so this is (in the view of this study) epistemic information.

Hidalgo, meanwhile, claims that information is physical, and it expresses the embedded physical order or "arrangement of parts". This information is meaningless, because meaning is different from information. Meaning emerges when physical information encounters a system that can process it. It is the interpretation of physical phenomena or their properties through cognition. (Of course, we may extend the concept of meaning to include biological organisms and artificial systems. Here, meaning denotes roughly the same concept for cognitive systems in that information has some impact on the structure and processes within these systems.) Thus, we distinguish two concepts of information: information that is devoid of meaning and information with meaning. The former information is perceived as the form, the structure in things, or ontological information in the sense of this study. The latter form of information, information with meaning, which is referred to in this study as epistemic information, has partial origins in ontological information, with meaning being added through cognition. The information in things (i.e., ontological information) is physical in the sense of being embedded in, or a part of, the matter–energy complex. Incidentally, the term "complex" denotes *a group of obviously related units of which the degree and nature of the relationship is imperfectly known* or *a whole made up of complicated or interrelated parts* (Complex 2018), and it is used here to avoid using the difficult term "hylemorphism", which is loaded with many interpretations.

In fact, a qualified form of "hylemorphism" is used by several authors, such as Turek and von Weizsäcker, to indicate the relation between matter–energy and information. Certainly, the literary interpretation of a complex as a composite of parts, in light of how information is conceptualized, is not correct for the matter–energy–information complex. How information is embedded in matter–energy is not resolved in this study, in the studies we have reviewed, or in any other study for that matter, so it remains open.[5] This problem is as old as philosophy itself. It originated with Plato's Forms and Aristotle's *eidos*. These two philosophers somewhat charted the course for this discussion over the coming millennia. Meaningful information is an intentional object, a product of cognition. How meaning becomes added to sensory information is an issue for cognitive sciences, and we currently have a limited understanding of how meaning for intentional objects arises in cognitive systems, although some claim we know it all (e.g., Dennett 2017). A simplified, or generalized, concept of meaning in artificial cognitive systems has algorithmic explanations, but this is bound within the concepts of artificial minds, knowledge bases, and Turing machines, so it is of limited import for the philosophy of the mind, much like with formal models that relate to reality. (See what import Tarski's semantic theory of truth has for understanding what truth is.)[6] Some will recognize the Chinese Room problem in the discussion and the ensuing controversies.[7]

PE: Information is a physical phenomenon

The claim that "ontological information is a physical phenomenon" means several things. Ontological information is not an abstract concept in the way that mathematical objects, ideas, or thoughts are abstract. Ontological information does not belong to the Platonic

---

[5]Some studies (e.g., Landauer 1996, Bennett 2003, Moore 2012, Lutz 2012, Hong *et al.* 2016, Ladyman *et al.* 2001) point to the Maxwell demon and Landauer's (erasure) principle for the information–energy connection.

[6]See, for example, the comments on Tarski's semantic theory of truth by John Searle in his Berkley Lectures on the Philosophy of Language (Searle 2013a). In short, Tarski's theory of truth does not explain the metaphysical meaning of truth, but only truth in an artificial language system. We do not learn much about truth in our everyday and metaphysical meanings from Tarski's theory.

[7]To understand the discussion, see, as starting points, the Chinese Room Argument in (Hauser 2018) or Cole (2015).

realm of Forms in either the classic or neo-Platonic sense. Ontological information is real, observable, and measurable. Thus, we can claim that information exists much like other physical phenomena exist, because they exhibit the same class of properties. Furthermore, it seems that whatever exists in a physical sense contains information, so there is no physical phenomenon without information, i.e., by being physical, we mean being an integral part of physical objects and being disclosed in physical phenomena. As well, by being physical, we mean being an integral part of physical objects and being disclosed in physical phenomena. It took time for the concept of information to emerge as a separate, differentiable aspect of reality, much like how the concept of energy as a separate physical phenomenon also took time to be recognized. One may speculate that the concept of energy emerged once we learned how to use it to our benefit. A similar situation may be claimed for information. The concept of information emerged once we learned how to use it, and this process of discovery has coincided with, or been precipitated by, the advent of the computer, an information-processing tool *par excellence*. Through information technology, we learned to see information all around us as this information became accessible for our manipulation. We have also begun to see ourselves as information-processing systems, because we take in information from the environment and produce knowledge. We also recognize that the homeostasis of our bodies includes "information stasis".

The claim that information is a physical phenomenon guards us against attributing some nonsensical qualities to information. Von Weizsäcker claims that information should always be understood within the context of a matter–form composite, where information is quantified by measuring the multiplicity of forms that matter–energy can take on. Physical processes are processes of information exchange. Turek, meanwhile, states that information *is what is realizable in substance*, while Collier observes that information is a property of physical objects, one that *is contained in their physical structure*. Next, Stonier claims that information is embedded in different forms of matter, while Heller claims that mathematical models of nature decode the information that is encoded in natural structures. Dodig–Crnkovic, meanwhile, postulates that information is what constitutes the structure of the universe, so information is always embedded in matter–energy phenomena. In other words, there is no information without a physical representation, so all information is carried by some physical medium. Hidalgo also claims that information is always physically embodied and that information is physical. This information is inherent in all physical objects, because they embody physical order, and physical order is information. One must be careful not to identify information with the organization of things itself, though. If information were a table, it would not be four legs, a tabletop, and whatever other components. It would not even be the arrangement of atoms that form the wood that in turn forms the table (Russell's famous table view (Russell 1959)). Information is the order of things on multiple levels of organization. Without a table, this information would seem not to exist, because we can identify it only when it is in something.

If we attribute some causal power to ontological information, information must be "of this world" to preserve the causal closure of nature. Something other worldly cannot be the cause of things in this world, unless it is some kind of deity, but we will stay away from this solution in this study (see the section on the General Theory of Information (GTI) later in the book, on possible causal interpretation of information).

Closely related to the physical nature of information is OO. OO postulates that I_O as an entity exists objectively. Objectivity in this context means that the object exists independently of an observer (i.e., it is mind-independent). This is how physical objects and physical phenomena exist.[8] The existence of physical entities is also the position of scientific realism or conceptual realism in combinatorial ontology (e.g., Brock and Mares 2010, Cocchiarella 1996), so OO

---

[8]Objective existence of information has nothing to do with objective existence attributed to Being vs being. In this perspective, objective information is still contingent as physical world is.

claims that information is just like physical objects or physical phenomena and part of the mind-independent reality. Von Weizsäcker claims that information has an "objective character". He claims that because information is related to the combination/composition of elementary particles, all interpretations of the mass–energy complex apply to information as well. Heller, meanwhile, claims that information may be seen as a material of the world, where "material" is used here in the sense of a physical substance that things can be made from (Material 2018), with it having synonyms such as substance, stuff, and medium. Dodig Crnkovic, for her part, claims that information is an "ontologically fundamental entity of the physical reality". Hidalgo, meanwhile, observes that what is left after separating meaning from information that is perceived as having meaningful import is a physical phenomenon that can be seen as physical order.

The consequence of information being a physical phenomenon is the concept of PE. This property means that I_O always exists in a physical carrier and as a physical phenomenon that is subject to the laws of physics. The claim that "I_O is a physical phenomenon" is necessary and obvious if we want to see information as a part of the physical world, and if this is indeed the case, and we presume that it is, this information must be subject to the laws governing the physical realm. However, we are not sure exactly which laws apply (e.g., the law of gravitation, the law of conservation of momentum, the three laws of thermodynamics, the theory of general relativity, or some other yet unknown laws for information).

Some insight into the sort of laws we may be talking about can be gleaned from the concept of pancomputationalism or natural computing, where all natural processes are seen as information processing. Thus, information would be subject to all laws that we think govern the fundamental properties of the physical universe. We obviously do not know all of these, because if we've learned anything over the history of science, it is that what we know today is never the last word (at least, this has been our experience so far). The claim that "I_O exists always in a physical carrier" prevents us from conceptualizing information as some unknown esoteric thing or mysterious phenomenon of sorts, but this is not an endorsement of material monism and certainly not material reductionism. There are philosophies of the mind that consider the mind as not reducible to matter while still recognizing that it has a material base.[9]

FN: Information as an organizing factor in nature

Ontological information is responsible for the organization of the physical world. Organization is a fairly broad concept that may be, and is, interpreted as structure, order, form, shape, or rationality (if perceived by a cognitive entity). We do not posit that information is structure, although this has been claimed several times. The problem with such a statement is that we do not know precisely what a structure is and what kinds of structure we would associate with information, as well as how this would be achieved. Information is certainly not the visible structure or shape of an object, but we concede that the shape or structure of an object is how information discloses itself or how we sense its presence. Thus, the shape of a tea cup is not information, but information is being expressed in the shape of a tea cup.

If we try to attribute to the concept of structure some domain-specific meaning, such as mathematical structure or the structure of physical laws, information would simply acquire the characteristics of that domain (i.e., information would be a mathematical structure or a physical law). We may risk conjecturing, though, that quantifications of structure, such as Shannon's ToC probabilistic model of the structure of the message, are not information but rather "numbers" assigned to the consequences of information interacting with physical media. It seems that quantifications of information quantify the "shapes" rather than the information. We want to avoid these domain-specific information claims, because ontological information is domain-neutral.

---

[9]Despite claims by some researchers to the contrary, the nature of consciousness has not been resolved. See, e.g., Kandel (2006, pp. 376–390), Searle (1998, 2002, 2013b, 2015a, 2015b).

If we say that information is a "deep" structure, it becomes even more ambiguous, because we do not know what we mean by these "deep structures". Finally, if information is a structure, why do we not identify ontological information with structure? Or, conversely, why do we posit the existence of information separately from the existence of structure? It would therefore be simpler to say that information is structure, and this is where we would end up with structural realism or informational structural realism. Moreover, structures in structural realism are passive, and they do not carry the meaning of *informare*, namely, to shape; or, at least nobody in the structural realism literature has attributed such causal power to structures. We also have other terms like *eidos* or Form for the internal shape of things, which is what gives them their individuality, but these ancient terms are loaded with many interpretations and declaring information as Form or *eidos* could not be regarded as progress in the understanding of the concept of information. After all, some would say the Greeks knew it long ago. The term organization seems to encompass the meaning of form, the meaning of structure, as well as allowing for the causal interpretation of *informare*. Thus, we posit that information is a factor responsible for the organization of the physical world.

Information is expressed by, is responsible for, is equated with, or is considered a structural property of natural and artificial objects. The structural property of information is attested to by all of the authors we have studied, although as we mentioned, structures are defined in many ways depending on the context and the discourse domain.

We may again ask whether the structural property of information is intrinsic to information, or is it just the way we perceive information or the way that information reveals itself to us. To help answer this question, we may look at energy and work. We often confuse energy with work, claiming that energy is work. The reality is that work is just a way in which energy is perceived. We perceive energy as a factor of "work". By analogy, the structural aspect of information is maybe just the way that information reveals itself, but not the information itself. Thus, information is "a principle of organization" that is seen, or at least its effects are, as a structure. Von Weizsäcker conceives information as a structure, the shape of a natural object of an artifact, but information is not simply a geometric shape. Information for von Weizsäcker goes beyond shape—it is something common across different substances and objects with different shapes. He gives the example of a message written on a sheet of paper or printed on a telegram. For Turek, information is a *subset of forms reducible to structures*. Information may be realized in prime matter (in Turek's view, information is imposed prime matter), or it is inherent in the form–matter composite. This information can also be represented through mathematical formalism. Collier, meanwhile, claims that things have a definite structure. There must be something that gives them this structure, or it is contained within it. He calls this factor "information". Stonier states that all structures have or contain information, and a change in the information content of an object results in a change in its structure. Information may also be encoded in different structures, because it is matter-independent. Heller, meanwhile, postulates that the world is a structure, and this structure contains encoded information. Information structures are therefore fundamental to existence. The more complex a structure, the more limitations it has and the more information it contains. While information is expressed in structures, it is not what fills these structures. Furthermore, Heller claims that structures in nature are beyond the capabilities of modern mathematical–empirical methods. Jadacki and Brożek claim that information is a certain state in the internal structure of an object. Dodig Crnkovic, meanwhile, claims that information forms structures, which in turn form nature. She defines information as structures on different levels of resolution, with successive levels forming the entirety of nature. Furthermore, she states that reality is built of information structures. She does not explain what these information structures are, though, so we must speculate that they are either structures interpreted as information or structures built from information. Hidalgo defines information as structures, the order or arrangement of parts in a system, and these structures are manifestations of information. In other words, physical order is structure that expresses information. In Hidalgo's example, order (i.e., the information contained in an object) explains the difference between the car before the crash and the same car after the crash.

Corollaries C1 and C2

We have formulated two corollaries for three characteristics of ontological information: (C1) information is quantifiable and (C2) changes in the organization of physical objects are denoted as computation or information processing. So, why were these characteristics singled out?

Corollary (C1), namely, that information is quantifiable, is supported in almost every study we reviewed. Functions quantifying information are almost foundational for the idea of information, even if they do not represent what information is but rather how it discloses itself. These quantifications are used to measure certain utilitarian aspects of information, such as optimal communication channel coding (Shannon), error recovery, optimal computer program size (Chaitin), and such like. They have many important applications, but they do not explain the nature of what they seek to quantify. This corollary is supported by claim (11) in that measures of information provide quantifications of sensible structures that reflect information but are not information itself.

Corollary C2, meanwhile, states that changes in the organization of physical objects can be denoted as computation, but what does this mean? Computing refers to information processing, and most would agree with this. Computers process information (i.e., they compute). Computing by computers is essentially a form of symbol manipulation with a set of rules. This is the case for a Turing machine, which is our general model for symbolic computing. The information we seek to manipulate is encoded into symbols that we can then manipulate. This is obviously epistemic information or semantic information, however, because a Turing machine interprets symbols that we define in the way we have defined them. In other words, we impose syntax and semantics on the input to computing systems—it is not the case that they create it. Computers do not add their own interpretation or even their own syntax. For example, we may say that the specific form of a specific electromagnetic wave is "0" or "1". We may say that "01000001" is the letter "A" in ASCII or "100" is the number 4, and then we tell the computer what to do with these symbols through a program. In principle, the computer can add "A" to "4" as 01000001+ 100, because this is a valid binary operation. We would be rather unlikely to do this, though, because it would make little sense to us, and consequently computers, to add a number to an ASCII-encoded letter.[10] (One exception might be if you wanted to transform the "A" into an "E" (i.e., move forward four letters through the alphabet), but that would be a specific intention on the part of the human programmer.) To refer to Searle again, computing is in the eyes of the beholder (Searle 2015b). Physical processes in computers compute because we set them up to do what we call computing.

In contrast, when information is seen as ontological information and this in turn denotes the organization of physical things, the concept of information processing changes. In this case, information processing is a change to the organization of a physical system. Information processing acquires the meaning of computing, but not in the sense of symbol manipulation using a strictly defined limited set of rules—it refers more to changes in the organization of a physical system. As a specific case of information processing is TM computing (realization of the abstract Turing Machine), but the more generalized sense of computing concerns changes in physical organization or the processing of ontological information. In reality, what computers do is enact controlled changes to the organization of the physical systems underlying them. These computers are in essence (in the sense of a physical artifact) von Neumann-type machines with a TM interpretation superimposed on them.

---

[10]In some sense, neuromorphic computing models that are potential replacements for current digital computers (i.e., von Neumann's (1945) computer architecture in silicon) provide some proof that nature computes. If neurons compute, then why not extend this idea to cover all biological systems? For references, see, for example, Furber (2016) and Hylton (2018). For the new concept of computing, see also, for example, Adleman (1998).

However, does this generalized concept of computing trivialize this concept, because it means that everything computes and computers are everywhere, at least in this extended definition of computing? If we are claiming that everything is a digital computer, this is obviously false. It would muddle the concepts of digital computing and general computing rather than clarify them. If we say that information is an organization of physical entities and information processing is the manipulation of organization, however, it logically follows that nature computes, so natural processes in this sense are computing processes, but not in a TM sense.

We must highlight that nature is not a computer in the sense of TMs or the von Neumann architecture, even if the latter does also fit into this extended sense of computing. Thus, if we assume that information as organization is a part/aspect of the physical world, physical processes are, in this sense, computing processes. Alternatively, we may say that information processing is computing in this extended sense. Again, however, we must emphasize that this does not claim that nature is a computer, at least in the TM sense. Corollary (C2) is supported by claim (10) in that natural processes are information processes that we may denote as computing (in the extended sense),

4.2.2 *Two or one property?*

Now, how many properties do we need to characterize ontological information? Do we need all three properties? Maybe we can characterize ontological information with just two, or maybe even one, of them? Let us test the possible options. In this exercise, we use the following notation for the properties of ontological information: Ontological information is epidemically neutral (P1), ontological information embedded in a physical carrier is physical (i.e., embodied in physical phenomena) (P2), and ontological information is formative with respect to nature (P3). These are subject to the following interpretations:

- P1: Ontological information has no meaning. Meaning is defined as representing some value for the cognitive agent. From ontological information, an agent derives something that has some significance for its existence, thus creating meaning.

- P2: Ontological information is not an abstract object in the way that mathematical objects or thoughts are abstract. Ontological information does not belong to the realm of Forms in either the classical or neo-Platonic sense. Ontological information is real, observable, and measurable. It exists like other physical phenomena exist, and whatever exists in nature contains information. There are no physical phenomena without information.

- P3: Ontological information is responsible for the organization of the physical world. Organization may be, interpreted as structure, order, form, shape, or rationality (if perceived by a cognitive entity), but it is none of them.

We have the following six options with respect to the various selections of properties: (A) P1 and P2; (B) P1 and P3; (C) P2 and P3; (D) P1; (E) P2; and (F) P3.

Option (A) with P1 and P2 would claim that ontological information has no meaning (P1) and is physical in nature (P2). This, however, would omit the critical aspect of ontological information being expressed in structure/organization. All things that are physical in nature have no meaning. For example, the whole of nature—including the cosmos with its stars and galaxies and the smaller things on Earth like the rivers, oceans, and volcanoes—would qualify as ontological information if we would use only these two properties. Thus, a volcano or a star would be information. Thus, accepting only P1 and P2 as characteristics of ontological information would not be a meaningful proposal, so this option is rejected (the whole of nature is characterized this way).

Option (B), P1 and P3, would claim that ontological information has no meaning but has a FN. We assume that things in nature have no meaning because they do not. The P1 + P3 option would leave the door open for the status of ontological information, so it could be an abstract notion rather than a strictly physical phenomenon. Their incomprehensibility is of a different nature though. Forms and eidos are complex in details but yield conflicting interpretations.

Tao is so condensed as the Ultimate principle that cannot be even comprehended or expressed (by definition). Thus, the P1+ P3 option would not address the abstract–concrete tension encountered by such as Davies and von Weizsäcker, among others. It would leave the ontological status of information unresolved, so this option is also rejected.

Option (C), P2 and P3, would claim that ontological information is a physical phenomenon with an FN. This option may be a possible candidate for describing ontological information, because the meaningless character of information can be deduced implicitly in that anything objective (existentially and epistemically) is obviously independent of a cognitive agent. Now, as agents are the source of meaning, anything agent-independent must be meaningless. Thus, we could argue that ontological information has the P1 property by implication, yet this would mean the critical difference between epistemic and ontological information is not explicitly accounted for, making this variant less accurate than the original.

Options (D), (E), and (F)—the individual properties P1, P2, or P3 by themselves—would not designate any specific phenomenon. These descriptions would be of course correct in that they assert nothing that is incorrect, but they would also be incomplete. By way of analogy, we could characterize an electron as a particle with a negative charge. This would be correct, of course, but it would also cover negatively charged ions rather than being limited to a single subatomic particle. Thus, any designation of ontological information with a single property would be correct but incomplete, because it would cover other phenomena. For example, option (D), P1, would claim that ontological information is epistemically neutral, but many things have no meaning to us, so P1 is not specific enough. Likewise, option (E), P2, would claim that ontological information is physical, but so many things are, so phenomena with this property include a variety of things that are very different in many other respects. Again, designating ontological information purely with this property would be incomplete. Finally, option (F), P3, would potentially reduce ontological information to structure, such that ontological information is the structure or shape of things. Everything we talk about has some kind of structure of form, though. If we would accept that ontological information is P3, we could discard ontological information as a redundant concept and simply claim that ontological information is just another name for structure.

We may also look differently at the properties of information: Instead of selecting a set of three, two, or one property, we could seek to create a super-property that encompasses all three of the selected properties into one. We assume that the three properties do express the essence of ontological information, so this hypothetical super-property cannot add any new features but only express the meaning of these three. In fact, we may have such a possibility: The single property could be like Plato's Form or could be Aristotelian *eidos*, Platonic Form, or Tao-Te-Ching Tao. These do, in their conceptualization, combine the concept of form/structure, nature, and the independence from any cognition. These proposals, however, have suffered from centuries of critique, and proposing them anew would not change their value. The concepts of Aristotelian *eidos*, Platonic Form, and Tao-Te-Ching Tao are so condensed and abstract that they are incomprehensible, and they are certainly not quantifiable or measurable. Thus, they do not pass the tests for modern scientific reality. For example, could we accept the claim that Shannon's ToC measures the *eidos* of a message? We think not.

Thus, it seems that the three properties P1, P2, and P3, plus the two corollaries, provide the most complete description of ontological information that we have been able to identify. We therefore propose this option as being characteristic of ontological information. Future research may change how we see and conceptualize ontological information, however, because scientific hypothesis, as this indeed is, can never be proven right but only wrong (Chalmers 1994).

Chapter 5

Ontology and Epistemology: Two Perspectives on Information

In this chapter, we present two perspectives for considering information: ontological and epistemic. The meaning of these terms is explained following Searle's ideas. This binary perspective permits, in the author's opinion, a means to reduce the many definitions of information to two categories. But are the boundaries between these two perspectives clearly defined? Not necessarily, because it all depends on our understanding of concepts such as meaning, consciousness, information processing systems, message, existence, and so on. However, if we establish some boundaries for the meanings of these terms, we may be able to classify most information concepts into these two groups. Finally, we propose that epistemic information depends on an ontological basis for existence. This would make ontological information, as defined here, more fundamental than epistemic information.

5.1 The Dilemma of Information

We have classified information into two types, namely ontological and epistemic. Ontological information is information without meaning, and it does not need a sender or a receiver to exist. It is a physical phenomenon that is perceived as an organization of something. Ontological information has found applications in cosmology, thermodynamics, physics, quantum mechanics, and metaphysics, and it has begun to manifest in information sciences. With ontological information, quantified models of information are reinterpreted as different takes on the informational structures. No one quantified model of information is supreme, and some are just more useful than others depending on the application. Ontological information may also justify a generalization of the concept of computing into one where computing transforms structures rather than manipulates symbols, as is the case with the universal Turing machine (UTM) (Dodig-Crnkovic 2012, Hidalgo 2015). Such a view would align the theoretical models of computing (i.e., the UTM-centered ones) with advances in natural computing systems, such as neuromorphic computations (e.g., Shanahan 2015). We refer to ontological information as structural information or the organization of natural and artificial phenomena.

Epistemic information, on the other hand, is information related to concepts of knowledge, a cognitive agent, or meaning. Epistemic information is "about" something and is intended "for someone". For epistemic information to exist, it requires a conscious agent to create and/or receive it, and it exists with that agent. Epistemic information represents what is meant by information in communication sciences, cognitive science, library science, biology, social sciences, and information technology. We may also refer to it as cognitive information (stressing its dependency on cognitive systems), semantic information (stressing meaning as a defining feature), or abstract information.

Epistemic information does not recognize the presence of ontological information, yet it cannot disregard the physical reality and the physical stimuli that forms a large source of epistemic information. Thus, in the definitions for epistemic information, we find data, physical signals, infons,[1] or something else filling this gap (e.g., the GDI definition of Floridi 2010). Simply speaking, the concept of epistemic information tends to disregard its physical basis. Thus, epistemic information, as it is, is not a complete description of the concept of information.

In contrast, ontological information does account for the organization of natural objects and artifacts, but it cannot have meaning

---

[1]See, for example, the work of Stonier (1990), Devlin (1991), Floridi (2010), and Martinez and Sequoiah-Grayson (2014).

and knowledge. It is by definition meaningless, so it is also an incomplete description of the concept of information.

Ontological and epistemic information are closely connected. Ontological information "gives shape" to natural phenomena. It may then be "intercepted" by a cognitive agent and become epistemic information. In other words, epistemic information is ontological information as comprehended by a cognitive agent. This process of "comprehension" is complex and irreducible.

In a sense, both types of information exist, ontological as something concrete and epistemic as an abstract view of knowledge. From this perspective, ontological information acts as the carrier of what can potentially become epistemic information. Indeed, it is its main source, with the cognitive faculties of the mind itself being another source. I_e is contingent, dependent, and relative because it is located in the mind. I_o, meanwhile, is objective and meaningless, because it exists as a physical fact. We may need I_o to get I_e, but I_e acquires its own "persistence" once created. While there is an obvious bottom-up causation from I_o to I_e, there is also a top-down causation from I_e to I_o. This means that in many cases, the forms and organization in physical reality (e.g., man-made objects) are expressions of mental concepts (I_e). We may therefore imply an emergence relation between the two forms of information. However, this emergence must be properly understood. I_e emerges from I_o as a non-reducible "entity". I_e cannot be explained purely in terms of I_o, because it acquires features that do not exist at the I_o level. Another interpretation would involve regarding I_o as representing the level of physical reality, which is in itself a multi-level reality with complex structures at different levels of organization for nature. In fact, we have multiple levels of I_o to reflect nature's complexity. I_e, meanwhile, represents the reality at the level of a living conscious agent. This reflects I_o, but the agent creates its own specific representation. Which particular interpretation of I_o and I_e is most accurate should be the subject of future research.

So, what is the conclusion? If we accept that information is epistemic only, we are ignoring the discoveries of modern science and limiting ourselves to the anthropocentric (or agent-centered) perspective of information. However, this concept of information is incomplete, as we have endeavored to demonstrate.

In contrast, if we postulate that information is ontological only, we imply that epistemic information can be reduced to, and expressed fully by, ontological information. This would be a grave error, because while epistemic information is largely derived from ontological information, we would be disregarding the fact that epistemic information has a certain individual presence, so it cannot be reduced to ontological information.

However, we could accept that both forms of information exist, albeit in different ways, and both are required for a complete understanding of the concept of information. We could then further accept that these two types of information have mutual dependencies, although they are not reducible to each other. It appears that this duality in the information concept cannot be fully understood until we resolve the nature of cognitive processes and knowledge. We could risk the statement (going against the naturalistic perspective) that for the full description of the universe and us in it (Tallis 2016) we need to recognize the existence of both types of information, epistemic and ontological, and may be "word" in John 1:1 meant that information is both.

5.2 Epistemic Information

The epistemic perspective is how information is understood in communication sciences, cognitive sciences, library science, biology, social sciences, some strands of pancomputationalism, and information technology. Indeed, this is how we most often perceive information these days. The concept of epistemic information has been through many incarnations, but there is no single definition that would be accepted by everyone or even some majority.[2] For some examples, see the works of Bar-Hillel and Carnap (1953), Brooks (1980), Rucker

---

[2]The number of supporters for an idea does not count, because in philosophy, ideas are not selected through democratic voting, and ideas that are rejected by the majority often contain the truth.

(1987), Buckland (1991), Devlin (1991), Losee (1998), Sveiby (1998), Dretske (1999), Casagrande (1999), Floridi (2010, 2013), Burgin (2003), Lenski (2010), Vernon (2014), DasGupta (2016), and Carroll (2017), among others. Each of these authors painted a somewhat different picture of epistemic information. We therefore grouped conceptualizations of epistemic information into classes related to human cognitive agents, biological agents, artificial cognitive agents, and formal models, including logical models and quantitative models. These formal models include the one of Shannon–Weaver–Hartley and other related proposals, Chaitin models, statistical models, and Devlin information logic. A common element in all these conceptualizations, however, is how information is conceived as having some meaning to a receiver or sender, where information comes in a message that is communicated to a system. The receiving system can be a human being, a biological organism as simple as a cell, or an artificial cognitive agent, such as an autonomous robot. Table 5.1 summarizes the main elements of some selected models for epistemic information, but this is certainly not exhaustive.[3]

Epistemic information is conceptualized within a range of domains, applications, and methods.

These conceptualizations include human cognitive agents, biological systems, artificial cognitive systems, and logical and formal conceptualizations. The common element in all these concepts, however, concerns how information is being conceived as something relative to an agent or other cognitive systems (i.e., the knowledge of that agent/system). Of course, what an agent, cognition, and knowledge are must be understood in relation to the context. Epistemic information in any of the above definitions does not exist on its own, because its presence must be recognized by some reference system (i.e., an agent with some sort of cognitive capacity). Therefore, how do we define an agent, cognition, and knowledge? No single definition

---

[3]One should also mention the "classification of schools" of information, with each school taking a different view on what information is. This list of schools was created by Dodig-Crnkovic (2006).

Table 5.1. Summary of selected models for epistemic information.

Category of model	Author	Main claim
Human cognitive agent	Beyond-Davies (2009)	Information is data + meaning.
	Bateson (1979)	Information consists of differences that make a difference.
	Dretske (1999)	Information is sharply distinguished from meaning, at least for the concept of meaning relevant to semantic studies.
	Floridi (2013)	Information is data + meaning.
	Buckland (1991)	Information-as-a-thing, information-as-knowledge, information-as-a-process
	Ratzan (2004)	Information is meaning.
	Davenport (1997)	Information is "data endowed with relevance and purpose".
Biological agent	Smith (2000)	DNA transmission is equivalent to a human communication channel.
Artificial cognitive agent	Vernon (2014)	Information is what an artificial cognitive system extracts from the environment.
Formal models, including logical and quantified models	Shannon (1948) and other models related to Hartley–Shannon–Weaver entropy	$H(X) = \sum_{i=1}^{m} \frac{p(xi) \log 1}{p(xi)}$ (measure of information entropy in the communication theory)
	Solomonov, Kolmogorov, and Chaitin	String complexity measures based on the UTM model
	Fisher and Klir Models	Statistical measures

would suffice due to the fact that we need to deal with natural agents (human and non-human organisms) and artifacts (computers, robots, etc.). One may refer to the literature for reference,[4] and there are

---

[4]For a general definition of an agent, see, for example, the work of Poole and Mackworth (2019).

plenty of examples showing the relativity of epistemic information. For example, forgotten scriptures, such as the Egyptian hieroglyphs or Assyrian cuneiform writings, are just symbols with no meaning without the continuity of tradition.

Epistemic[5] information is associated with knowledge, semantics, belief, a communication process, or other more broadly understood meaning.[6]

Epistemic information exists only if someone or something—such as an artificial or biological system, although we need to be careful what we assign epistemic processing capacities to—recognizes it as information after receiving or creating it. Epistemic information exists specifically in, and for, the mind, which can be broadly understood as a complex of cognitive faculties of the receiver or the originator.[7] This information exists when communicated (i.e., created, sent, and received) as a message or a sequence of symbols. The dependency on the sender, receiver, and their cognitive functions therefore makes information epistemically subjective, even if meaning of information is shared among the group of individuals. Thus, this information depends on something else to exist and to denote something. We may also claim that epistemic information is relative to the cognitive faculties of the receiver or sender. Interpreting information as

---

[5]*Epistemic [...] describes anything that has some relation to knowledge* and *Epistemology, or the theory of knowledge, is that branch of philosophy concerned with the nature of knowledge, its possibility, scope and general basis* (Honderich 1995). For this specific domain of discourse (e.g., computer systems and artificial cognitive agents), the concept of knowledge may be defined in domain-specific terms while retaining the generic meaning.

[6]Meaning has many interpretations. For this study, unless otherwise stated, we follow the definitions from the philosophy of language, where the term "meaning" denotes how language relates to the world. A review of theories of meaning is beyond the scope and purpose of this work. An extensive list of references can be found in Speaks (2018) and other sources. The theories claiming that meaning is the correlata to the world are contested with good arguments (Chomsky 2013, 2016). This statement does not say anything about creation of meaning.

[7]The originator or receiver may here have an extended meaning that includes natural (i.e., not man-made) and artificial systems. We may also use the term "cognitive system" rather than "the mind" as a more general term.

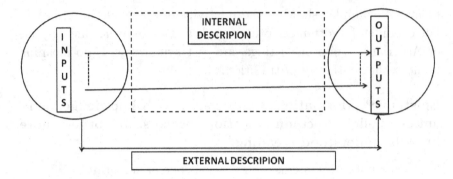

Figure 5.1. A communication system (following Casti 1989, p. 255).

an epistemic concept somewhat reflects the current mode of philosophy, where epistemology (the theory of knowledge) is regarded as more important and fundamental than the concept of metaphysics or ontology, so it holds that an important concept like information should be primarily regarded as epistemic.[8]

Epistemic information is defined in the context of a communication system between sender and receiver.

This system may have many realizations—such as those of Cherry (1978), Shannon (1948), Shannon and Weaver (1964), Smith (2000), and Vernon (2014)—but the general format of the model described by Casti (1989) is shown in Figure 5.1. How epistemic information arises in a cognitive system is a separate issue that is not discussed here.

In a superficial description, the communication system processes inputs into outputs. In the internal description, on the other hand,

---

[8]This epistemic turn in philosophy is attributed to Descartes and Kant, among others. The roots of this change in philosophical focus may also be traced to the fact that we cannot explain the fundamental causes of reality. We can only describe the reality and then only in a rather superficial way. You can see this problem emerging in the Newton–Leibniz discussion about the interpretation of calculus (Guicciardini 2018).

the input is a message that is processed into outputs through the following steps: (1) Inputs are interfaced with the communication channel M. (2) The internal rules for encoding input are applied to the inputs to produce an internal representation of them. (3) This new representation, through a set of rules, is decoded to produce the outputs (Casti 1989). The internal rules or the internal encoding representation is not specified, so the model is generic, and it is equally applicable to humans, biological agents, and computers. This model is important for understanding epistemic information, because its elements, although not always all of them, always play a role in defining epistemic information.

The meaning of epistemic information is relative to the cognitive agent (i.e., the sender or receiver).

Thus, epistemic information depends on the state of a cognitive agent and its cognitive faculties, which some may call previous knowledge, and information-processing capacities and abilities. The same sensory stimuli may or may not be information for different agents. In addition, an uninterpreted stimulus is often denoted as data, despite the fact that data assumes some prior interpretation. The cognitive agent may be a human agent, a biological system, or an artificial cognitive system with the ability to change its internal state in response to stimuli or create a message by modifying a physical carrier under specific rules. The exact boundary between cognitive and non-cognitive information-processing systems is not entirely clear.

If we want to consider information as an essential element of nature, as information is indeed understood in this study and the referenced works, epistemic information clearly has significant shortcomings. These shortcomings indicate that information must in essence be something other than epistemic information, because our intuitive understanding of information is not matched by concepts of epistemic information. This list of specific problems is rather long.

(I) The epistemic concept of information is incomplete because it requires, as was mentioned above, additional concepts to explain its presence. These auxiliary concepts are usually called data or raw information, but data are again interpretation-dependent, so where is the basis for saying that data do not depend on anything? Are they raw physical phenomenon? It seems that with epistemic information we are on shaky grounds, because its foundations are elusive.

(II) Epistemic information always misses something about the state of nature. Cognitive systems (CS) are (reductive) filters, so they select and interpret the physical sensory stimuli in a selective matter. In other words, what is missed is in principle physically the same as what is absorbed by a cognitive faculty. For example, human hearing detects only air pressure waves within a certain frequency range with sufficient amplitude, but what is registered and what is omitted is the same physical phenomenon. The difference is the filter function of the CS. Epistemic information does not recognize this unity of nature but rather divides it into "meaningful" information and everything else. It artificially bifurcates nature into meaningful and neutral elements even though they are part of the same phenomenon.

(III) The different concepts of epistemic information lay out several contradictory claims, so one may even say there are many epistemic "informations [sic]", How can such a multifarious confused concept be regarded as foundational for nature as indeed the claims about information proclaim?

(IV) If we are information systems geared toward surviving in our environment, our information cannot just arise from us or exist only as an interpretation of what is out there, because we would be unable to evolve and survive. Information must therefore be out there first, and then we interpret it for our own needs. We are shaped by our environment, and information exists in it whether we are there or not.[9] We do not project our intentions into the external world—it works the other way around.

---

[9]It seems the role of information in evolution is mostly discussed within the context of inheritance (Goodfrey-Smith and Sterelny 2016) and the role of DNA. However, other voices indicate the role of environmental information acting upon the organism. Madden (2004) realizes that an organism is an information-processing system paired with an environment: "*It is proposed that information was derived from the environment as a direct result of the evolution of organisms that used other organisms as a food source*". However, for Madden, *for there to*

(V) Information, if it is indeed a foundational factor in nature, cannot be probabilistic in Shannon's sense. The probabilistic nature of information would mean that information either may not exist or that information may only exist at certain times. However, if information is part of the fabric of reality, how can we reason that there is no information or that it only exists at certain times, which would be the case if information were intrinsically probabilistic? It would be a rather disturbing ontology if we made Shannon's claim ontological. Such information does not make claims about what it is or how it exists. This does not mean that probability calculus cannot be used to describe information under epistemic interpretation, because it is used to describe many deterministic phenomena in classical physics (e.g., entropy), but here probability is used *in lieu* of precise knowledge. If we later prove that on the sub-particle level, the world is indeed intrinsically random, we may have to amend this claim.[10] We need to clarify, however, whether the intrinsic randomness of nature (i.e., at the QM level) denotes ontological randomness (it exists randomly) or epistemic randomness (its properties can be described with random calculus) at the macro level. It seems that at our present state of knowledge, the first view is true (Lukasik 2017) with respect to some aspects of QM.

(VI) Epistemic information is an abstract concept. Information, as it is defined in this study, cannot be an abstract notion. Abstract

---

be information, there must be something or someone to inform; to be capable of "being informed". Thus, information is epistemic. Ontological information and its role in the evolution of life and organisms is expressed in the following line from Avery (1993, p. 72): *we discuss the work of Maxwell, Boltzmann, Gibbs, Szilard, and Shannon. Their research established the fact that free energy contains information, and that it can thus be seen as the source of the order and complexity of living systems.* Here, information is seen as a factor in creating life forms, not just an interpretation of nature by an organism. The literature on information, entropy, energy, and chaos is extensive, but this line of research will not be pursued here except when absolutely necessary. (For additional information on this topic, see, for example, Weber (2018), Bishop (2017), Avery (1993), and Schrödinger (2012), as well as Nagel's discussion in Chapters 3 and 4).

[10]For ideas about randomness as an intrinsic property of nature, see, for example, Mścisławski (2014) and Acin and Masanes (2016).

notions do not exist in the same sense and in the same way as concrete things exist. After all, abstract things are abstract because they lack a physical or concrete existence, so they cannot be foundational factors in nature. Information that is foundational cannot be just "in the eyes of the beholder", like subjective notions of beauty or knowledge, unless this beholder is some supreme creator, which is obviously Berkeley's theme and to some extent Newton's.

5.2.1 *In search of the locus of epistemic information*

Ontological information is a part of nature, but where is epistemic information and where does it come from? The dependency, or relative nature, of epistemic information on the background knowledge/state of the cognitive agent has of course been recognized by several researchers attempting to define epistemic information (e.g., Bar-Hillel and Carnap 1953; Dretske 1983; Jadacki and Brożek 2005; Floridi 2013). Ontological information, on the contrary, is free from this dependency on interpretation. The differences between ontological and epistemic information are illustrated in Figure 5.2.

Figure 5.2 shows how nature is organized and structured into objects and phenomena with various forms and shapes. Flowers exist whether we give them a name or not and so do the mountains,

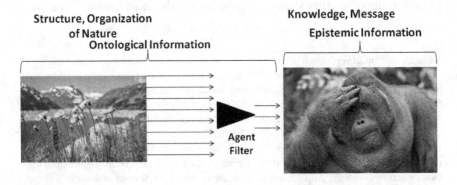

Figure 5.2. Differences between ontological and epistemic information.
Credits. CC0 Public Domain; Free for personal and commercial use; No attribution required. Image on the left: https://pxhere.com/en/photo/655865. Image on the right. https://evolutionnews.org/2014/12/court_declares/.

seas, and volcanoes. Nature's organizational factor is ontological information—this is our claim. A cognitive agent filters physical stimuli in its environment and with it ontological information, through sensory apparatuses, and then organizes it through cognitive processes into knowledge or epistemic information in the mind.

We denote the process in which ontological information is absorbed into the agent's mind as a filter. We may more specifically call this filter a semiotic filter,[11] because it imposes an interpretation on the received and translated physical stimuli. By organizing ontological information into knowledge about the world, the agent derives meaning for itself from something meaningless, namely physical stimuli, which is ontological information. Different agents can derive different meanings from the same ontological information. To sum up this process, we say that nature provides ontological information in the form of physical stimuli to an agent, which then creates for itself knowledge about nature not nature itself, so this knowledge is epistemic information. The nature of this knowledge is not clear. It is certainly not any sort of image or a copy of reality.

The source of "information about the world" (i.e., the raw input) for a human agent are the senses. This information about the world is transformed by the mind, at least in the case of human agents, to inform us about how the world is. The purpose of the cognitive apparatus and cognitive processes is to tell us how the world is based on the input of our senses. We denote the information (knowledge) created in this process as epistemic information, so it is information about something or knowledge of the outside world.

Epistemic information is not what comes to us through the senses of sight, hearing, smell, taste, equilibrium, and somatic senses of

---

[11]The term "semiotic filter" is understood here as the ability of a system (biological or artificial) to create signs, which in general are abstract references to the specific features of the world or other signs. Semiosis was originally attributed to living systems, but it may now be extended to artificial agents (e.g., Ferreiria *et al.* 2013).

touch, temperature,[12] pain, and proprioception.[13] What comes to us through the senses is variously denoted as sensory information, stimuli, external stimuli, or a form of physical energy (e.g., Rock 2015, Silverton 2007). This is in no way exactly analogous to the representation of reality. It is a series of pure physical flows of energy in different forms. Where then does epistemic information in the form of colors, houses, trees, flowers, cars, faces, sweetness, sourness, heat, cold, smooth come from if it does not come through the senses? Let us look at the perception process as we understand it, which is mostly guesswork for now, and see where epistemic information emerges.

The sensory systems, at least in higher level mammals, generally have a common architecture for responding to different stimuli.[14] The stimulus acts on a sensory receptor, a transducer. This transducer converts the stimulus into an intracellular signal and then builds up action potential until it reaches a certain threshold that triggers a sensory neuron along the central nervous system, which integrates the incoming signals. Some stimuli proceed up to the cerebral cortex where they reach conscious perception, while others remain on a subconscious level. The sensory organs differ in form and biological composition, as does the transmission of sensory stimuli. Sensory information, the action potential passed on through sensory

---

[12]Temperature is understood here as a subjective feeling of cold or hot rather than as a thermodynamic property of physical systems in the sense of the Zero Law of Thermodynamics (e.g., Guggenheim 1985, Atkins 2010). Thermodynamic temperature is related to Kelvin temperature as $k\beta = 1/T$, where T may be called conventional temperature and k is Boltzmann's constant expressed in J^{-1} units. k is a conversion parameter between the common measure of temperature in K and the thermodynamic properties expressed by β. β is a more natural measure of temperature as it is more meaningful in that it is related to the physical state of the system. From the molecular perspective, temperature expresses *the most probable distribution of populations of molecules over the available states of a system at equilibrium* (Atkins 2010). Temperature in the thermodynamic context is a state function or, in other words, a property of a system independent of how that state was achieved. A state function is the internal energy of a system, and we may risk conjecturing that information as system organization is a state function as well, but such a claim would require further exploration.

[13]An awareness of body movement and position in space.

[14]This description follows closely that of Silverton (2007).

pathways, can be modulated and reshaped during its transfer from the receptor to the cerebral cortex. The receptors in sensory organs respond to particular forms of energy, and the passing of stimuli is not like the flow of current through a wire. It is a series of events triggered by an outside stimulus (in the case of external events) and the activation of the transducer receptor, ending with the signal reaching the cortex or other site of awareness, according to our current knowledge (see, for example, Kalat 2007, Passer and Smith 2007, Coon and Mitterer 2013, Kandel *et al.* 2013).

The process of perception can be represented as follows: A physical stimulus of type "i" (Phi) is detected by a sensory organ. It is converted through biochemical processes into a biochemical stimulus (BCi) and transmitted along nerve pathways to the appropriate area of the brain. In the brain, the BCi undergoes a process of integration of which we currently know little about, and it then sometimes reaches consciousness, making us aware of the sensation (Si). That is the sequence of processes for sensory stimuli to trigger conscious experiences, and this is where epistemic information, or information about something, is created. The pathway may be presented as the sequence:

$$\text{Phi} \rightarrow \text{BCi} \rightarrow \text{BCi}' \rightarrow \ldots \rightarrow \text{Si}.$$

There is no physical equivalence between the stimuli originating the perceptual process and the stimuli in the sensory pathways. These stimuli are recorded, albeit in a specific way rather than randomly. The lack of physical equivalence can be symbolized as follows:

$$\text{Phi} \neq \text{BCi} \neq \text{BCi}' \neq \ldots \neq \text{Si}.$$

The "$\neq$" sign should not be interpreted as the mathematical symbol of "not equal to" but as a symbol denoting non-equivalence. Likewise, the "$=$" sign should be interpreted as symbolizing equivalence rather than as meaning "equals to". Finally, the "$\rightarrow$" sign should be interpreted as a symbol meaning "transformation" rather than mathematical implication.

By "physical equivalence", we refer to similarity in the type of the physical phenomenon stimulating the perceptual process and stimuli in the sensory pathways. This does not mean that these signals (i.e., the stimuli and signals in the neural pathways) are random, because they are highly correlated. Indeed, they are a function of the stimulus and tightly coupled to the stimulus itself, and they are repeatable and reproducible. However, their physical form, as a sort of physical carrier, is not same as that of the external stimulus. More specifically, the various external stimuli have different physical forms in nature (e.g., electromagnetic radiation for vision, biochemical content for taste, airwaves for sound, etc.). A visual stimulus is very physically different from the corresponding biochemical signal in the visual path, and the same goes for the other senses. They are mediated by specific processes $(F(x))$ that transfer some aspect of the stimuli (i.e., a certain subset of it) from one stage of the perceptual process to the next:

$$\text{Phi} \neq \text{BCi} = F'(\text{Phi}); \ \text{BC}'j = F''(\text{BCi})$$

and

$$\text{Si} = F'''(\text{BCi}'') \text{ or } \text{Si} =''''(F''(F'(\text{Phi}))),$$

where F' is the stimuli mediation function between sensory pathways.[15] Phi $\neq$ BCi$\neq$ F' (Phi) means that the mediated physical stimulus $\{F'(\text{Phi})\}$ is not physically equivalent to the original sensory stimulus (Phi) or to the physical signal in the neuronal pathway (BCi). Si = $F'''(F''(F'(\text{Phi})))$ means that the awareness of sensation (Si) is a result of several stages of mediation (i.e., $F'''(F''(F'(\ ))))$ for the input stimulus (Phi).

Now, if Si is epistemic information giving us knowledge about the world, what is Phi? We know that Phi is a specific type of physical phenomenon, such as light, heat, pressure, or a chemical compound. Each of these phenomena has its own specific structure/form to which the sensory organs respond, but the sensory apparatuses do not respond to any phenomenon in its entirety. For example, we do not respond to every electromagnetic wave but rather only to those within a narrow frequency range (i.e., the visible spectrum).

---

[15] Details about sensory pathways, transfer mechanisms, and biochemical signaling in neurons can be found in, for example, the work of Kandel *et al.* (2013).

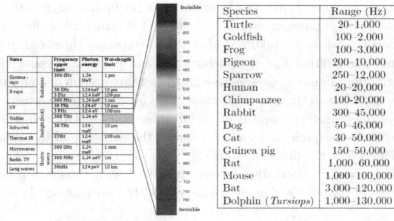

Species	Range (Hz)
Turtle	20–1,000
Goldfish	100–2,000
Frog	100–3,000
Pigeon	200–10,000
Sparrow	250–12,000
Human	20–20,000
Chimpanzee	100–20,000
Rabbit	300–45,000
Dog	50–46,000
Cat	30–50,000
Guinea pig	150–50,000
Rat	1,000–60,000
Mouse	1,000–100,000
Bat	3,000–120,000
Dolphin (*Tursiops*)	1,000–130,000

The visible spectrum of electromagnetic radiation by a human agent   **Hearing ranges of animals**

Figure 5.3. Perceivable ranges for vision (Danila *et al.* 2016) and hearing. *Note*: A comparison of the audible ranges of various species can be found in ("Before it is" 2019).

Therefore, a sensory apparatus responds only to a narrow subset of a selected phenomenon (see Figure 5.3). This could be determined by the frequency of the electromagnetic waves in case of vision, the shape of molecules for taste sensation and specific concentration, the kinetic energy of the molecules in a substance for the sensation of heat, or the frequency of air pressure waves. No human sense responds to the full range of possible stimuli. What is more, the human consciousness acknowledges only a portion of the received stimuli (e.g., Augusto 2010, Hasher and Zacks 1984). Evolution in this case is very frugal, and we only get what we need or sometimes not even that. For example, endowing humans with an energy-intensive and functionally overdesigned brain seems "unevolutionary" in a way, seeing as we usually only get what we need from evolution, if that.

It seems that in the case of the brain, we got more than simple survival would require.

A common aspect among different physical stimuli that trigger a chain of physical processes in sensory pathways that eventually result in the emergence of epistemic information is the form or organization of the physical phenomenon. If you change the structure of the phenomenon, such as by taking it above the perception threshold, you change the awareness of the phenomenon and the related epistemic information. In most cases—although the sensory system of an agent does not react to changes in all cases—this is related to the sensitivity of the sensory apparatus or certain inertia in sensory response. Of course, epistemic information requires the existence of the mind in addition to the physical stimuli.[16]

If epistemic information is conceptualized as a thought or the content of the mind and many studies explicitly state this, ontological

---

[16] Can we say that a radio receiver sees radio waves? The interesting question is whether a smartphone processes epistemic or ontological information. A smartphone certainly has a wider range of senses of physical stimuli than a human agent. It senses electromagnetic waves in its transmission range (cellphone signal) and visible range (camera). It also processes signals from GPS satellites, magnetic fields, heat, pressure, position in the gravitational field, movement, touch, and even recognizes a voice, and this is only a small portion of what a modern smartphone can "know". All these signals change the internal status of the smartphone by affecting its counters, memory, and the internal state of its software (e.g., Bharadway and Sastry 2014, Fong 2019, McGonigle *et al.* 2019). So, does the smartphone have a state of mind? It certainly "knows", in some sense, more than a plant about its *umwelt* in that it has internal states that reflect the outside world according to how the smartphone "sees" it? But if a smartphone has a mind, then so does every piece of computer machinery to some degree. How far can this analogy be pushed? Three responses are possible. One is that yes, smartphones exhibit all or most features of a cognitive agent, so smartphones process epistemic information. This position could be held by those who are prone to attributing cognitive abilities to plants and primitive life. The second response is a little more restrained in saying that computers in general model the mind, and eventually they will have consciousness, so current smartphones are like an early form of primitive life with some rudimentary consciousness that can produce/process epistemic information. This position is held by Daniel Dennett, Jerry Fodor, Gualtierro Piccinini, D. J. Chalmers, Edelman, and many others (e.g., Rescorla 2017). Finally, the third answer recalls Searle and the Chinese room argument in that the computer model of the mind is simply a categorical mistake and computer devices (i.e., UTMs) will never have a mind and become conscious beings in the same sense as humans and animals, so they process only ontological information. This position is held by John Searle, Roger Penrose, and others. See, for example, the discussion of Hauser (2018). All three positions are argued for in the literature, and on this matter, I am with Searle.

information is described here as a causal factor in shaping the mind or its structure if we say that the structure of the mind is its thoughts. This can be expressed as

$$I_O \to M(I_O) \to I_E,$$

where I_o is ontological information, M () is a mediation process described before as $\{F'''(F''(F'( )))\}$, and I_E is epistemic information. Of course, the I_E for the same I_O will be different for different individuals, at least to some degree.[17]

The claim that I_O is physical (located in nature), while I_E is mental (located in the mind/brain) is not, as will be explained later, such a good differentiation, because it may be controversial. To be more precise, we should say that I_O is not dependent on the mind, while I_E is. This commonly accepted division can be the source of many problems with regards to interpreting the nature of information, so it should not be taken as a declaration of the dual nature of reality. It simply means that ontological information is found in nature regardless of the mind, while epistemic information depends on the mind for whatever its nature is. (Note that this is also physical in the sense that it is hosted in a physical system, namely the brain. Disembodied mind is rather out of the question in this discussion.) Thus, I_O is embedded in a physical carrier as its structure or form, so it is a physical phenomenon. I_E, on the other hand, is located in the mind and described as the content of the mind. The term "located" is misleading, however, because it incorrectly implies that I_E occupies some physical space, but it is only "located" in the sense that the content of the mind is "located" in, or associated with or dependent on, the mind, to our best knowledge.

---

[17] *Because people have widely different experiences throughout their lives, it follows, that no two people will process a given piece of information in the same way* (Kandel *et al.* 2013, p. 319). There should be no doubt that the essence of conscious perception (the M() function, i.e., is a mediation process) depends on the complex functions of the mind or, as some may have it, the brain. There is nothing like Hume's fleeting impressions. The lectures in Oliver Sacks's books, such as in the book *An Anthropologist on Mars* (Sacks 1996), should dispel any doubts as to what is seen and what is perceived, although this is restating a rather obvious fact.

Of course, nature's physical structure is a complex multilevel organization. Which levels of organization interact directly with the sensory apparatus is not always obvious, even if these levels are closely dependent. This dependency means that, for example, the frequency of light depends on the shape of the light wave, which in turn depends on the properties of a photon, while the molecular shapes that the sense of taste responds to depend upon the atomic properties of its constituent elements, which in turn depend on the structure of atoms and their subatomic particles. From the individual atoms themselves, one cannot deduce their taste, because they have none. Thus, to say that taste buds respond just to the external shape is a gross simplification. The existence of different levels of organization does not imply these properties can be reduced, because the sensory system responds only to a portion of the available natural stimuli. I_E is not a response to everything in nature or even to everything detected by the sensory organs. As we said earlier, I_E represents I_O in a mediated form, so I_E is always just a fragment of the I_O. This should be an obvious conclusion from analyzing the mechanics/physics of sensory systems in cognitive agents. (For more details about the sensory apparatus, see the works of Kalat 2007, Passer and Smith 2007, Nolen-Hoeksema *et al.* 2009, Coon and Mitterer 2013, Kandel *et al.* 2013).

In clarifying the distinction between epistemic and ontological information, we need very precise terminology. The notions of the mind, intelligence, knowledge, meaning, messages, and communication may be interpreted in many ways. With these interpretations, we may assign epistemic capacities to a human agent, an artificial agent, complex animals, lower animals, cellular organisms, plants, and even entities on the border of life and the material world, such as viruses. But why stop there? We may say that physical systems communicate. We may also state that all these systems are organized complexes, some inanimate and some animate, and they exchange organized matter–energy elements with the environment. Some systems do it as a chain of physical processes, while some involve what we call cognitive functions, which also seem to be physical processes of some kind, or to put it differently, processes based on the physical properties of biological matter. Epistemic information emerges when cognitive functions come onto the scene. But where does it occur? Where do we position cognitive functions in the range of information processing performed by natural agents? This question is not trivial, and an incorrect answer trivializes the question and the problem, because we will see cognitive functions everywhere or merely only in humans. Both options seem to be incorrect.

This discussion is more than just a search for some minimally conscious life. It is actually a reflection of the fact that biological information-processing systems existed before consciousness emerged. In other words, information in nature existed before information in consciousness appeared on the scene. Attempts to extend the cognitive abilities to biological processes in plants (somewhat backwards, or *post factum*), for example, were met with strong criticism from biologists who were less prone to such flights of fancy.[18] Nobody denies the information-processing capacities (in the sense of ontological information) of these lower organisms on the phylogenetic tree. What is denied is that this represents consciousness. Thus, the existence of information-processing capacities in biological systems means that information in nature, or ontological information, existed long before epistemic information emerged, because biological life emerged eons before human consciousness.

There is a danger in extending the concept of meaning without qualification over unrelated or vaguely similar cases. Such generalizations impair our ability for rational discourse. If everything is alike, and if everything is like everything else, how can we have a discussion about anything? This is what trivialization means. Now, take the case

---

[18]In the recent study of Tiaz *et al.* (2019) on plant biology, the authors state, *There is no evidence that plants require, and thus have evolved, energy–expensive mental faculties—such as consciousness, feeling, and intentionality—to survive and reproduce.* It seems that the whole plant "neurocontroversy" has hinged on a liberal interpretation of the meaning of words like intelligence and cognition and the somewhat irresponsible use of terms like "machine intelligence" by computer scientists and AI researchers. The latter observation comes as a surprise seeing as these two occupational groups are not well known for flights of fancy, so we would expect some reservation from them in their overly poetic use of language. This is why we may have been duped about AI's possibilities.

in point: If we use the term "intelligence" without qualification, all terms like machine intelligence, human intelligence, intelligent systems, intelligent animals, artificial intelligence, and animal language are meaningless (see the comments of Chomsky 2014). Likewise, if we employ the unqualified use of the term "information", we fall into the same trap. We need to be wary of the differences and apparent similarities.[19]

Epistemic information comes in different degrees, so its presence and content vary from system to system. The boundary (locus) between epistemic information and ontological information may be tentatively placed when or where the system interprets "the physical aspects of the world" not as the physical aspects of the world but rather some abstract, generalized interpretation that has been associated with them. (Would we ascribe this interpretation to a phenomenological perspective?) We may say that meaning, or the creation of meaning, is a distinguishing human feature that is not present in the same form in non-human animals.[20] By diluting the concept of meaning, we can extend it to even include stones, but then the concept of meaning becomes meaningless.

One suggestion for the "boundary condition" separating epistemic information from ontological information is provided by Strawson in his discussion of perceptual experience. Strawson says that when speaking about conscious experience, we talk about something that is *not merely sensitive to its environment. So much can be said of a plant or an instrument. But we are speaking of something which is*

---

[19]From time to time, we hear news that someone has succeeded in storing data in a DNA strand or used DNA to process some data. This should not be interpreted as proof that DNA is information or stores information, but rather that any biological, physical, or chemical structure (including DNA) can store what we would interpret as information.

[20]We are meaning-seeking animals (Armstrong 2006, p. 2). It may seem that the talk about artificial agents, plants, and animals creating meaning is a gross categorical mistake propagated by a rather shallow, technically focused perspective. To really put the discussion in the right perspective and place, we need to read books like *A Short History of Myth* by Armstrong (2006), which exposes the layers and layers of meaning created by millennia of humanity, something that does not apply to other biological systems that we know of.

not merely sensitive to its environment [...] but of which the sensitivity takes a form of conscious awareness of its environment. We are speaking of subjects who employ concepts in forming judgments about the world, judgments which issue from the experience enjoyed in sense perception (Strawson 1992, p. 62). Strawson saying that *subjects who employ concepts in forming judgments about the world* is another way of saying what we said earlier about attributing abstract notions to the physical aspects of the world. Do autonomous robots with Artificial General Intelligence (AGI), trees, and plants count as epistemic agents according to these definitions? They probably do not. The same likely applies to other simple forms of life. But information agents or *inforgs* (see what follows) include all living things, not necessarily just those processing epistemic information. We may risk the claim that semantics, semantic information, or epistemic information appear when symbols appear (i.e., when ontological information is "symbolized" or tokenized) or, using Strawson's ideas, when an agent forms a judgment about the environment.

In this sense of symbolization, the DNA and RNA exchange between viruses and a cell is not cognition because what are being exchanged are direct physical structures, or so it seems. However, interpreting a written language is a process that Carl von Weizsäcker puzzled about, because we interpret shapes as letters with some abstract concepts associated with them. In this cognitive process of understanding a language, the physical structures in nature act in some way as pointers to the abstract features of the physical (i.e., real, concrete) world that exists in the brain. This structure–abstraction relation is never precise, so the match is approximate and not always unique.[21] What is more, the physical structure is never like the numeric address for a memory location in the brain, as in modern computer memory technologies[22]—such as in RAM, ROM,

---

[21] See the discussion of human cognitive functions in (Chater 2019, pp. 192–223). Of course, the book expounds the point of view that the mind is a computer. See also the work of Steward and Cohen (1997) for a similar discussion.

[22] In humanity, the physical organization of memory and the memory retrieval process is nothing like in computer memory or even ANN constructs. More details can be found in, for example, Schacter *et al.* (2009, pp. 167–209) or Passer and Smith (2007, pp. 232–273).

or on a hard drive—it is not even remotely similar to this (e.g., Squire and Butters 1992).

The progress in information-processing capacities is in no way a linear path. As a rule, biological systems possess information-processing capacities to a degree that matches their survival needs. For example, dogs have a better sense of smell than humans, while bats are better in sensing "sounds", because it suits their functions in nature. It may seem an anthropomorphism to place a human agent on one end of the spectrum and non-living systems on the opposite end, yet I would argue that only human agents have managed to augment their sensory capacities beyond the evolutionary imperative of survival, and this has given us a somewhat privileged position as information agents or inforgs.[23]

A point to observe is that concepts of cognition, cognitive function, and knowledge, which are so critical to the concept of information, are highly anthropomorphized. Even when we talk about machine cognition, we talk indirectly about human capacities, because human capacities are always, or at least very often, used as a reference point in these discussions, because we lack any other reference point for these capacities. It is rather difficult to find a conceptualization of cognition that is not "informed" by the human perspective. (This should not be a surprise as cognition is a distinctly human feature. But, the anthropomorphizing of cognition is not the same as anthropomorphizing the cosmos or the solar system.) Would this mean that human cognitive faculties are the only reference point for the cognition we possess, barring some fringe views about extraterrestrial cognition, whatever that may mean, or superhuman faculties that are not new but rather just human faculties infinitely expanded (not a very clear goal)? From some not-so-recent

---

[23] The term "inforg" is coined by Floridi (2013). The term denotes entities made up of information and existing in the infosphere. One may admire Floridi's penchant for creating catching neologisms or remain puzzled by this (con) fusion and long for Ockham's parsimony. The infosphere is another one of these newspeak terms. The first documented use of the word was in a 1971 *Time Magazine* book review by Sheppard ("Rock Candy" 2010). Both terms have been subsequently "legitimized" through the use by other authors.

studies there emerges the concept of cognitive functions in single and multicellular organisms like bacteria and plants (e.g., Trewavas 2016, 2017, Van Loon 2016). However, whether we can accept such an extended concept of cognition is dubious.

While we are not going to attribute human-level cognitive abilities to these simple organisms, we do attribute to them several analogous capacities, although an open question is how analogous they are and what "analogous" may mean in this case. It seems that a sign of life is active engagement with the environment. Some may denote this as "information exchange" in one or both ways, while others may claim there is no life without information exchange, so in this view, all living organisms are information systems of sorts. Thus, within this perspective, some level of "active engagement with the environment" or cognition (if one wants to call this function of a biological system this way) may be determined based on a continuous scale for everything alive. However, assigning cognitive capacities without precisely defining what they mean here would be overly cavalier (Firn 2004). In addition, what "information" exactly means in this context is not so clear.

Shifting the boundary between cognitive and non-cognitive systems may lead to panpsychism, which is the view that *mentality extends from humans to animals, insects, plant cells, and other natural bodies exhibiting persisting unity of organization* (Clarke 2004). Panpsychism is rarely accepted these days, yet it was supported by the ancient Greeks, modern poets, and even prominent scientific figures like Leibnitz and Whitehead. Aside from the magical attraction of this idea, it seems that it does not stand up to the facts, so panpsychism is certainly not a view supported by this study. Finally, panpsychism is not the same as paninformatism, where information is considered an organizational element of nature.

So, what is the conclusion then? If we conceptualize information as knowledge or Information$_E$, we must admit that everywhere where this information exists, there is, underlying it or carrying it, a physical stratum. This stratum is the source or carrier of I_E or something that may become I_E. Some may say this carrier is information *in potential*, but we would say that this information *in potential* that underlies epistemic information is actually ontological information.

5.3 Ontological Information as a Bearer of Epistemic Information

Epistemic information is always derived from some sort of stimuli, because epistemic information can be seen as the complex stimuli response of a cognitive system. This stimuli may be a signal in a telecommunications channel (e.g., Shannon–Hartley–Weaver and related models), or it may be an environmental stimuli interpreted by the cognitive system of a cognitive agent, or it may be an exchange between chemical complexes. In all these cases, there is a physical phenomenon that is called a signal, data, message, or such like underlying the generation of epistemic information. The characteristic of this phenomenon that makes it a source of epistemic information is its structure or physical organization. Due to the complex hierarchical organization of physical objects, which are often denoted as structures of structures, it is not always clear which level of organization plays the role of information carrier for a given cognitive agent. Or, it is not always clear which level of structure is interpreted as epistemic information. In smoke signals the receiver interprets a large-scale shape of a smoke cloud, not its micro molecular organization, even if these two are somewhat dependent. Thus, epistemic information is an interpretation of some level of organization in physical objects.

Now, if we accept the conclusions of this study, this structure, order, or arrangement is an expression of ontological information. We stay clear of stating that these structures—or at least the structures for a particular domain like physics, biology, or chemistry—are ontological information. However, this is what ontological information is seen as. Thus, epistemic information is an interpretation of ontological information being carried in a physical system as its organization. We do not need to postulate data, data structures, or *infons*. Data are, in reality, just stimuli that have already been interpreted. Thus, were we to postulate that epistemic information is derived from data, as is often assumed, we would be postulating that epistemic information is derived from epistemic information, thus creating an infinite regress. But where does the buck stop? We have a schema:

(1) (infons ?) → epistemic information (as data)

→ ... → epistemic information

Schema (1) reads as follows: Some unknown pre-epistemic phenomenon (infon?) is perceived by a cognitive agent and converted into data. This process is then repeated until the data are converted into, or recognized as, epistemic information. This study proposes the following schema:

(2) Ontological information: structures visible or recognizable → interpretation of physical stimuli **by a** cognitive system → epistemic information

Schema (2) reads as follows: Nature has a specific organization denoted as ontological information, which is seen as visible or detectable structures. These visible structures are perceived by a cognitive agent's sensory apparatus and converted into epistemic information. With the proviso that structures can be imposed on physical objects by some cognitive system (via mediation of physical processes) and these structures will be interpreted as epistemic information (we call it " sending a message").

How information is imposed on physical media, in the case where an agent is the originator of epistemic information (i.e., a message), where it comes from, and how meaning is associated with it by a cognitive system are different matters that we will not be pursuing here.

We have attributed to ontological information three properties:

1. EN: Information has no meaning; meaning is derived from information by a cognitive agent.
2. PE: Information is a physical phenomenon (by being physical we mean being an integral part of physical objects and being disclosed in physical phenomena).
3. FN: Information is responsible for the organization of the physical world.

Table 5.2. Comparison of ontological and epistemic information.

Information$_O$	Information$_E$
1 Information$_O$ is a physical phenomenon, so it exists objectively and is not relative to anything.	Information$_E$ is a (artificial or biological) cognitive agent's interpretation of physical stimuli, which may be a signal, the state of a physical system, or some other physical phenomenon.
2 Information$_O$ has no intrinsic meaning.	Information$_E$ exists for a cognitive agent, or it is relative to a cognitive agent. In other words, Information$_E$ is agent-relative or ontologically subjective. Information$_E$ has meaning for a cognitive agent.
3 Information$_O$ is, in a sense, responsible for the organization of the physical world.	A cognitive agent may be a human, a biological system, or some artificially intelligent system.
4 For Information$_O$, existence implies existence in the physical world, somewhere in the space–time continuum.	For Information$_E$, existence denotes the presence of an abstract notion somewhere outside of space and time.[a]

Note: [a]In this sense we talk of existence of thought.

A phenomenon with these properties could not be epistemic information, because the characteristics of ontological information exclude it from being epistemic information and vice versa, because something that is objective cannot be subjective, something that has no meaning cannot have meaning, and something that is subject to the physical laws cannot be not physical, which epistemic information seems to be. Likewise, something that is foundational in nature cannot depend on the cognitive faculties of some agent for its existence (God excepted). Thus, epistemic information cannot be the thing that satisfies the properties of ontological information.[24] Thus, epistemic information and ontological information represent two different

---

[24]The identity of indiscernibles is usually formulated as follows: if, for every property F, object x has F if and only if object y has F, then x is identical to y. Or, $\forall F(Fx \leftrightarrow Fy) \to x = y$ (Forrest 2016).

concepts, because two things can be the same only if they have the same properties (following Leibnitz Law of The Identity of Indiscernibles). Table 5.2 compares the proposed main features of ontological (concrete) and epistemic (abstract) information.

So, what is the conclusion? Well, we have said it several times over already. Ontological information that "gives" shape to nature is intercepted by a cognitive agent and interpreted as epistemic information. In this schema, ontological information is a carrier of epistemic information and its partial source.

Chapter 6

Applications and Interpretations of Ontological Information

In this chapter, we look at several consequences of accepting the concept of ontological information. We observed that preferring a concept of information based on semantics (i.e., epistemic information) would exclude information as an element of nature. However, many studies, including those cited in this work, indicate that information in nature is a concept with a solid scientific basis. But, epistemic information fails to account for this significant aspect of reality and the related concept of information. We also observed that a precise demarcation between epistemic and ontological information relies upon how we define cognitive function, meaning, and cognitive agents. While these definitions continue to be in a state of flux, it will be hard to establish a firm boundary between epistemic and ontological information. We also observed how epistemic information may be conceptualized as being partially derived from, and thus dependent upon, ontological information. In the following section, we discuss several topics, including quantified models of information. We point out that while these models offer significant operational benefits, they do not explain the nature of information, and this point is frequently missed by researchers. We also discuss the concept of data, which is usually positioned as something of primary importance to epistemic information, but we point out that in reality, data are already a form of epistemic information or interpreted ontological information. The division between data and information has been followed for operational reasons rather than being based on any inherent difference between these two concepts.

We then move on to discuss *infons*, which have been mentioned in some studies as an ontological basis for information. We show that the concept of the *infon* is poorly defined, however, and lacks an ontological, metaphysical, or scientific basis. Thus, once more, the *infon* is an operational concept that plays a role by standing in for some unknown quality, but it cannot be regarded as being ontologically fundamental. We also discuss the abstract–concrete dichotomy in the information debate. We point out how this dichotomy stems from the misuse of the verb "to exist" and the lack of a concept of ontological information. Once we recognize that we are dealing with two types of information, one abstract and one concrete, and when we recognize their interdependence, we see how these two concepts represent different modes of existence, with concrete information existing in space–time and abstract information existing outside it. We believe that this perspective resolves the conflict. We also discuss Popper's three worlds and his idea about information. This discussion arose somewhat in response to the critique that in this study, we deny the existence of the whole realm of human culture and thought, although we do not do this at all. Indeed, we simply cannot deny that the products of human thought exist, but we collectively call them epistemic information. We also do not deny that these products can be represented or embedded in physical things to create ontological information. We also cannot deny that the world of concrete things exists, and this is where ontological information persists. However, we also have to agree that the world of human products needs at least one agent, because without an agent who "understands" the content of world three, there would be no causal link between world three and the concrete world of embedded ideas. Even we, as humans, are defined by our ideas, and we need to recognize the fragility of our world. The objects of the Popperian world three do not exist without a "knowing" agent. For example, an ancient scripture that is rediscovered would just be a series of meaningless symbols without an agent who understands the language in which it is written. Indeed, the fate of lost civilizations testifies to the fragility of our humanity. We also present Burgin's General Theory of Information as a unifying concept for information, outline Perzanowski's combinatorial ontology, and briefly discuss Millikan's natural information.

The concept of ontological information has illuminated many of the current discussions about the nature of information, because it questions the role of information in nature. It also questions how we conceive nature itself and the role of information in specific sciences, such as computing, communications, physics, biology, social sciences, cognitive sciences, philosophy, and metaphysics, for example. The range of problems that the concept of ontological information may affect is quite broad, as can be seen from the literature. Topics discussed here are selected as they touch on often discussed aspects of information.

6.1 Ontological Information and Quantified Models of Information

Our discussion of quantified models of information will not focus on the details of the models themselves, because enough has been written about them and replicating these efforts would serve no purpose (Brillouin 2013, Klir and Folger 1988, Avery 1993, Stone 2015, Floridi 2016). The discussion therefore focuses on the impact these models have on our understanding of information and how ontological information places these models (or what they represent) in a different light. In discussing the quantified models of information, we need to keep in mind the ontological separation between the quantified phenomenon and its mathematical representation.[1] These are entirely different things, although not everyone would agree with this view.

Now, let us begin with Shannon's Theory of Communication (ToC). Claude Shannon's concept of information has been elaborated many times over,[2] so there is no need for a further rehash of Shannon's work—a brief review will be sufficient. Therefore, we will focus on aspects of the theory that seem to be overlooked but are important to understanding Shannon's concept and the view of information implied in his work.

Shannon's ToC describes the functioning of a communication system comprising a sender, a communication channel, and a receiver. This is a standard communication model (e.g., Cherry 1978, Fiske 1990, Holmes 2005, Littlejohn *et al.* 2017), but obviously, in Shannon's case, the context is that of a digital communication system. The sender forms a message (i.e., encodes it into the signaling media) in an attempt to convey something, which we call information, about himself or something else for someone else. The sender sends it through the communication channel in some physical form,

---

[1]We need to recognize the fact that the mathematization of a phenomenon does not constitute its explanation.

[2]See, for example, Shannon (1948), Shannon and Weaver (1964), Pierce (1961), Klir and Folger (1988), Avery (1993), and Stone (2015), but the list is much longer. Also see Hartley (1928) as the originator of the idea of digital communication that is used in Shannon's work.

and the message is received by a receiver. The receiver decodes the received message in an effort to recover the original information encoded by the sender. In Shannon's model, the channel supports the binary encoding of the signal (i.e., the physical media carrying the message), so the message comprises strings of zeros and ones (binary encoded). In other words, the physical phenomenon forming the channel is modulated (shaped, organized) according to some predefined rules that were agreed upon by the sender and receiver. These coding rules allow the receiver to decode the binary sequence from the physical media and recover whatever has been encoded by the sender. Without the same imposed encoding and decoding rules at both ends of the communication channel, there would be no communication.[3] The establishment of an encoding/decoding method is usually assumed in simple communication models like Shannon's.

The sign that can take 0/1 values is conventionally denoted as a bit. Shannon's measure of information (i.e., the amount of information) is the number of bits required to encode the message. So, if a message has only two possible values, one bit would suffice. If a message has "n" possible values, one needs 2^n bits. Therefore, a message that can be encoded with one bit contains less information (according to Shannon's definition) than a message that requires 2^n bits. For example, two values requires 1 bit, four values require 2 bits, eight values require 3 bits, and so on. The bit metric should be read as "the message has fewer bits" rather than as some metaphysical claim that the message has less "information", because Shannon's measure of information is a number of bits, nothing more. In Shannon's measure of information, there is not much beyond this for the concept of information. In addition, this "amount of information" is for this message only, not for the channel, the communication process, the world, or the sender. We have such concepts as channel information

---

[3]Recall the fate of ancient scriptures where the encoding rules of the sender have been lost to the receiver. This is in fact the principle behind encryption, where the encoding rules are known only by the selected ends of the communication channel.

capacity (Cover and Joy 2006), but these are derived concepts not primary ones.

As a model of "information" (as it is often interpreted), the Shannon–Weaver–Hartley model seems to have a problem with the assumptions that are (by the definition) behind the underlying probability model. One assumption is the statistical independence of the modeled probability space. Such an assumption seems to contradict the inherent features of any language, because the elements of language always have highly correlated structures, with uncorrelated linguistic-like utterances being a sort of gibberish or cipher. Shannon's model, however, assumed no such correlation. Later attempts to reinterpret the Shannon–Weaver–Hartley formula for information content in terms of thermodynamic entropy have led only to confusion (e.g., Pierce 1961). Despite syntactical similarities between Gibb's formula for thermodynamic entropy and Shannon's formula for measuring information, these two varieties of entropy are not the same phenomena, so conclusions about one of them do not necessarily translate to the other.[4]

Where is the probability in Shannon's formula coming from? After all, the messages are rather intentionally (in the Searle's sense of intentionality (Searle 1996)) structured objects—they are not random. The probability in the messages comes not from the apparent random nature of the source or randomness in the receiver's perception of the message content. The source of the messages in Shannon's ToC is the repository of the English language, which is a well-organized collection of signs that are highly correlated internally. Indeed, it is only because they are so well organized that they can be used in communication. The probabilities in the message in the ToC arise from the faulty assumption that the message is a kind of random pooling by the source, with some elements being more probable than others. However, the assumption of a random pooling in the case of

---

[4]To make this more obvious, we could say that two phenomena, even if they can be quantified by the same mathematical structure (e.g., a linear equation), are not necessarily similar or the same.

language is clearly wrong. The assumption that some elements are more probable than others is right, though. The assumption that elements are highly correlated is missing from Shannon's model, and Shannon's simplified model of communication results in a simplified model of information transfer and misconceptions about the nature of information. So, why does Shannon's formula work? It works when applied as a coding and decoding recovery strategy in digital systems, but it does not function as a general model of information of any sort if we impart some epistemic, semantic, or metaphysical properties to information, which, by the way, Shannon excludes from his theory. Can he really exclude all these properties by decree, or are they being implicitly unstated? It may be that this assumption is quite justified and acceptable for the engineering model of communication, but it may not be for philosophical considerations.

Discussing the probability space of the ToC model is critical if we want to apply the ToC to other physical phenomena such as DNA structure or cosmic phenomena. The conclusions about the results and the significance of the results applied in Shannon's model can only be generalized to other phenomena if both phenomena have isomorphic probability spaces. It is questionable whether this is the case with thermodynamic entropy, with DNA, or quantum information (e.g., Lukasik 2017).

The measure of the amount of information defined by Shannon is the entropy of the information source (symbolized as H (X)) of a message (X), and the more bits that are needed for encoding a message, the more entropy that is attributed to the message. The sender has a pool of signs from which the message is composed, and each sign has an associated probability (defined over the pool of available signs) of being in a message. In the original formulation of the theory, the pool of signs and assigned probabilities were the letters of the English alphabet, with the frequency of occurrences for each letter corresponding to its use in English (Shannon 1948),[5] but

---

[5]It really does not matter whether the language is English or some other set of symbols, because they all encode semantics in syntax if they are to function as a language.

the specific language is not important of course. Information entropy is the average number of bits to encode the sign. In addition, *the concept of information applies not to the individual messages, but to the situation as a whole* (Shannon and Weaver *op. cit.*, p. 9).[6] The term information, in the context of Shannon's theory, is used in the special sense of *meaning that it measures freedom of choice and hence the uncertainty as to what choice has been made. Uncertainty arises by virtue of freedom of choice (limited) on the part of the sender or errors (noise)* (Shannon and Weaver *op. cit.*, p. 19).

Shannon's formulas are defined over the probability space under the assumptions for probability calculus (Kolmogorov 1965):

- All probabilities pi is $<= 1.0$ and$>= 0.0$.
- Particular events are not correlated.
- Individual events are additive.

The formula for information entropy (of a discrete source) is as follows:

$$H(X) = \sum -p(x) \log(p(x))$$

where X is a variable with probability density distribution $p(X)$ and $H(X)$ is the information entropy of $p(X)$. For $p(xi) = 0$, which means that this particular event-message is improbable, the formula is undefined, while for $p(xi) = 1$, the entropy or amount of information is zero (implying no coding is possible so it is not information in Shannon's sense). This obviously requires some explanation, because assured information is information. So, why is this? The explanation seems obvious. As the source has only one message to send, there is no shortest coding (or no coding at all) to encode this message, but this is obviously flawed, because the message is sent in some form of encoding. The meaning of Shannon's model at the outer limits is therefore not well defined when looking at information as a concept; it may be acceptable as an engineering solution (In fact, the boundary interpretations of Shannon's entropy of information were

---

[6] "The situation" is a process of pooling signs from a predefined collection of signs with a specific frequency of occurrence that is characteristic of the given language.

arbitrarily assumed and did not come from the model itself or from the concept of information).[7] These results are the artifacts of the mathematical model used to represent information, but who worries about what happens at the boundaries of the definition space?[8]

Shannon clearly states that his concept of information, which is represented by a measure of information, has nothing to do with semantics, which is a property usually associated with information. This would seem to exclude Shannon's entropy of information from the class of epistemic information, but does it really? Shannon's entropy, or measure, of information is defined over the probability space of events that are intentional in origin, so they have semantics in language communication. They therefore exist only as expressions of human cognitive faculties, at least in the original formulation (Shannon used English as an exemplar language). What is more, the encoding of the message is not some random process but rather a carefully designed intentional action. Thus, Shannon's claim that his model is semantic-free is incorrect when we talk about the larger picture of the communication model. It is, however, correct if we restrict the model to pure technology.

Probability is generally regarded as a measure of ignorance, a lack of knowledge for predicting events. But, one may ask for whom this predictability is—it is for us? Events in nature just occur, and uncertainty (as an epistemic concept) does not come into play. For purely random events (ontologically random) in nature, if any do indeed exist, such as atomic decay or particle creation,[9] what would

---

[7]Someone may also notice that the analogy between information entropy and thermodynamic entropy breaks at these boundaries as well. Physical systems with entropy equaling zero (a crystal may have zero entropy only if the crystal has a ground state with only one configuration (see, e.g., Kozliak and Lambert 2008, Atkins 2010)) represent concrete physical systems, not something non-definable (Atkins 2010).

[8]The necessity of thorough examination of the assumptions of the mathematical models representing a physical phenomenon is emphasized by Ziman stating that "it is all too easy to derive endless strings of interesting—looking but untrue or irrelevant formulae instead of checking the validity of the initial premises" (Ziman 1991, p. 14).

[9]The problem of randomness in nature is still an open question. See, for example, Nicolic (2007).

Shannon's measure give us? Probably not much, because the information entropy of one specific event would tell us nothing about another event (see the case of measurements in QM), if they are indeed truly random, nor would it say much about the state of the source. So much for the "reduction in uncertainty" interpretation of Shannon's metric of entropy of information.

The concept of information buried in Shannon's ToC conflicts with the intuitive understanding of what information is. Thus, it is difficult to accept it as a general conceptualization of information (Cherry 1978, Pierce 1961). We may see it as an index or measure of structures that can be identified with information, and certainly it is safe to attribute this to Shannon's entropy of information as a purely probabilistic interpretation of the properties of a coding channel. In other words, it considers the content of the channel expressed as a formal measure of the probability density function (PDF) of the signals transferred over the channel, much like other measures of the PDF, such as the average, median, standard deviation (and other moments of higher order). Such an interpretation agrees with von Weizsäcker's interpretation of information.

A purely numeric interpretation of information (based on Shannon's theory) would have the following definition: Information is a certain measure of the PDF of the encoding media and expresses for discrete variables the average (expected) value of logarithms based on the probability of individual messages. All interpretations of this information should then be related back to the specific event probability space in which the specific PDF is founded. Information, the entropy of information, or the measure of the amount of information in the ToC is essentially an abstract measure/number assigned to a certain probability density defined over the space of certain uncorrelated random events. Shannon's interpretation of the concept of information is therefore tied to the probability space of the events in his model of communication. As we said, an interpretation from one probability space cannot be automatically carried over to another space if these spaces are not isomorphic (e.g., Yokey 1999, p. 70). One problem, although not the only one, in carrying over interpretations from Shannon's theory from one context to another is that, for Shannon, the most important message is the one with the lowest probability of occurrence, because it yields more information (in terms of bits) than messages with a higher probability. This is certainly an important feature for decoding the signal and reconstructing the message in a known language, and this was the basic assumption of Shannon's model. However, in the general case, information with a very small probability of occurrence may have no significance for the receiving agent.[10]

So, what is Shannon telling us about information in his ToC? First, he tells us only about the coding complexity of a message in the binary channel and not the semantics or meaning of what is encoded. We talk about semantics in the model itself, as explained earlier, but not about the semantics in the message. It tells us about the state of the source sending the message, and it tells us how to decode/encode the message efficiently but not accurately, because the signal is presumably based on random choice. It is based on implicit coding rules and probability axioms (see Kolmogorov 1956). In addition, it is in no way unique in representing a coding schema.

The question needs to be asked as to whether ontological information is probabilistic? The reality is that it is not probabilistic, at least on a macro-scale. Probability is a measure of some uncertainty of knowing, some inability to accurately predict something, but not a measure of what that something is. This is an epistemic metric par excellence, even in the case of QM. Nature is not random in a metaphysical sense; it just is the way it is. If one takes Shannon's communication channel as a reference point, the signal is a deterministic, physical phenomenon. Only the interpretation with respect to the original source and the pooling process makes

---

[10]When decoding ciphers, one looks for repeated, recurring patterns. The least probable occurrences of signs do not tell us much about the cipher (as it is how ciphers are designed). See, for example, Sutherland and Koltko-Rivera (2009). There are cases where the highly probable information is not informative (in epistemic sense). For example, if it rains, the road will be wet. For someone who has experienced the rain frequently, this is not news. But, for someone with no experience with the rain and roads, it may be. Thus, it seems that whether "information" or message is informative is not the function of the message but of the context.

it probabilistic.[11] Thus, one may venture to suggest that Shannon's ToC with its measure of information is not measuring some objective feature but rather the effects of the message creation and communication processes (barring the case of white noise).

We also need to discuss the relation between Shannon's entropy of information and the entropy of physical systems, because the discussion of entropy as a kind of information and information as a kind of entropy pervades the literature. Some examples of this can be found in the first part of this study. A few saner voices have advocated restraint in these analogies, but to no avail. To close the door on this issue for this study, we refer to the work of Ingo Muller (2007) about entropy, Shannon, and information entropy.

Muller points out that entropy (thermodynamic) is not something unknown or poorly understood, as it was suggested by von Neumann. Thermodynamic entropy is a well-understood physical phenomenon that has little to do with chaos, disorder, and message as used in the context of Shannon's entropy of information. Extrapolations of well-defined physical concepts (i.e., thermodynamic entropy) to other fields do not explain anything. On the contrary, such (ungrounded) extrapolations make these explanations more obscure (vide Schrödinger's cat. See Mann 2020).[12]

As Muller suggests, mixing the concepts of information and entropy brings more confusion and harm than help in explaining

---

[11]With the "reduction in uncertainty", a typical interpretation of information makes sense only against the deterministic and well-defined source of the signal. If the source is random (completely unpredictable), such as we assume atomic decay to be, there cannot be any reduction in uncertainty with additional information. Thus, this interpretation of information only makes any sense, if at all, for a deterministic signal source.

[12]*For level-headed physicists, entropy—or order and disorder—is nothing by itself. It has to be seen and discussed in conjunction with temperature and heat, and energy and work. And, if there is to be an extrapolation of entropy to a foreign field, it must be accompanied by the appropriate extrapolations of temperature and heat and work. If we wish, we can now assign an entropy to the message which Shakespeare sent us when he wrote Hamlet: We look up the probability of each letter of the English alphabet, count how often they occur in Hamlet and calculate Inf. People do that and we may suppose that they know why* (Muller 2007, pp. 133–134).

anything about the nature of either concept. Information as ontological information does not dissipate in chaos. Indeed, information
in this sense pervades both highly organized and highly disorganized
phenomena. Organization and disorganization are simply part of our
insignificant anthropomorphic perspective. Information in the sense
of organization exists everywhere all the time. The following passage
from Mott-Smith (1964, p. 172) explains this clearly: *To say that the
entropy of the universe tends to a maximum is simply to say that the
universe is passing from an interesting, useful and significant state,
to an uninteresting, useless and meaningless state. Apart from us
human beings, that is quite indifferent. There is just as much going
on in a chaos as in what appears to us as an orderly universe—only
it means nothing to us. We cannot make head or tail of it; we can
do nothing with it; we have no use for it; we do not like it. And of
course we could not live in it.*

It may also be the case that we tend to attribute names to abstract
objects or ideas, not necessarily using some logical justification, so
this naming may cause problems in the long term. This is the case
with imaginary numbers, which have nothing to do with the imagination or incommensurable numbers which are numbers as other
numbers are, but with some unique properties. Such names were certainly chosen to signify something, yet they do not necessarily reflect
the nature of the named object. The names may have been chosen
for entirely different reasons. This may be the case with information entropy, which bears some formal similarities to thermodynamic
entropy but little beyond that.[13] Maybe we should stop uncritically
identifying entropy with information and vice versa.

Chaitin (1997, 2004) and Andrei Kolmogorov (Kolmogorov 1965,
Solomonov 1997)[14] independently developed the concept of an information metric based on the Universal Turing Machine (UTM)

---

[13] *But the essential principle involved (in naming) was quite clearly enunciated to
Alice in Wonderland by Humpty Dumpty, when he told her, apropos of his use of
words I pay them extra and make them mean what I like* (Whitehead 1911, p. 61).
Of course, Humpty Dumpty's response bears an uncomfortable similarity to von
Neumann's advice to Shannon.

[14] Ray Solomonov is also referred to as a co-inventor of algorithmic complexity.

model, and they called this algorithmic information complexity (e.g., Baldwin 2005). Algorithmic information complexity is the minimum size of a computer program that can reproduce a given string. The link to the UTM is there because the programs having their algorithm complexity considered are Turing machines. There are different formalizations for this measure. Algorithmic string complexity ($H(S)$) for a string S for a given UTM is the shortest program "p" that reproduces string S (Baldwin 2005). The algorithmic complexity for S depends on the UTM type. For a completely random string,[15] the size of the program approximates the size of the string, while for less random string, the program has a lower algorithmic complexity, because the Turing computational model (UTM) represents the complexity of strings or a series of symbols. As such, it is similar to Shannon's measure of information (Baldwin 2005), and its interpretation of the type of information resembles that of Shannon's measure of information.[16]

For the sake of completeness, we should mention Fisher information and Klir's concept of information. Fisher information is a statistical measure of how much information one may obtain about an unknown parameter from a sample. Technically, Fisher information is the inverse of the variance of the Maximum Likelihood Estimator (MLE) for a parameter Θ from a sample X (for a normally distributed X). (The MLE is the maximum of a function of a specific parameter Θ given a random sample.) To simplify this, the concept of Fisher information allows us to find the value of the parameter(s)

---

[15]The word "randomness" reflects an absolute lack of predictability, and it is a rather elusive phenomenon (Prömel 2005), particularly in computer-generated structures: *Anyone who considers arithmetical methods of producing random digits is, of course, in a state of sin* (von Neumann as quoted by Frantzen 2007).

[16]For the sake of completeness, we need to mention/list the mathematical models related to Shannon's measure (Shannon's entropy of information), such as Reniy Entropy, Tsalis Entropy, Hartley Entropy or Max-Entropy, Collision Entropy, and Min-entropy. See, for example, Hartley (1928), Tsallis (1988), Da Silva and Rathie (2008), Cho (1961), and Rényi (1960). These are mathematical variants of which Shannon's entropy is just a specific case. An analysis of these is beyond the scope of this study, nor would it further the objectives of this research because they are all probabilistic metrics.

of a function fitted to the experimental data such that it minimizes prediction error.[17] Fisher information has found many applications in experimental studies in fields like astronomy, biology, and social sciences (e.g., Friden 1998, Ly *et al.* 2017). For George Klir (Klir and Folger 1988), information is a reduction of uncertainty. Uncertainty may be considered as ambiguity or vagueness. Such uncertainty may be measured by Shannon's entropy of information (a measure of ambiguity), the Hartley measure (H),[18] or measures of fuzziness. Both Fisher and Klir define information as a reduction in uncertainty based on information from perceived observations,[19] so these concepts clearly belong to the class of epistemic information.[20]

A quite extensive list of quantified models of information is also provided by Burgin (2010, pp. 131–132), but the sheer number (32 formulas) of models for measuring information does not translate into clarity about the nature of what is being measured. In fact,

---

[17] *Fisher information essentially describes the amount of information data provide about an unknown parameter. It has applications in finding the variance of an estimator, as well as in the asymptotic behavior of maximum likelihood estimates* (Intuitive explanation 2004). The website provides a simple demonstration of the relationship between Fisher Information I and σ as the Gaussian likelihood for the mean. It has been also suggested that Fisher information can be a unified concept for all of physics (Fisher information 2018), but this claim did not gain support (von Baeyer 2005, p. 216).

[18] According to Hartley, *'H' is the information as the message is the logarithm of the number of possible sequences of symbols, which may be selected as H=s log (s), where n is a number of symbols selected, and s is the number of different symbols in the set from which symbols are selected.* See Pierce (1961, p. 40).

[19] The question is what does this reduction in uncertainty amount to? It is not uncertainty about this or that event, but rather an uncertainty about the structure or composition of the probability space to which particular events belong. Uncertainty is the opposite of knowledge. Thus, uncertainty measures our knowledge of something, a situation, or a process, and a reduction in uncertainty increases our knowledge of the process.

[20] *A reduction of uncertainty by an act is accomplished only when some options considered possible prior to the act are eliminated after it. This requires a semantic connection between the prospective outcomes of the act involved (observations, received message, experimental outcomes) and the entities to which they are applied* (Klir and Folger 1988, p. 188). This "semantic connection" is what makes Shannon's entropy of information measure, in its original formulation, epistemic.

the models listed by Burgin measure quite different properties of abstract constructs, usually probability spaces, so they do not necessarily convey the same concept of information. To clarify this point through an analogy, the numerous measures of mass led to multiple interpretations for the concept of mass, and these did not necessarily converge on a single concept of mass. Indeed, the concept of mass as we now know it has evolved significantly over the history of science.[21] These measures pointed to varying conceptualizations of mass, but they did not address the question of what mass actually is. Likely, multiple measures for information do not translate into a better understanding of what information is—it only shows a range of possible interpretations (Hintikka 1984, pp. 175–181).

We can now draw some conclusions. With ontological information, Shannon's and other quantified measures of information can be safely interpreted as just some measure of the organization of physical phenomena associated with ontological information. These measures reflect the form or structures that characterize ontological information for particular objectives (e.g., digital communication channel decoding (Shannon), experimental uncertainty (Fisher), and program size (Chaitin)). How these quantified measures are interpreted, however, is immaterial to the definition of ontological information. They are just interpretations of a measured phenomenon, with the formal aspects of the metric (like probability assumptions or boundary conditions) being imposed on these interpretations. Depending on what structures/forms they are applied to, their interpretations may be more or less in agreement with the nature of ontological information, but they were not designed to do this, nor were they designed to reflect the phenomenon of ontological information as it is but rather only as far as it is applicable for some purpose.[22]

---

[21]Wikipedia lists 107 different units of mass (Units of mass 2019). Multiple measures of mass are also listed in the Wikipedia entry Mass (2019). The evolution of the concept of mass is discussed by Jammer (2000), Okun (1989), Mashood (2009), and Hecht (2006).

[22]In formal or quantified model of information one may also include logical models of information as in (Allo 2016).

6.2 Ontological Information and Data

Why do we question the relation between ontological information and data? After all, what do data have to do with ontological information? When we look at definitions of epistemic information, these definitions often, if not almost always, claim that information (i.e., epistemic information in this study) is "data + meaning" (Floridi 2013). There are similar claims that "information is derived from data" or "information is data endowed with relevance and purpose" (Davenport 1997, Drucker 2001), "information is organized data" (Saint-Onge 2002, pp. 28–29), or it is "interpreted data" (Terra and Angeloni 2010). It somehow seems that we need data to get information, that data are some kind of input to the process of creating information, that data differ from information, or that data are some "primitive stuff" from which information is formed. Data certainly seem to be not information—they are different. But, are these claims warranted? Could it be that data can be considered the primary stuff of the universe, a position we reserved in this study for ontological information? Let us look at how data are defined and where this fits in our conceptual schema of the world in relation to epistemic and ontological information.

According to Drogan (2009), *data are a prerequisite for information and information is a prerequisite for knowledge*. Liew, meanwhile, defines data as *recorded (captured and stored) symbols and signal readings. Symbols include words (text and/or verbal), numbers, diagrams, and images (still and/or video), which are the building blocks of communication. Signals include sensors and/or sensory readings of light, sound, smell, taste, and touch* (Liew 2007). Another definition tells us that *Data is the term used to describe the information represented by groups of on/off switches* (Surbhi 2016). From three authors, we have three definitions, and these do not necessarily converge. Even though the terms data and information are often used interchangeably, there is an important distinction between them. Data consist of the raw numbers that computers process to produce information. We also get very elaborate comparisons and a clear differentiation that *data and information are interrelated. Data usually refers to raw data, or unprocessed data. It is the basic form of data, data that hasn't been analyzed or processed in any manner. Once the data is analyzed, it is considered as information. Information is 'knowledge communicated or received concerning a particular fact or circumstance.' Information is a sequence of symbols that can be interpreted as a message. It provides knowledge or insight about a certain matter* (Ackoff 1989, pp. 3–9). Furthermore, Ackoff states that *Data are symbols that represent properties of objects, events, and their environment. They are products of observation. To observe is to sense.* Yet another take on data is given by Machlub (1983), who states, *Data are the things given to the analyst, investigator or problem-solver, they may be numbers, words, sentences, records, assumptions, just about anything, no matter of what form and what origin* (Ackoff *ibid.*). Table 6.1 (Machlub 1983) shows the many possible interpretations of data and information, where information is interpreted here in its semantic meaning.

Based on Table 6.1, it seems that the differentiation between data and information is somewhat arbitrary, a matter of interpretation as to what constitutes raw data versus analyzed data, no special meaning versus assigned meaning, collected versus processed, formal formats (tree, tables, graphs) versus linguistic interpretations, symbols versus ideas, and so on. These differences are not very well accentuated, so the boundary between data and information seems to be somewhat fluid, and the multitude of definitions of data only confirms this impression. Zins (2007) documents no less than 130 definitions for data. It seems that we are in the same situation as we are with trying to define information, namely, that we have so many definitions that we do not know what we are defining. The multitude of definitions supplied by experts is positioned as an important scientific feat, but I would claim that for science and philosophy, it is more of an embarrassment.

Including data in some conceptualizations of information is a sign, in my view, of not being able to see the forest for the trees. Whatever is denoted as data already has some meaning imparted on it.[23]

---

[23]There is a separate section in Chapter 4 about data and information.

Table 6.1. Comparison between concepts of data and information.

	Data	**Information**
Definition (Oxford Dictionaries)	Facts and statistics collected together for reference or analysis.	Facts provided or learned about something or someone; Data as processed, stored, or transmitted by a computer.
Refers to	Raw data, stimuli, signal.	Analyzed data.
Description	Qualitative or quantitative variables that can be used to propose ideas or draw conclusions.	A group of data that carries news and meaning.
In the form of	Numbers, letters, symbols, or a set of characters.	Ideas and inferences.
Collected via	Measurements, experiments, etc.	Linking data and making inferences.
Represented through	A structured format, such as tabular data, a data tree, a graph, etc.	Language, ideas, and thoughts based on the data.
Analysis	Not analyzed.	Always analyzed.
Meaning	Carries no specific meaning.	Carries meaning that has been assigned while interpreting data.
Interrelation	Information that is collected.	Data that has been processed.

Whatever information is, from this perspective, already has some additional meaning imparted onto already processed data. Knowledge is therefore processed information. The distinction between data, information, and knowledge can be therefore made, and this is certainly operationally useful in certain areas of research or technology, such as computing, artificial agents, Big Data, cognitive artificial systems, and artificial intelligence. Indeed, it is helpful whenever we want to denote or differentiate one narrow aspect or stage of information processing, especially with computers. However, these divisions overlook the strong similarities and stress the rather relative differences (e.g., Dasgupta 2016, Floridi 2013). This division into data, information, and knowledge is often referred to as the DIKW (data, information, knowledge, wisdom) hierarchy, wisdom hierarchy, knowledge hierarchy, information hierarchy, or the data pyramid (e.g., Zeleny 2005, Livesley 2006, Rowley 2007, Zins 2007). A detailed discussion of the DIKW lies outside the scope of this study, however.

Unfortunately, this (con)fusion of data, knowledge, message, meaning, and so on is how information has been largely understood in the 20th century, which will be referred to in the history books as the age of information or the age of something we are not sure of yet. As we have said, we refer to this information as epistemic information—thus emphasizing the relation to, or reliance on, knowledge—or information$_E$ or I_E for short. Of course, the reader may find others who refer to this information as cognitive information, thus highlighting information's dependency on cognitive systems, semantic information, emphasizing meaning as a defining feature of information, or most often just as information.

On trying to find some firmer ground for the concept of data, we may say that data are a sort of epistemic information, symbols imposed on natural stimuli, elements in communication, numbers stored in digital form, or some kind of information (i.e., interpreted stimuli). The boundary between data and information is fluid and not very well defined. Thus, in some cases and for some purposes, data will be data, while in other cases, the same data will be information or information will be data. It seems that how we refer to data depends on where we are situated on the spectrum of information processing, from stimuli to knowledge.

Now, let us try to position data and information within the perspective of this study. To begin with, we cannot say that data are uninterpreted stimuli, because data must have been interpreted under some symbolic convention, because they represent stimuli through symbols, data structures, and suchlike. Every stimulus we receive has already been interpreted by our sensory/perceptual system. The moment we attempt to record something, we interpret it again in some kind of formal language with its own symbols, grammar, and syntax. Thus, if stimuli are interpreted, someone or something must have interpreted them, either directly by recording symbolic representations in a sort of note-taking or indirectly through the use of some equipment or apparatus, such as the digital recording of sound waves. There is no data without interpretation, there is

Table 6.2. Data vs. epistemic information.

	Data	Epistemic information
Meaning	Data are raw, unorganized observations, being recorded on some media and in need of processing. Data can be something simple and seemingly random, and are useless until they are organized.	When data are processed, organized, structured, or presented in a given context so as to make it useful and they are called information.
Example	Each student's test score is a piece of data.	The average score of a class, or of an entire school, is information that can be derived from some given data.

no interpretation without an interpreter, and there is no interpreter without a format or language to interpret stimuli into. Imposing a format on something is to impart meaning, or at least some form of it. Following this logic, we see that the concept of data is clearly one of epistemic information. It is physical phenomena interpreted by a system or ontological information interpreted by a cognitive agent. Data are not elements or components of nature, nor are they in any way fundamental to the physical world. They represent, however, a link in the process of interpreting natural stimuli, the process by which cognitive agents process ontological information, albeit an early link in this process. Table 6.2 presents a comparison between data and epistemic information (Data vs. Information 2019). The differences here are somewhat arbitrary, often being imposed due to operational concerns rather than their inherent properties.

One may argue that in this comparison, data are the information for a particular student and the average score is of lesser importance to this individual, so the difference between data and information is rather arbitrary and relative, a matter of preference. We do not deny that this division can be useful or even an operational requirement, however. In computer information systems, knowledge systems, and computer decision systems, information is usually defined as the result of processing data, the outcome of bestowing meaning on what we call "input data". In his book on business information systems, Beynon-Davies (2009) states that *data are concerned with form and representation of symbols in storage and transportation. Information is concerned with the meaning of symbols and their use in human actions. Hence, information is data + sense making* (Beynon-Davies *op. cit.*, p. 75). This statement is inaccurate, because imposing form and representation, as we pointed out earlier, is already imposing some level of meaning or interpretation. Within this technical or operational definition, data are already classed as epistemic information.

From the perspective of computer information systems, however, this differentiation into data and information plays a useful role. Akerkar and Sajja (2010) provide definitions of data and information and point to the differences. For them, data and information are *factual, discrete and static things, and raw observations of the given area of interest. Information can be generated after systematic processing of such data* (Akerkar and Sajjaa 2010, p. 13). However, they do not realize that information for some may be data for others, making this distinction again relative. There are no interpretation-free data, just as there are no assumption-free scientific theories. What they are actually telling us, without realizing it, is that information, however they mean it, is processed/interpreted data or that data are information minus some processing. This is true even if they later say that information is not data because information is data that have been processed and connected with some meaning. Such claims assume that data have no meaning, but we recall the previous definitions of information (or semantic information) as "data+ meaning", but in this view, data have already had some meaning imparted on it, so we have the following dependency:

$$\text{"?"} \rightarrow \text{data} + \text{meaning} \rightarrow \cdots \rightarrow I_E$$

where the question mark represents some undefined "original" source of an uninterpreted physical process.

That said, Akerkar and Sajja's book is not written by, or for, philosophers, so such distinctions may not be visible or even needed

Table 6.3. Comparison between epistemic information and data.

Epistemic information	Data
Epistemic information is an interpreted physical stimulus—call it data, a signal, a state of a physical system, or some physical phenomenon—by a cognitive agent.	Data are interpreted stimuli in some format or language.
Epistemic information exists for a cognitive agent or is relative to one, so epistemic information is agent-relative or subjective.	Data are specific to an interpretation system and interpreting agent.
The cognitive agent may be a human agent, biological system, or an artificial cognitive system.	The interpretation of data may be performed by a biological or artificial agent/system.

for their narrative. The concepts of data and information must be stated simply in a clear, technical way that computer heads can understand, and there is no place for metaphysics here.

We need to state this to avoid any attempt to assign an objective, ontological status to data. There are no data out there, nor is the world a stream of digital data like it is presented in *The Matrix* movies. Data are interpreted, theory-laden observational facts.[24] The world is full of the uninterpreted or as we call it ontological information. Data are just as subjective as epistemic information is. Something is not data by its very nature, but rather because some agent denoted it as data. Thus, any definition of information that claims that this information has at its foundations data is committing a circular fallacy (*circulus in demonstrando*). The answer begs another question *ad infintum*, because in actuality, these definitions claim that epistemic information is founded on epistemic information or that epistemic information is the source of epistemic information. Table 6.3 compares the characteristics most often attributed to epistemic information and data to illustrate their similarities.

---

[24]This resembles the problem of "pure" observation in experimental sciences as it was initially imagined (e.g., Chalmers 1994), where every observation is theory-laden.

For the sake of completeness, we also need to mention the so-called metadata. Metadata, as a concept, represents data about data.[25] It usually describes the origins, the processing context, the originating systems, and other information about some data. Metadata is therefore nothing more than data about data—it does not enjoy any special metaphysical status, let alone granting such a status to data. The concept of metadata does not bring any new arguments to the discussion of data, at least from the perspective of this study.

6.3 Ontological Information and Infons

The *infon* is a concept described by Stonier (1990), Devlin (1991), Floridi (2013), and Martinez and Sequoiah-Grayson (2014). Infons are positioned as "elemental (natural) units of information", not as something like binary bits but rather in the sense of the elementary constituents of matter, much like quarks. In other words, they are elements that are fundamental to the construction of information.[26] Thus, much like how nothing is smaller than a quark, at least with our current knowledge, no information is smaller (whatever that may mean) than an infon.

Stonier claims that there may exist *a class of hypothetical particles which consist of only information. Such 'infons' might not show up in traditional physical experiments since such particles would possess neither mass nor energy—they could, however, manifest their effect by changes in organization* (Stonier 1990, p. 126). The physical interpretation of an infon provided by Stonier is just conjecture, however. He does not propose how we could conduct an experiment that could prove the existence of infons. After all, if they exist, we should be able to detect them. Thus, Stonier's infons are not like bosons in the way they were conceptualized (in terms of their properties) before

---

[25] *Metadata is simply **data about data**. This means it is a description and context of the data, which in turn helps to organize, find and understand data* (Metadata 2020). See also Snowden (2019).

[26] We compare infons to bits because a bit is the smallest unit of data in digital computer information systems. But, what is the smallest processing unit in analogous systems?

they were detected. Indeed, Stonier's infons have been conceptualized without a chance of ever being detected.

Floridi (2013, p. 84) uses the term infon in his General Definition of Information (GDI) stating, *GDI σ (an infon) is an instance of information, understood as semantic content.* He also explains that an infon *refers to the discrete item of information, irrespective of its semiotic code and physical implementation.* Furthermore, he also says that *the term 'infon' and the symbol refer to discrete items of factual semantic information quantifiable in principle as either true or false, irrespective of their semiotic code and physical implementation* (Floridi *op. cit.*, p. 110) and that *infons are messages formulated by a source* (*ibid.*, p. 111). Floridi's infons are clearly elemental units of semantic information, so they are foundational to the semantic conceptualization of information. Thus, Floridi's infon is the smallest form of an interpretable something, and it is not physical, so it must be abstract.

Infons have been also defined by Devlin (*op. cit.*, p. 35) in many ways. For example, infons are not physical objects. It is an "item of information" that is theory absolute or representation-independent; they are like real numbers and independent of the form they are in. Infons are semantic objects within the theory they are in. Their nature is that of numbers. For Devlin, information comes in infons, elementary bits of information for a specific agent. Infon information essentially comprises propositions about the state of the world, or facts if you will. The source of this information is perceived stimuli processed by a cognitive system, and each cognitive system may have its own infon-based ontology that suits its needs. (Note that ontology here refers to preexisting information/knowledge that enables the interpretation of stimuli.) For example, a cat will have a different infon-based ontology from a bee, as would a fish and an autonomous car.

Yet another definition of infons is proposed by Martinez and Sequoiah-Grayson (2014). They define an infon as *informational issues that may or may not be supported by particular situations; what is expressed as* $s \models \sigma.$, *with s being a situation and σ being an infon.* This definition is developed in the context of the situation theory of information (Martinez and Sequoiah-Grayson *op. cit.*).

The lesson to take from this discussion is that the infon is clearly an attractive concept, as many people seek to define it. Indeed, the infon seems to enable the quantification or discretization of information, thus making it measurable. Yet, the infon is not a clearly defined concept like electrons and protons, assuming we regard them as being clearly defined. It is not elemental in the sense that an elementary particle is in physics, nor is it sufficiently well defined to use it without qualification. The infons of Stonier, Martinez and Sequoiah-Grayson, and Devlin are clearly not the same, even if they all seek to play the role of *elementary units of information.*

From the perspective of this study, an infon must be smallest quantity of identifiable information, much like today's opinion that quarks are the smallest identifiable form of matter. From the perspective of epistemic information, an infon appears to be a unit of thought, so it is a unit of epistemic information.[27] We do not know what this unit is, though. For example, what is an elementary thought? Is it a simple Humean impression? The search for it seems rather pointless. From the perspective of ontological information, though, we may see the infon in a different light. With ontological information, we assume that information is always embedded in a physical carrier, so the simplest ontological information relates to the simplest organizations of nature or to the fundamental elements of nature, much like elementary particles do. As we recall, some authors in the reviewed publications do mention that matter and information cannot be considered separately, with there being no priority between matter and information. Thus, if information is always carried by a physical phenomenon, the smallest physical

---

[27] As the smallest amount of matter that we know of today, this complex object is somewhat reflected in the combinatorial ontology of Perzanowski (1965), where objects appear only after reaching some level and some structural complexity from the fundamental ontology realm. In other words, the simplest objects that exist are already complexes.

element, elementary particles like the muon, may be also the smallest "quanta" of ontological information, although this is just conjecture.

6.4 Ontological Information and Natural Information

The concept of natural information has many renditions. Natural information seems to have close relation with physical phenomena (this is where the qualifier "natural" comes from). Thus, it is worth exploring its possible connection with ontological information. We focus primarily on the work of Ruth Millikan (2013, 2017). We pose the question, one that has puzzled others as well,[28] as to whether natural information is ontological information or a kind of epistemic information. After all, we talk about ontological information as a part of nature, so it is in some sense natural.

Millikan defines natural information through a series of descriptions and analogies without explicitly defining it, as she admits herself. She claims that natural information *is carried by natural signs such as a sign of fire or ambient energy patterns that initiate perception* (Millikan 2017, p. 110). Furthermore, she states that *natural information is carried by informative human language, by maps or diagrams. Electronic patterns or neural patterns that are involved in information processing by computers and brains **can also carry** natural information* (*ibid.*). She also writes that *natural information resides only in sign vehicles. It is not something that is first generated at a source and then carried by the sign. Being housed in an infosign— having a vehicle—is intrinsic to natural information* (*ibid.*). Infosigns (intentional icons or representations) in Millikan's work mean events, objects, or phenomena (such as black clouds, wooden frame, the direction of the North Star, actions of some agent, situations (see Millikan 2013, 2017)), carrying intentional information (intentional means "ofness" or "aboutness (Millikan 2017)). Not all infosigns have to be intentionally created signs. These non-intentional signs are

---

[28]The question was posed by the audience during one of the presentations of the concept of ontological information. Private communication (2019).

called natural root signs. If infosigns are not produced by human agents, these signs carry natural information. Moreover, natural information in infosigns may be disjunctive information or information about probabilities. The example given by Millikan of this type of natural information, aka. disjunctive information, aka. information about probabilities, is information one may gain from unspecific symptoms of some illness; unspecific symptoms like a red rash may indicate some type of illness, but not one specifically. Furthermore, she says that *natural information does not have a privative form. There is no such thing as natural misinformation (ibid.,* p. 111). According to Millikan, natural information is not quantifiable.

Thus, what is natural information for Millikan? Natural information is created in communication processes. It is a certain message with meaning or meaning that can be interpreted by a cognitive agent (human or non-human). The source of this message may be a natural phenomenon like a fire (natural root sign). Or, it can be a human agent (language, a map, a diagram). In all cases, messages ride on some kind natural phenomenon, or physical carrier, or a vehicle, interpreted as an infosign. Natural information does not exist outside the carrier. The carrier of natural information is an infosign.

Now, what do we do with such a concept? On the one hand, natural information exhibits the properties of ontological information (e.g., *being housed in an infosign* and *does not have a privative form*). It is also carried by *ambient energy patterns,* so natural information is embedded in a carrier and not something subjective. Millikan's natural information is somewhat related to the state of physical systems as the state of physical systems carries natural information. On the other hand, natural information exists only when it is interpreted, as seen in this claim: *Electronic patterns or neural patterns that are involved in information processing by computers and brains* **can also carry** *natural information.* This means that the same physical patterns may or may not carry natural information.

It appears that Millikan's natural information is a concept that combines some notions of epistemic information (i.e., for an agent, communication process) and some recognition that information is carried by the patterns of physical systems, which are objective and independent (i.e., natural information *does not have a privative form*). Thus, we would not call natural information a new concept but rather a recognition that this information has a physical basis, i.e., a state of a physical system, and is derived from the state of this system by a cognitive agent. Thus, it is in our definition epistemic information.

We should not read too much into the Millikan's reference of *electronic patterns or neural patterns that are involved in information processing by computers and brains*, because the nature regarding the information-carrying role of these two carriers is not the same. The states of these carriers (electronic or neural physical signals) and the possibilities for carrying information in a given system (human brain and computer) are completely different. Yes, both these patterns are involved in information processing, though in completely different ways, so the analogy is misleading. The individual neuronal states, in all probability, do not carry any meaningful information, and only their totality within the specific system, i.e., the brain, may in some sense do this. But, how meaning arises from individual neural signals is as yet unknown (see, e.g., Zeki 1999, 2009). Conversely, the individual flows of electrical currents in wires or light pulses in optical communication conduits in computers and computer networks are encoding a specific meaning or, if you prefer, a message (with of course some level of noise) (e.g., Laughlin 2006).

Summing up our discussion, we may conclude that natural information in Millikan's explanation is a kind of epistemic information bound with much generalized concept of a sign, communication, and cognition, and it has little in common with the concept of ontological information as defined in this work.

Note that Millikan's concept of natural information is based on Dretske's work on semantic information (Dretske 1999). In this study, Dretske's concepts of information are classified as epistemic information (as semantic information is by definition (Dretske) related to knowledge). Dretske's work gained some commentaries resulting in concepts like nomic, factive information, counterfactual theory of information, or thermometer information (!) (Baker 2021). These variants of information belong to the class of epistemic information, as well. When talking about natural information, one should also mention not-Dretske-related definitions of natural information. Sweller (2006) defines natural information as information governing the activities in natural entities. This type of definition is related to the concept of morphological computing and biological information processing.[29] While coming from the different perspectives, the concepts of information proposed by Dretske, Millikan, Baker, and Sweller do have obvious similarities, allowing us to classify them in this study as the same type of information. The detailed discussion of computing and information in natural systems is outside the scope of this work.

6.5 Ontological Information: Abstract or Concrete?

6.5.1 *Dilemma of existence*

What is this dilemma about? It was posited by Davies, Mynarski, von Weizsacker and others, and it emerges when under the single heading of information, we group concepts of information being conceptualized as objective, having physical presence and having meaning. In other words, information conceptualized as objective is something concrete while information conceptualized as knowledge is associated with thoughts and the mind, so it is an abstract thing. Davies claims that information is on one hand abstract, but on the other hand it has a physical presence (Davies *op. cit.*, p. 35). He asks how something can be at the same time abstract and concrete.[30]

Similar ideas about the immaterial nature of information are expressed by Wheeler. His solution to the puzzle was the idea of participatory universe (Wheeler *op. cit.*, p. 331).[31]

---

[29]The similar concept of natural information is proposed also by Xavier and de Castro (2013).

[30]The separation of objects into abstract and concrete as understood in this study is so called in philosophical parlance a classical perspective in metaphysics, not necessarily agreed to by all philosophers (Rosen 2020).

[31]Participatory universe is an idea that the universe or reality is created by an observer (see, e.g., Nesteruk 2013).

Such views are fascinating, yet they would imply a "Berkeleyism" of sorts, which is a rather difficult concept to accept today. These ideas come from the search for the ultimate foundations of reality and the fact that the deeper we delve into the hierarchy of physical phenomena,[32] the less solid are the things we find, at least in our everyday concept of solidity. However, a lack of knowledge does not justify such flights of fancy, and modern "Berkeleyism" is a discussion that lies well outside the scope of this work.

We claim here that the problem of information being split between abstract and concrete concepts is actually nonexistent, contrary to the claims in some previous studies. Information clearly cannot be both at the same time and in the same way. If something is abstract, it cannot be concrete, and vice versa. So, how is this dilemma resolved? Ontological information is purely natural, and it exists in nature, in the physical world. There is nothing esoteric about it. Epistemic information, meanwhile, exists in the mind and has in this view, which incidentally has been tainted by Descartes and others to implying some "metaphysical" side to physical reality, "existence" in the mind of the beholder, whatever that may mean. Thus, in the same message written in a letter, spoken in words, or coded in a telegram, there is no magic "substance" that is common among these messages and transferred with them from one physical state to another. The attraction of some magical dust that bestows meaning on an otherwise inert substance is what led von Weizsäcker and others astray. They were looking for some "transcendent thing" over and above the media in question, something that is "preserved" between forms of physical media. Clearly, as this thing is not physical, it must be abstract in this view (*tertium non datur*). Let us look into the details of this thinking (Figure 6.1). A piece of music may be carried by through sound as "air pressure waves" with a physical structure S_A, by the physical organization of groove on a vinyl record with a physical structure S_B, or another transport media with a respective physical organization. They can all be interpreted as the same

---

[32] By "deeper", we refer the scale of the universe in the sense described by Lamża (2017), which is in some approximation the scale of resolution.

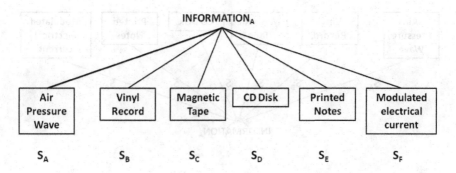

Figure 6.1. Perceived existence of epistemic information.

piece of music (i.e., the same information), so it seems obvious that this information must be common among them. It cannot be physical, however, because there is nothing common between structures S_A and S_B or any other physical structure conveying this music. The only commonality between these carriers is that they are physical substances with some form. There is no similarity between these structures. Thus, because the common factor is not in the structures, it must be abstract. This is information$_A$, and it is obvious from this argument that it must "exist" in some form. How otherwise could completely different physical structures carry the same information? We claim, however, that it is nothing like this, and the whole premise is simply wrong.

The correct explanation, we think, goes as follows: The various structures $(S_A, S_B, \ldots, S_Z)$ mean the same thing because we, as people, shape them in a certain way and interpret them in a way that is common to us. The music is in the ears of the listener, meaning that it is in the mind. There is no "abstract information" floating around in some extra-physical space that we tap into when needed. Indeed, it is possible that someone with a different mindset would interpret these physical structures entirely differently. This perspective is represented in Figure 6.2.

This figure illustrates what is actually happening with the piece of music. Everything is in the head (the mind) of the listener or composer. The music-carrying physical structures $S_A \neq \cdots \neq S_F$ are dissimilar, as are the different physical carriers. What makes

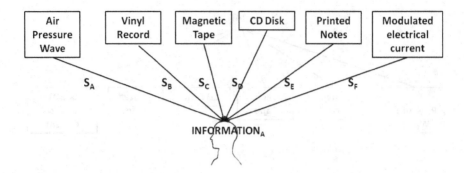

Figure 6.2. Perception of epistemic information as proposed in this study.

them the same music is the interpretation of the agent, not some information$_A$ transcending the physical realm. An agent imposes a proper structure, encodes it, and decodes it through the appropriate physical process. The sequence of dots in a CD disk becomes music only after we learn how to encode and decode "music" in the physical media. The same applies for any other physical carrier of music. How the mind is actually achieving this we do not yet understand. We more or less know about neural perceptual processes, but we do not know how we perceive music; music is in this case epistemic information.

The process of recovery of information$_E$ from different information$_O$ presented above is highly simplified. The relation between epistemic information and ontological information in different carriers is much more complex than it is suggested in Figure 6.2. If we assume, as in the example, that information$_E$ is a specific piece of music, none of the ontological information in different carriers in principle encodes exactly the same information$_E$. Every change of carrier result in the changes in ontological information. The conversions of structures (i.e., ontological information) between physical carriers are not lossless. Thus, strictly speaking, a specific piece of music recovered from S_A is not the same as the piece of music recovered from S_B. They are only similar. It is a human mind that allows us to say that these different pieces of music are the same. Of course, only if a certain degree of similarity is preserved. The key in this process is a function of the mind that seeks commonalties and similarities in received stimuli. How this process is carried out exactly is for now only a guess.[33]

We assume here that the mind is a non-reducible biological phenomenon, even if we cannot explain what precisely it is at our current level of knowledge. We obviously try to avoid Descartes' duality, and we do not need to postulate the existence of abstract information. This relieves the concrete–abstract dichotomy that was indicated by Davies. Of course, this argument can be applied only if the concept of the mind is posited as the *locus* of the epistemic information being created from different physical signals.[34]

While this explanation removes epistemic information from its "abstractness", it does not explain how epistemic information in our mind gets created and "transferred" into our artifacts. There is no natural law that directly shapes a car, a table, or a watch.[35] We must state that we simply do not know and that our theories of the mind do not provide conclusive explanation.[36] The only thing that we may assume is that the natural world, including the mind and its artifacts, is closed, and there is no "bifurcation" of nature as was implied by Descartes and denied by Whitehead (Whitehead 2015), as well as modern philosophers of science (under the various brands of naturalism)[37] who regard thoughts and the mind as being parts

---

[33]This important remark was suggested by Prof. Paweł Polak.

[34]See, for example, *human behavior is determined by physical processes in the brain* (Shanahan 2015, p. 18). Similar views are widespread in the literature.

[35]I refer to the 747 junkyard argument. The details may be found in (Junkyard Argument 2019).

[36]Mercier and Sperber refer to information "about some state of affairs" (i.e., epistemic information), when this state of affairs produces a unique cognitive state in an organism (Mercier and Sperber 2017, p. 339), falling short of denoting this "unique cognitive state" as a neurological state of the brain. The theories of the mind or of consciousness offer quite a rich field of studies with a variety of "products", thus offering a real intellectual feast but falling short of supplying the solution. The publications are too numerous to list them here.

[37]Some may think that the essence of naturalism is expressed in the phrase *The Cosmos is all that is or ever was or ever will be* (Sagan 2002). Yet, under close scrutiny, this phrase is too vague to mean anything specific. It is so unspecific that it lacks the intended gravitas (e.g., Papineau 2020, Gillet and Loewer 2001).

of this physical world, much like the other phenomena we experience and observe.

A Short Commentary

Information is mostly perceived as an abstract idea that is closely associated with knowledge, cognition, or communication. It has meaning, intentionality, and purpose, and its presence depends upon the existence of a cognitive agent. Information may also be regarded as a physical phenomenon. Such information does not need an agent to exist, but it has no meaning, purpose, or intentionality. So, how can information be, at the same time, abstract and endowed with meaning while also being concrete and physical yet meaningless? Paul Davies (2019) identifies this abstract–concrete dichotomy as a fundamental problem of information. Carlo Rovelli (2016), meanwhile, also highlighted this gap between information as a physical phenomenon and information with meaning. In his paper, Rovelli (2016) outlines how to close this gap. This commentary examines Rovelli's claims and asks whether his concept of information offers a fundamental solution to the abstract–concrete dichotomy, the concept of information in general, and the concept of meaningful information. Note that this discussion is intentionally brief, so several ideas are only conveyed through references and not elaborated in detail.

Rovelli (2016) presents a "purely physical definition of meaningful information", but how? First, Rovelli uses Shannon's ToC concept for measuring information and derives from this the "relative information" between two physical systems. He denotes it as "a purely physical version of the notion of information" or a purely "physical correlation". But, what is Rovelli's pure correlation? Pure correlation is defined as the correlation of two probability distributions (in compatible state spaces) or as the difference between (information) entropies of two probability distributions. As Rovelli states, "[these] correlations can exist because of physical laws or because of specific physical situations, or arrangements or mechanisms..." Therefore, a "purely physical correlation", which is information for Rovelli, represents some (co-)dependence of the (two) states of physical systems.

In other words, the two states are correlated, and the entropy difference and joint probability are formal expressions of this relation.

Second, Rovelli proposes (following the Wolpert and Kolchinsky paper [2016]) that Darwinian evolution provides the essential mechanisms to endow the natural/physical processes related to the evolution of organisms with some notion of meaning, purpose, and intentionality. From this viewpoint, environmental/physical stimulus has meaning for an organism if it increases its chances of its survival (or preservation). As a very rudimentary example, if bacteria are able to avoid a harmful environment by sensing it through some sort of physical stimuli, interpreting it correctly, and initiating evasive action, it creates meaning out of the physical sensory input. In other words, it creates meaningful information for itself. This is how environmental stimuli acquire meaning, intentionality, and purpose. (In the original text, the meaning of information is tied with an organism's ability to stay outside the "thermal equilibrium", that is, to keep a low entropy state.) By combining a Darwinian-based interpretation of meaning, purpose, and intentionality with information perceived as a correlation between physical states using relative information (Shannon 1948), Rovelli defines purely physical meaningful information. In his own words, he creates "the crucial first link of the chain" for connecting physical information with meaning, as expressed in the paper's title: "meaning=information + evolution".

So, what is Rovelli's "purely physical definition of meaningful information"? Rovelli used Shannon's information measure— Shannon never defined information but rather a measure of information and information entropy—to define the relative information (the information element of Rovelli's definition) and then applied this to the physical aspect of evolutionary processes, thus obtaining the Darwinian element responsible for meaning in Rovelli's definition. However, in his definition, Rovelli implicitly adopts the whole framework of Shannon's communication model (ToC) and the formula for the amount of information in messages between agents (i.e., information entropy). Why is this important? First, the model of relative information derived from Shannon's ToC information entropy implicitly includes at its basis the concept of the communication model. This implies that (physical) information is created by agents or exchanged between them, so the communication context is essential for the creation of meaning.

Another consequence implied in Shannon's model of information entropy is the probabilistic nature attributed to information. This serves a purpose in the optimization of communication channels, or it may be acceptable in specific cases that deal with very large state spaces, such as the entropy of a black hole (Barrow 2017). We can ask, however, is information in its very essence really probabilistic, or is probability introduced to characterize how information is really an expression of the epistemic opaqueness of the phenomena (i.e., the case under study) rather than a feature of the information itself?

There is also a question as to whether we can attribute meaning, intentionality, and purpose to probabilistic evolutionary processes. What do these terms mean in this context? What is more, do we not indirectly invoke the notion of intelligent design or God's hand in creation by assigning meaning, intentionality, and purpose (even in a reduced form) to natural processes? Of course, we may propose highly reductionist interpretations of these terms, and this is indeed what Rovelli did, but in this way, these terms would not mean what they purport to denote and what they would then denote in reality is unclear.

Why is such a (over) use of the terms' meaning, intentionality, and purpose not recommended? This is because when claims of meaning, even when qualified, are associated with physical or biochemical processes, it distorts the meaning of meaning. These claims reinterpret the very concept of meaning, which in turn may result, as is often the case, in misinterpretations or misuse. There is also always a danger of running the Sokal affair in reverse. As a reminder, the Sokal affair involved using terms from one domain (e.g., physics, mathematics) in another completely different context (e.g., social sciences, philosophy).

We can observe that Davies sensed he was on rather unstable grounds when blending the TOC, physical phenomenon, meaning, and intentionality, and he admits that his ideas are merely proposals.

Rovelli also points out that this sort of meaning is a very primitive one. The distance between the theoretical models of the cosmos or Bach's fugues and a bacterium's reaction to its environment is light years apart, yet the reaction of the bacterium is, at its core, the seed for others. This is conceptual quicksand for sure. Granting meaning, intentionality, and so on to natural biological systems is, it seems, an anthropomorphization of nature. Restricting these concepts to human agents runs the risk of incurring human exceptionalism. The proper approach is probably somewhere in the mythical middle, such as recognizing the exceptional human cognitive ability, but viewing it as an emerging function in a higher-level biological system. Another approach is to simply bite the bullet and stick to more widely recognized definitions.

Summing up Rovelli's view, information is correlation (pure correlation) between two physical systems (as defined above) and meaningful information is pure correlation in the above sense within the context of an evolutionary process being viewed as a communication process. This approach excludes, in principle, the concept of information where it is an intrinsic, not agent-relative, feature of physical phenomena.

Rovelli's meaningful information is certainly an interesting idea and worthy of study. However, its novelty and import must be placed in perspective. Shannon's TOC naturally lends itself to the concept of physical information in evolutionary processes, because communication is a physical process at its foundations and the very essence of evolution is based on communication between the environment and living agents. It must be said, however, that Shannon probably did not intend to make an association between purely physical processes, evolution, and information (Shannon 1956). As we said, Darwinian evolution is in some sense just a specific instance of a communication model being adopted for an evolutionary process. It is rather obvious that we are the creations of evolution (and therefore created through communication), and our cognitive faculties are the product of this (see, e.g., Nagel 2012, Searle 1998).

Now, does this proposal solve the abstract–concrete divide? Perhaps it does, but at the cost of stretching the meaning of meaning itself and forcing the concept of physical information into the TOC framework. Is this a price we want to pay, though? It seems that the solution to the "divide" lies somewhere else.

It has been suggested that the abstract–concrete dichotomy of information is caused by a misconceptualization of what information is (Krzanowski 2020a). One possible solution to resolve this abstract–concrete tension could be based on recognizing that information at the fundamental level is an organization or other form of physical phenomena (Krzanowski 2020), and it does not require the communication model framework to be defined, so there is no need for the TOC. This information exists everywhere where there is physical reality, as anything in reality takes some form, so in this view, information is fundamental. In addition, this information is ontologically objective in Searle's sense (1998)—it exists independently of anyone "sensing it" but is meaningless. The meaning in, or of, information is created by a cognitive agent, for an agent, or in the agent's cognitive system. From this perspective, the dichotomy dissolves, because information is fundamentally physical, but meaning is created by an agent and stays with him or her.

Assuming that meaning and intentionality are properties created, or attributed, by cognitive capacities, the presence of an agent with cognitive ability endows physical information with meaning. In other words, the agent derives meaning from neutral physical stimuli. Meaningful information is then simply agent-relative or ontologically subjective (Searle 1998), even if it is shared among many agents. How meaning is created by cognitive agents is not precisely known at this point, but we may assume that meaning has a biological basis, because cognition is a biological phenomenon. We need to avoid dualism, however, because this would take us into the never-never land of Descartes.

Now, does this agent-originated meaning correlate with physical information? Yes, it does, because cognitive natural/biological agents evolve to respond to the external environment by interpreting it as something meaningful for them. However, can we assign meaning to any response by a biological agent to environmental stimuli like in (Rovelli 2016)? If we were to, we would run the risk of trivializing the concept of meaning, because we would assign meaning, knowledge, and intelligence (or some derivatives thereof) to plants, single-cell organisms, and so on, which is a trend in biology that is actually happening (see, e.g., Trewavas 2017). Can we really say that meaning is a well-defined concept that spans the continuum from the primitive responses of simple biological systems to complex human-based meaning? We could say so, and some are indeed doing precisely this (Trewavas 2017), but it is tantamount to proposing some form of panpsychism.

In summary, we can see how introducing the concept of relative information based on the TOC and associating with it a meaning of sorts created through the evolutionary process dissolve the alleged gap, albeit only superficially. Indeed, it prompts more questions about meaning and information, particularly physical information, than it resolves. Introducing this new concept of meaning does not necessarily help to explain what comprises meaningful information and what meaning is, and defining physical information in the context of the TOC renders physical information relative rather than absolute (ontologically objective), which is what physical phenomena like information are.

6.6 Minimal Information Structural Realism

Minimal Information Structural Realism (MISR) claims that information (signified by I) is an ontologically and epistemologically objective physical[38] entity[39] (signified by R) and is perceived as a

---

[38] "Physical" as understood f.e. in Vocabulaire Technique at Critique de la Pilosophie, A. Lalande, Press Universitaires de France, 1956—"belonging to the world of perceptual phenomena and may be the subject of experimental research"— (fr.*artenant au monde phenomenal, qui peut etre objet de connaissance experientielle*) (p. 780).

[39] These claims are about the mode of existence (apart from the type of knowledge). Epistemic (or having to do with knowledge) objectivity means that the object of knowledge is/exists independently of the mind. Ontological (ontology or having to do with existence) objectivity means that the object is/exists as observer-independent. Epistemic and ontological objectivity in the case of information means that information is not dependent on the existence of the mind.

structure[40] (or form)[41] of nature[42] (signified by S). The term minimal
(M) is added to ISR, meaning that no other claims, epistemic, ontic,
or others, are associated with MISR. MISR may be seen as a version
of Structural Realism (SR). However, MISR goes beyond structures
conceived in SR[43] and postulates that behind them lies information.
MISR is not a claim about pancomputationalism though, along the
views of, for example, Fredkin (1991), Lloyd (2007), or Muller (2008).
The paper is not a comparison of MISR with SR but rather an
explication of MISR, and SR is providing solely the context for the
discussion.

The chapter is organized as follows. First, the basic claims of SR
are reviewed. Second, the concept of information is discussed, and
the basic assumptions of MISR are explicated. Finally, the conclusion
section collects the claims formulated in the discussion and suggests
some areas for further work.

Structural Realisms (SR)

SR, as explicated in the works of Psillos (2004), Brading and Laundry
(2006), Frigg and Votis (2010), Ladyman (2016), and many others,[44]

The statements like "this is a beautiful painting" are epistemically subjective.
Tectonic plates exist in this sense objectively. The examples are from Searle's lecture (2005). See lecture at Google Academy by John Searle (2015) for the detailed
explanation.

[40] "Structure" is notoriously difficult to define. One way to tackle this is to understand structure as "Configuration of parts forming some whole" after Vocabulaire
Technique at Critique de la Pilosophie, A. Lalande, Press Universitaires de France,
1956 (p. 1031). However, this is a very general definition and does not reflect the
multifarious role the term "structure" plays in the philosophy of science.

[41] In some SR papers, the term "form" is used exchangeable with "structure". For
example Worrall writes, ... *There was continuity or accumulation if the shift, but
the continuity is of form or structure* ... (Worrall 1989, p. 117). Such examples
may be found in other papers on structural realism.

[42] "Nature" as understood f.e. in The Oxford Companion to Philosophy.
T. Honderich. OUP, 1995: ... *everything that there is in the physical world of
experience, very broadly constructed. The universe and its contents, in short*
(p. 607).

[43] This concept of structure obviously assumes that it is a representational or
abstract (or abstracted) structure.

[44] SR and related ideas extend well into last century and traces of it can be found
in much earlier works (for example, see Ladyman 2016).

claims that nature is structural (roughly speaking because structure is what seems to be invariant in scientific models of nature; it is what survives theory changes). The two main currents in SR are ontic and epistemic. Ontic Structural Realism (OSR), as defined by Ladyman (1998) and French (1998), embodies the view that structure is the ultimate reality and ontologically basic. In the strong version of OSR, structures are "all the way down" (Frigg and Vostis 2010). Epistemic Structural Realism (ESR), defined by Worrall (1989), claims that structures are all that we can and may know about nature. There can be more to nature than structures, but ESR does not say what this "more" could be. The differences between ESR and OSR go much deeper, but they are omitted here as having no importance for this discussion. Another version of SR that is interesting from the perspective of MISR is Information Structural Realism (ISR).

ISR has been defined by Floridi (2004, 2010). It does not change basic SR_S claims, rather it admits that nature is structural, but structures are informational objects or information structures. Information structures supervene upon data (or data structures). Data structures, in order to be information structures, must have meaning, which in turn depends on the presence of the scientific agent.[45] Elementary data structures form "infons" or "elementary information particles" (Floridi 2010). At the core of ISR is the GDI which describes the foundational assumptions behind data, infons, and information structures (a more detailed description of data and infons is given in the following sections). ISR, because of its epistemic claims, can be seen as a variant of ESR.[46]

Information

Most of the definitions of information relate it to knowledge, belief, or a communication process (for example, see Capurro 2009, Floridi

---

[45] Dependence of informational structures on the mind gives to Floridi's ISR a Berkeleyan touch, so it seems.

[46] The problem for SR is that the definition of structure and its ontological meaning are open; SR structure is often left unspecified (Vostis 2010, Floridi 2004), or assumed to be logical, physical, or mathematical in nature, or claimed that it is an information object of the sort defined in the OOP paradigm (Floridi 2005), but there is no single version of a structure accepted in SR.

2010, Nafria 2010). This makes information epistemically and onto-logically subjective; information exists if someone recognizes it as such, it exists specifically in and for the mind of the receiver or an originator, or it exists when communicated (such as created, sent, and received). Epistemologically and ontologically subjective information is the one specified by GDI, elaborated by Floridi (2010) or information defined by Bar-Hiller and Carnap (1953), Brooks (1980), Loose (1998), Sveiby (1998), Dretske (1999), Casagrande (1999), Burgin (2003), and Lenski (2010), to list just a few examples. Shannon's concept of information as being a measure of the PDF over some probability space (Shannon 1948, Shannon and Weaver 1964, Pierce 1968) may have subjective or objective properties depending on how probability is defined (Gilles 2000). If we accept Shannon's informa-tion[47] for what it is (a moment of PDF), we may think of it as some measure of patterns, which may be natural or manmade. However, how Shannon's concept is related to other definitions of information is disputable (see, e.g., the discussion of Shannon's information by Shannon Weaver 1964, Pierce 1968, Cherry 1978, Casagrande 1999, Hidalgo 2015, Krzanowski 2016, and Schroeder 2017).[48]

In recent decades, the perception of information as an ontologi-cal[49] element of nature has become quite widespread in physics, cos-mology, computing sciences, biology, and other sciences. Information seems to be a unifying concept connecting these diverse domains. The success of computing models of natural phenomena can be explained by postulating that computing models and nature share a common element—information (see, e.g., Polak 2017).

---

[47]To be precise, Shannon never explicitly defined information. However, his con-cept of measure of information was later interpreted (correctly) as the definition of it, so there is not much inaccuracy in saying "Shannon's information" as most of those working in the field understand this term for what it is—a mental shortcut.

[48]For example, Hidalgo writes, ...*the interpretation of entropy and information that emerged from Shannon's work was hard to reconcile both with the traditional use of the word information and with the interpretation that emerged from Boltz-mann's work* (Hidalgo 2105, p. 15).

[49]"Ontological" means here pertaining to ontology or "things in themselves" (fr. ...*les chose ells-memes*...) following Vocabulaire Technique at Critique de la Pilosophie, A. Lalande, Press Universitaires de France, 1956.

One may argue that the concept of information as an ontological element of nature goes back as far as the pre-Socratic Greeks and Ancient China (Curd 2011, Oldstone-Moore 2011). However, it is safer to focus on the 20th-century authors; the incomplete, selective, and rather idiosyncratic list would include the following:[50] Zuse (1970), von Weizsäcker (1970), Turek (1978), Wheeler (1982), Heller (1987, 2014), Collier (1989), Batenson (1979), Stonier (1990), Toffoli (1990), Thagard (2000), Barwise and Ethemendy (2000), Steinhart (2000), Jadacki and Brozek (2005), Seife (2006), de Castro (2007), and Hidalgo (2015). These authors claim in some way or another that information is at the center of nature (Dodig-Crnkovic), as energy is (Seife), and is related somehow to structure of nature (Collier), patterns (Dodig-Crnkovic), or physical order (Hidalgo); it is a property of objects and a property of the universe (Stonier). For Hidalgo, Seife, and others quoted above, information is as real as any physical phenomena can be; it is objective, it is structural.

Why Minimal Information Structural Realism?

Presented here are two informal arguments for MISR. The arguments propose that interpreting natural structures as information or representing information is consistent with the findings of physical sciences and that epistemic interpretation of information and structures (as in ESR and ISR) is not sufficient for the description of nature, thus postulating that ontological interpretation (of information and structures) may be more constructive.

Isomorphism of mathematical models of nature. The research in physics and cosmology provides evidence that different mathematical structures of natural phenomena support the same experimental results (Heller 2014, p. 85). This would suggest that behind different mathematical models, or structures, there is an unchanging physical reality, and mathematical models are just reflections, or approximations, of this reality. Heller, a cosmologist and a philosopher, gives the example of how the evolution of quantum states is modeled by

---

[50]Dates of publication refer to the edition cited, not to the original date of publication of the work.

three different mathematical representations: those of Schrödinger, Heisenberg, and Dirac.[51]

Heller observes that, as these three models support the same experimental results, they must then refer to another invariant structure, to which we do not have access, but that is representing a true reality or is a reality in itself. Heller (2014) also writes, *This is not an exceptional situation in physics* (p. 65), meaning that multiple mathematical structures describing successfully the same physical phenomena exist, as well, in other areas of physics than just QM.

Epistemic incompleteness. In epistemic definitions, information always supervenes on datum or data. The existence of data in addition to information is what may be called epistemic incompleteness. Epistemic incompleteness means that epistemic definitions of information recognize the necessary existence of something beyond epistemic information itself for the complete description of nature. An exemplary case for epistemic incompleteness is offered by the GDI. In GDI, data are primary "stuff" of the universe and occur prior to information (Floridi 2010, p. 84). Data are denoted as "lack of uniformity", diaphora de re, didomena, or "a fracture in a fabric of being" (Floridi 2010). Information forms structures composed of data in a certain specific way that is meaningful to some observer. As Floridi (2010) writes, "...General Definition of Information (information is defined) in terms of data + meaning" (p. 83). Thus, information supervenes on data structures. In addition, between information structures and data, Floridi includes *infon*—an elementary particle of information; as Floridi (2010) writes, "the parallel with fundamental particles of physics the electrons, protons, neutron, photons, and so forth" (p. 85). Infon is a strange concept, as, on one hand, it is conceived to be similar to elementary, physical particles and

---

[51] *There is a proof that these (Schrödinger, Heisenberg, Dirac) mathematical models are unitary equivalent, meaning that they lead to the same empirical predictions. To say it differently, there is an isomorphism between these models with respect to all observables. Thus, it is not the case that one mathematical structure corresponds to something we would call the structure of the world* (Heller 2014, p. 64).

objective ontologically, while, on the other hand, it has an epistemic, subjective quality.

Minimal Information Structural Realism

MISR combines intuitions about the structural character of reality and the ontological and foundational role of information in nature. Structures in MISR are the order behind the abstract structures of ESR or OSR. Information in MISR is not something waiting to be recognized by the mind but rather an organizational principle pervading nature. This view of structures and information is not present in current strands of SR (ESR, OSR, and ISR).

MISR claims also that information is an objective aspect of reality and it is perceived or apprehended through (or as) patterns or structures. No data and no infons are necessary to define what information is.

MISR is not associated with ESR and OSR directly, but it does not contradict them. MISR is somewhat related to the concept of Floridi's ISR, in that both ISR and MISR attribute importance to the role of information in nature, yet do so in different ways. Floridi's ISR claims that structures perceived in SR strands are informational structures, or can be interpreted as informational, similar to informational structures modeled by the Object Oriented Programming (OOP) paradigm (Floridi, 2004). MISR claims that structures in SR reflect, or approximate, the structure of nature that contains information.

Versions of MISR may support more nuanced versions of MISR along ontic, epistemic, mathematical, quantum, or computational perspectives. Of course, each of these versions of ISR must be refined and evaluated for its logical coherence and correspondence with the facts of physics.[52]

---

[52]One would have to mention the differences in the understanding of *realism* in SR and MISR. In SR, realism denotes the position of science and scientific theories toward nature (realism vs. anti-realism). In MISR, realism denotes the objective character (mind-independent) of information. Both realisms, in further interpretations, do, however, converge on the same claim that there is an objective (mind-independent) reality that we can study. Realism is a polysemic concept that

Final thoughts

SR and MISR take two different, but not completely contradictory, views of nature and our knowledge of it. SR claims structures are what is or what can be known,[53] but that they have nothing to do with information. In Floridi's ISR, information is epistemic and it emerges over structures composed of data. MISR sees structures that we conceive as representations, or approximations, of the structure of nature, which is what is invariant behind SR structures. This structure of nature may be thought of as information or composed of information.

6.7   Ontological Information and Popper's Three Worlds

One difficulty that arises in recognizing the existence of ontological information (i.e., information that is meaningless, objective, physical) is the deeply rooted notion that information is a human-centered concept akin to knowledge, meaning, and the mind in some form or mode,[54] as we have said many times in this study.[55] Thus, the argument goes that if information is ontological information, then what is

---

splits various versions of scientific realism (see, for example, Chakravartty 2007). It seems that MISR may add (regrettably) still another interpretation to what is real.

[53] A big problem for SR is how structures in ESR and OSR translate into the objects of nature. This problem seems to be so far unsolved, despite many propositions.

[54] This section was added after the suggestions from Prof. P. Polak.

[55] A similar idea about epistemic information and physical information was expressed by Landauer. He wrote that *The quaint notion that information has an existence independent of its physical manifestation is still seriously advocated. This concept, very likely, has its roots in the fact that we were aware of mental information long before we realized that it, too, utilized real physical degrees of freedom. Our intuition has misled us in other ways* (Landauer *op. cit.*). However, as we see in the next section, Landauer's claim that "information is physical" does not mean exactly the same thing as what the statement "ontological information is a physical phenomenon" denotes. See more on Landauer's principle (e.g., Landauer 1996, Bennett 2003, Moore 2012, Lutz 2012, Hong *et al.* 2016, Ladyman *et al.* 2001).

this epistemic information? We cannot reject the existence or reality (of sorts) of human knowledge in its various forms, such as history, culture, civilization, the arts, and so on—it would be like rejecting humanity itself—so it would seem we have to reject the concept of ontological information, because these two "informations" cannot coexist. However, ontological information in no way contributes to this conclusion. We can validly assume that both kinds of information, epistemic and ontological, exist but in different ways. These two forms of existence for ontological information and knowledge or epistemic information will be valid as long as we clearly define their modes of existence.

Karl Popper proposed the idea of Three Worlds (Popper, 1978). Popper's three worlds postulate that there are three realms of existence.[56] The first world *consists of physical bodies: of stones and of stars; of plants and of animals; but also of radiation, and of other forms of physical energy* (Popper *op. cit.*, p. 3). The second world consists *of our feelings of pain and of pleasure, of our thoughts, of our decisions, of our perceptions and our observations; in other words, the world of mental or psychological states or processes, or of subjective experiences* (Popper, *ibid.*). Finally, the third world comprises *the world of the products of the human mind, such as languages; tales and stories and religious myths; scientific conjectures or theories, and mathematical constructions; songs and symphonies; paintings and sculptures. But also airplanes and airports and other feats of engineering* (Popper, *ibid.*) and *the American Constitution; or Shakespeare's The Tempest; or his Hamlet; or Beethoven's, Fifth Symphony; or Newton's theory of gravitation.* More succinctly put, the third world consists *of the world of the products of the human mind* (Popper, *ibid.*). Such a distinction between physical things, the workings of the mind, and the products of the mind is not surprising. In fact, Aquinas and Aristotle did something similar in a different way. What is surprising is how Popper assigns the same ontological

---

[56]Popper posed his concept in the opposition to the monist view, where everything is physical, and the dualist view, where there is the mind and the physical world, and positioned his perspective as a pluralist view of the world.

status, the same meaning of "to exist", to the objects of these three worlds. He calls this construct "three worlds realism" as opposed to monism or dualism (*ibid.*, p. 151). Popper says that *the objects of world 3 may be in a very clear sense not fictitious but quite real: they may be real in that they may have a causal effect upon us, upon our world 2 experiences, and further upon our world 1 brains, and thus upon material bodies* (*ibid.*, p. 150). Furthermore, he says that *world 3 objects are real; real in a sense very much like the sense in which the physicalist would call physical forces, and fields of forces, real, or really existing* (*ibid.*, p. 152).

So, what is Popper saying here? To justify existence or coexistence with the same ontological status of the objects in his worlds, Popper redefines what it means to be real; he says *what is real or what exists is whatever may, directly or indirectly, have a causal effect upon physical things* (*ibid.*, p. 154). Consequently, the usual question of existence is morphed into a question about causality, although without defining how this causality can be understood. Popper states, *Thus we may replace our central problem of whether abstract world 3 objects, such as Newton's or Einstein's theories of gravitation, have a real existence, by the following problem: can scientific conjectures or theories exert, in a direct or indirect way, a causal effect upon the physical things of world 1? My reply to this question will be: yes, they can indeed* (*ibid.*, p. 155). I think this claim would leave most people with more questions. For example, Newton's theory of gravitation (Popper's example of something in world three) is only an approximation, so how can such a theory have a causal effect *upon the physical things of world 1*? To put it another way, what changed in nature's state with the introduction of Newton's theory? There must have been a difference in reality when this theory emerged as a new causal factor in the cosmos? We may ask similar questions about the other objects of world three. To leave no doubts, Popper adds that *scientific conjectures or theories can exert a causal or an instrumental effect upon physical things; far more so than, say, screwdrivers or scissors.* So what are the objects of world three? We learn from Popper that these are *Thought contents . . . conjecture, products of human language; and human languages, in their turn, are the most important and basic of world 3 objects* (*ibid.*, p. 159).

Now, why are these thoughts not the content of the mind? Popper claims that thoughts are processes in the mind rather than the contents of the mind. Thus, it is not clear whether these processes have content. If they do not have content, then are these thought processes just empty? In other words, are they about nothing? Alternatively, if they have content, what is this content? Popper claims that the products of these processes are the objects of world three, but we do not know where this world three exists. We know from Popper that it does not exist in the mind, because thoughts are empty processes, so where is it? He does not unequivocally explain what counts as the end product for a thought. Is it a theory, a conjecture, a false theory or a correct theory, an airplane, the idea of a book, a book, a belief, or a wish? We may ask whether we could accept the model of the mind as the seat of fleeting thoughts devoid of content. It seems a bit like Humean's model of the mind.

Popper also introduces the concepts of subjective and objective knowledge (knowledge in a subjective and objective sense). He explains that *Knowledge in the objective sense consists not of thought processes but of thought contents* (*ibid.*, p. 156). What this means is that objective knowledge is the content of world three, but what does "objective" mean for Popper? "Objective" for him means not independent of the observer, as it is usually understood when we talk about objective reality but rather something that is common between observers. As we read further, however, because the world three objects depend on world two agents, this objective knowledge is agent-dependent. Popper claims objective knowledge is the content of linguistically formulated theories that are translation invariant. Thus, objective knowledge in Popper's version of objectivity is not what is usually understood when this predicate is used in statements like "physical things exist objectively". This is in fact an epistemic claim, not an ontological one.

To make things clearer, Popper adds *Nothing depends here on the use of the word "real": my thesis is that our world 3 theories and our world 3 plans causally influence the physical objects of world 1; that they have a causal action upon world 1* (*ibid.*, p. 164). This claim is hard to accept, though, because we are not sure at this point whether we are talking about a complete abstraction, reality, or some shadow land of half-reality. If we are in reality (we still talk of *physical objects*), what kind of reality is it if reality, as he says, does not count? In his closing remarks, Popper explains that *This influence* [the causal effect of world 3 on world 1] *is to the best of my knowledge always indirect. World 3 theories and world 3 plans and programmes of action must always be grasped or understood by a mind before they lead to human actions, and to changes in our physical environment, such as the building of airports or of airplanes. It seems to me that the intervention of the mind, and thus of world 2, is indispensable, and that only the intervention of the mental world 2 allows world 3 objects to exert, indirectly, a causal influence upon the physical world 1. Thus in order that Special Relativity could have its influence upon the construction of the atom bomb, various physicists had to get interested in the theory, work out its consequences, and grasp these consequences. Human understanding, and thus the human mind, seems to be quite indispensable (ibid.,* p. 164). It seems that our everyday reality does catch up with Popper eventually. Popper needs an actor in the physical world for his causality to manifest, even if he states that *Nothing depends here on the use of the word 'real'.* It seems that the terms "ontology", "real", "causality", and "existence" have been somewhat confused or assigned obtuse meanings in Popper's worlds, such that they are too obtuse to avoid critique.

So, what about epistemic and ontological information and Popperian real–unreal worlds? We cannot deny that the products of human thought exist, and we call them epistemic information. We also cannot deny that these products can be represented in physical things, which we call ontological information. We cannot deny that the world of concrete things exists, and this is where ontological information persists. We also have to agree that the world of human products needs an agent, because without an agent who "understands" the content of world three, there is no causal link between the worlds, and the objects of world three do not exist without such an agent, like a lost scripture, which without an agent to read it is just a series of meaningless symbols. However, granting the same status of existence to the objects of these three worlds[57] seems rather doubtful. (Keep in mind what Popper said: *world 3 objects are real; real in a sense very much like the sense in which the physicalist would call physical forces, and fields of forces, real, or really existing.*)[58]

Despite these contradictions in Popper's claims, there are researchers that implicitly or not, support his views of three words (see, e.g., Mingers and Standing 2018). As we have indicated these claims hinge on interpretations of the terms "objective" and "to exist".

As an example, we may quote the entry on information from Audi's Dictionary of Philosophy (Audi 1999). In the first sentence, it states that *information is an objective (mind-independent) entity.* However, the next sentence, it says that *it (information) can be generated or carried by messages or other products of cognizers.* Clearly, the cognizers are originators or creators or carriers of information, i.e., information for its existence depends on them, so it is hardly objective. In a few sentences, the author states, *information would exist independently of its encoding or transmission.* These claims postulate some form of existence outside of the physical carrier, however, still dependent on the cognizer to recognize it (from sentences before). We see in this claim reflections of both von Weizsäcker and Popper's concepts of information.[59]

---

[57]Why do we have to give the same ontological status to worlds one, two, and three? The worlds should have the same ontological status to interact; otherwise, we again have a dualism problem, but this time with three rather than two worlds. As Popper says, world three depends on world two to impact world one. If world two had a different ontological status than the other two worlds, the objects of world three connecting with the objects of world one would have to pass through a kind of ontological no-man's-land in world two. Maybe, this is not a problem for Popper!

[58]Popper's three worlds view is not acceptable "as is". It is a useful conceptual tool for talking about different modes in which information can be perceived, but Popper's ontological claims (i.e., claims about existence) regarding the end product of thoughts are highly criticized (e.g., Carr 1977, Gilroy 1985, Albinus 2013).

[59]See also the less ambiguous and contradictory interpretation of Popper's Three Worlds by Ziman (1991, p. 106).

6.8 Ontological Information and General Theory of Information

Why GTI? We think that GTI presents the most comprehensive perspective on the nature of information. It encompasses ontological information, epistemic information, and quantifiable measures. It provides the foundations for the explanation of the causal nature of information and it provides the link to fundamental ontologies of the reality in the form of combinatorial ontology of Perzanowski and Cocchiarella.

6.8.1 *Elements of the general theory of information*

In the general theory of information, the definition of information in the broad sense is given in the second ontological principle, which has several forms (Burgin 2010, 2017).

Ontological Principle O2 (the *General Transformation Principle*). In a broad sense, *information* for a system R is the potentiality/cause of formations and transformations (changes) in the system R.

Thus, we may understand information in a broad sense as a capacity (ability or potency) of things, material as well as mental and abstract, to change other things. Information exists in the form of *portions of information.*

However, the common usage of the word *information* does not imply such wide generalizations as the Ontological Principle O2 implies. Thus, we need a more restricted theoretical meaning because an adequate theory, whether of the information or of anything else, must be in significant accord with our common ways of thinking and talking about what the theory is about, else there is the danger that the theory is not about what it purports to be about. To achieve this goal, we use the concept of an *infological system* IF(R) of the system R for the information definition. Elements from IF(R) are called *infological elements.*

The exact definition consists of two steps. At first, we make the concept of information relative and then we choose a specific class of infological systems to specify information in the strict sense. That is why it is impossible and, as well as, counterproductive to give an exact and, thus, too rigid and restricted definition of an infological system. Indeed, information is a very rich and widespread phenomenon to be reflected by a restricted rigid definition (cf., e.g., Capurro *et al.* 1999, Melik-Gaikazyan 1997).

The concept of infological system plays the role of a free parameter in the general theory of information, providing for representation of different kinds and types of information in this theory. That is why the concept of *infological system*, in general, should not be limited by boundaries of exact definitions. A free parameter must really be free. Identifying an infological system IF(R) of a system R, we can define information relative to this system. This definition is expressed in the following principle.

Ontological Principle O2g (the *Relativized Transformation Principle*). *Information* for a system R *relative to the infological system* IF(R) is the potentiality/cause of formations and transformations (changes) in the system IF(R).

When we take a physical system D as the infological system and allow only for physical changes, we see that information with respect to D coincides with (physical) energy.

Taking a mental system B as the infological system and considering only mental changes, information with respect to B coincides with mental energy.

As a model example of an infological system IF(R) of an intelligent system R, we take the system of knowledge of R. In cybernetics, it is called the *thesaurus* Th(R) of the system R. Another example of an infological system is the memory of a computer. Such a memory is a place in which data and programs are stored and is a complex system of diverse components and processes.

There is no exact definition of infological elements, although there are various entities that are naturally considered as infological elements as they allow one to build theories of information that inherit conventional meanings of the word *information*. For instance, knowledge, data, images, algorithms, procedures, scenarios, ideas, values, goals, ideals, fantasies, abstractions, beliefs, and similar objects are standard examples of infological elements. Note that all these elements are structures and not physical things. Thus, we can consider structural infological elements *per se* and use them for identifying information in the strict sense.

Ontological Principle O2a (the *Special Transformation Principle*). *Information in the strict sense* or *proper information* or, simply, *information* for a system R is the potentiality/cause of formations and transformations (changes) of the structural infological elements from an infological system $IF(R)$ of the system R.

We see that information in the strict sense is a particular case of relative information.

6.8.2 *The global world structure and information dichotomy*

Information in the strict sense is also stratified according to the global world structure (Burgin 2011). In the most advanced form, the global world structure is represented by the *Existential Triad* composed of the top-level components of the world as a unified whole and reflecting unity of the world (cf. Figure 6.3). This triadic structure is rooted in the long-standing tradition coming from Plato and Aristotle (Burgin 2010, 2017).

In the Existential Triad, the Physical (or material) World represents the physical reality studied by natural and technological sciences, the Mental World encompasses different forms and levels of mentality, and the World of Structures consists of various kinds and types of structures. The Existential Triad entails the differentiation of information into two fundamental classes: ontological information and mental information.

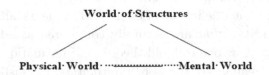

Figure 6.3. The Existential Triad of the World.

> *Ontological information* is the potentiality/cause of formations and transformations of structures in the physical world, i.e., of physical systems.
>
> *Mental information* is the potentiality/cause of formations and transformations of structures in the mental world, i.e., of mental systems.
>
> *Epistemic information* is the potentiality/cause of formations and transformations of knowledge (Burgin 2011b, 2014). Consequently, epistemic information forms a subclass of mental information.

As it is demonstrated in (Krzanowski 2020a), epistemic information and ontological information are complementary to one another.

It is possible to ask a question about how information belonging to the World of Structures can act on physical and mental systems/objects. The explanation is given in two more principles of the general theory of information.

Ontological Principle O3 (the *Embodiment Principle*). For any portion of information I, there is always a *carrier* C of this portion of information for a system R.

The substance C that is a carrier of the portion of information I is called the *physical*, or *material*, *carrier* of I.

Ontological Principle O4 (the *Representability Principle*). For any portion of information I, there is always a *representation* C of this portion of information for a system R.

To better understand the difference between the representation and carrier of a portion of information, let us consider the following example.

A letter is a carrier of a portion of information, while the text of the letter is a representation of this portion of information.

This example shows that a representation is also a carrier of a portion of information, while not any carrier is a representation of information.

Applying Ontological Principle O3, we see that when information has a physical representation, this representation act on physical systems. For instance, DNA is a representation (and a carrier) of the hereditary information. In such a way, hereditary ontological information acts on physical/chemical substances in the formation of the organism of a living being.

6.8.3 *GTI and ontological information*

Ontological information has been conceptualized as a part of the physical world (Krzanowski 2020) with the properties shared with other physical phenomena with the exception of its structure–formative character unique to information. The thing left out from the definition of ontological information was its causality or potentiality to cause changes to physical structures/forms of the physical objects. In (Krzanowski 2020), this active (or causal) characteristic of information was referred to as "forming principle". But, it was not further explored in that study. With the GTI, this "forming principle" obtains clearer expression and firmer logical foundations. Ontological principles (O2), (O2a), and (O2g) of the GTI define how this "forming principle" may be conceptualized and what is the meaning of the causality of ontological information in physical systems. Further, the Existential Triad of the World as formulated by Burgin locates ontological information in the context of two other elements forming the Triad: The Mental World and the World of Structures. In this context, ontological information belongs to the Physical world and "is the potentiality/cause of formations and transformations of structures in the physical world, i.e., of physical systems". Such positioning of ontological information addresses one of the open questions posed by Krzanowski (2020)—the question of whether ontological information is an active or passive component of nature and how this property should be understood. Finally, the Existential Triad of the World also establishes a dependency between three types of information: epistemic, mental, and ontological, the connection not explicated in the original description (Krzanowski 2020a) but necessary for comprehensive understanding of the foundational role of information in the universe.

6.9 Ontological Perspective on Information:
    A Proposal

What follows is a very speculative discussion. However, it opens the new perspective on ontological information. It suggests that certain types of foundational ontology may be conceptualized as information in the sense of structure and structure-forming elements. Of course, such a claim requires acceptance of speculative ontology and metaphysics beyond the usual framework discussed in the analytic philosophy of science. In the case of pure ontology, there is no way to say what is wrong or what is correct (this comment does not apply to applied ontology). We can only say what is coherent and logical and what is not. This is the way this section should be read. Because of its speculative character, this discussion was placed at the end of the work, somewhat indicating its distance to the main body of the book; one may even risk the claim that this is a metainformation discussion, meaning that it should be studied after the treatises dealing with information.[60] The concept of information discussed here one would be tempted to denote as meta-information, i.e., being beyond usual discussions of the concept of information.

6.9.1 *Introduction*

That information is a polysemantic concept has been repeated in these pages many times.[61] However, it seems that two major perspectives for information were being identified in the philosophy of information. First, the epistemic view claims that information is related to knowledge or that, at least, information requires the presence of the mind to exist. For example, look at the definitions of Bar-Hiller and Carnap (1953), Brooks (1980), Loose (1998), Sveiby (1998), Dretske (1999), Casagrande (1999), Burgin (2003), Floridi (2010), and Lenski (2010). Epistemic information (call it information$_E$) always needs a "carrier", sometimes denoted as data or other terms (e.g., Floridi 2010). The second, ontological approach claims that information (call this information$_O$) is a fabric of the universe, existing independently of the presence of the mind. For some example definitions, see Zuse (1970), von Weizsäcker (1970), Turek (1978), Wheeler (1982), Heller (1987, 2014), Collier (1989), Batenson (1979), Stonier (1990), Toffoli (1990), Thagard (2000), Barwise and Ethemendy (2000), Steinhart (2000), Jadacki and Brozek (2005), Seife (2006), de Castro (2007),

---

[60]The analogy to $\mu\varepsilon\tau\grave{\alpha}\,\tau\grave{\alpha}\,\varphi\upsilon\sigma\iota\kappa\grave{\alpha}$, *meta ta physika* is not accidental.
[61]This paper borrows several ideas and observations from Krzanowski (2017).

Hidalgo (2015), and Shroeder (2017). The first approach may date back to the mind–body problem of Descartes and an epistemic turn in modern philosophy. The epistemic turn is in fact a rejection of metaphysics. The roots of the second approach can be traced back to concepts of Arche, form, hylomorphism, monads, and the original meaning of the Latin word *informare*, which meant to mold, fashion, or give shape to (i.e., both formative and form-determinant factors).

Therefore, which concept of information (*information$_E$* or *information$_O$*) should we choose? Ockham would suggest using the one that does not need to postulate additional entities (data) to exist, indicating *information$_O$*. However, *information$_O$* has several renditions. It has been defined as a structure (as in structural realism), as a physical thing, as a mathematical structure, as a logical structure (expressed in set theory formalism), or as something beyond structures (such as perhaps an invariant element of mathematical models). No one coherent description of *information$_O$* has been formulated that expresses its fundamental role. This may be because the conceptual network used to describe *information$_O$* is always related to some specific domain, such as logic, physics, or mathematics. It always borrows terminology from some "other" phenomenon, domain, or conceptual apparatus. However, *information$_O$* is conceptualized as a foundational element of the Universe, so it cannot be rendered through concepts and methods from a specific domain. It must be described using concepts (using a conceptual network) that refer to the foundations of what is, because this is where information as an ontological element belongs in the order of being. After all, in this view, information is part of the fabric of the Universe. Such a goal may be achieved with a conceptual network of fundamental ontology. This refers not to the ontology of everyday (or phenomenal) objects, as is often the case in modern times, but rather to the ontology of being, of what is, of the totality of existence (i.e., the ontology as understood by Plato, Aristotle, some Medieval thinkers, and Leibnitz).[62] It would seem that an ontology qualified for this job

---

[62]Sytnik-Czetwertynski (2015) lists philosophers that influenced Perzanowski's philosophy, including Plato, St. Anselm, Descartes, Leibnitz, Frege, Wittgenstein, Russell, and Ingarden (a student of Husserl).

is the one formulated by Perzanowski, a well-known philosopher and logician with roots in the Lvov-Warsaw school of logic.

In the following sections, we present the elements of Perzanowski's ontology and employ them to outline the concepts of *information$_O$*. We hope this will demonstrate that the language of fundamental ontology can cover most of the concepts of information$_O$ and explain the profusion of definitions for information. In essence, we hope that the concept of information will be reduced down to the conceptual apparatus of fundamental ontology. This paper will not discuss the merits of the various schools of ontology or compare them. There are simply too many of them, and they are too distant in their claims. In this paper, the term *information* is used in its generally understood and commonly accepted form, while the term *information$_O$* refers to ontological information. Furthermore, the term *information$_P$* is used to refer to information as defined by Perzanowski.

6.9.2 *Ontology: Basic assumptions*

What follows is a summarized exposition of Perzanowski's ontology rather than a complete review of his ontological system.[63] It focuses on what seems relevant to the topic at hand. By the reference (J.X.x), we denote Perzanowski's (2016) work, and by the reference (R.X.x), we denote Perzanowski's (2015) work.

Claims	Perzanowski's Postulates
Ontological foundations	What is, is given to us not directly, like in a mirror, but through insight (R.19.1). What is given is given as a series of images. These images are obtained with different principles and described in different conceptual systems. What is given results from a superimposition of these images (R.19.3). We assume that images are forms of what is.

---

[63]The test is the author's translation of selected, relevant statements from Perzanowski's works.

Claims	Perzanowski's Postulates
	Investigation is when we analyze what is given to us. This analysis is made possible by the conclusions of several specific disciplines, such as physics, chemistry, biology, anthropology, neurology, psychology, informatics, mathematics, and so on. The conclusions of these specific disciplines do not provide answers but give data/material for philosophical reflection (R.19.4). Being (that what is) makes possible that which is possible, and in the next step, that which exists factually, that which lasts (J.112.150). Ontology is the theory of what is, the theory of being. It considers the totality of what is possible (*the universum*), describing and classifying its objects and reaching to the principles of its construction and principles and organizing ontic objects (particular beings) into the whole of being (J.29.1). The ontological space is a space of all possibilities (J.25.1).

Area	Perzanowski's Postulates
What is ontology? What is meta-physics?	Ontology and metaphysics are related disciplines, because both investigate possibilities. The first deals with the possibility of what is possible, while the second one is concerned with the possibility of what is factual. Ontology deals with the sphere of possibility, while metaphysics deals with the sphere of factuality (J.112.149). Ontology investigates being as is, while metaphysics investigates being in entanglement and fixed in phenomena and concretes/specifics (J.112.152).

Area	Perzanowski's Postulates
Ontological framework situation	This is the configuration or collection of mutually situated objects. The **ontological space** is the entirety of all possibilities, of all admissible configurations. **The world**, meanwhile, is the totality of existing situations, the **factual,** including processes such as changing events and time (including the order and direction of change), space, the order of coexistence, objects, stable events (in essence), and **facts** (J.154.7). An **element** is something simple and non-complex. The **complex** is what can be assembled, considering the given analysis. A **combination or union** is what is considered assembled in a given synthesis. A **configuration** is a set of combinations of objects. A **structure** is a way in which elements are assembled in a configuration, the totality of possible ordering relations. The **net** is a system of binding elements into a union, a structure for binding. **A fact** is an embodied combination, or union, with its secondary layers resulting from binding. **A form** is a possibility of combination that enables the positioning of elements (structure) and their binding (net). The differentiation between the complex and combination results from the separation of analysis and synthesis (R.48.109). **Form** is a cause (formata) of combination, which enables its structure and set (R.46.97). What constitutes a form is within the objects being combined (R.46.98). Every union has its carrier; it is a totality of its constituent elements, its structure, and a way of combining elements, their ordering,

and the net into a system for binding elements into
a whole. The **foundation of ontological space**
is a sum of the carriers of their complexes
(R.46.75). Elements forming unions or
combinations, creating the complex, create not
only a net of mutual bonds and a structure for the
complex but also a series of secondary layers. This
is the way that combinations materialize (R.42.78).

Ontology and   Epistemology must be based on the general theory
epistemology   of the universe, specifically ontology (J.10). The
object of cognition is information (J.21.10). The
basis of cognition is an assumption of fundamental
regularity (J.20.5).

Information   Information is an organized and ordered system of
and ontology   objects, the properties of some object, or a
situation (J.21.10).

Specific   Domain-specific ontologies (D-ontologies) are the
ontologies   ontologies of specific domains. For example, the
physical universe is the domain of what physically
exists (e.g., events, phenomena, objects) (J.31.5;
R.109.5). Physics investigates the world according
to physical possibilities that are consistent with
the laws of physics. Mathematical theories consider
the possibilities according to a given mathematical
apparatus, in terms of that which is consistent
with its basic axioms and rules (J.63.39).

6.9.3 *Ontology and information*

Now, let us try to interpret *information$_O$*, as understood in the
philosophy of information, through the concepts of Perzanowski's

ontology. Whenever the term ontology is used from this point on, it will refer exclusively to Perzanowski's ontological concepts.

6.9.3.1 *Information$_O$ as a constraint*

In the philosophy of information, *information$_O$* is often conceptualized as a constraint on possibilities (i.e., limiting the number of states a given system can be in). Heller (1987, 1963) states, "If information may be conceptualized as constraining options, every law of physics is information, as it constrains nature" (p. XX). In Heller's writing, information as a constraining factor on what can exist is reflected in Perzanowski's concept of being, in which the *universum* of being is the space of all possibilities, where metaphysics or the ontology of reality specifies what exists in the world (J.25.1) and thus limits the possibility of what can exist. What exists is then defined by complexes of elements and relations that are defined by the term *information$_P$* (J.21.10).[64]

6.9.3.2 *Information$_O$ as a structure*

Structural Realism (SR)—as explained in the works of Psillos (2004), Brading and Laundry (2006), Frigg and Votis (2010), Ladyman (2016), and many others—claims that nature is structural, because structure seems to be invariant in scientific models of nature and survives theory shifts.[65] Heller (2009) writes that, "...every (natural) structure has certain information; more constraints (by laws of physics) given structure imposes more information it contains. As the world is a structure, it contains certain information$_O$ or (we may say) the structure of the world encodes certain information" (p. 63). In a different work, however, Heller (1995) observes that "...modern physics suggests that the world does not have a structure but is a structure. This structure contains in itself certain information. Science decodes its fragments by fitting mathematical structures

---

[64]The term information$_P$ is defined by Perzanowski in (J.21.10).

[65]Structure is not very well defined in structural realism writings. Sometimes, its definition is even omitted and accepted as obvious, i.e., not required.

to the structure(s) of the universe" (Heller 1995, p. 170, see also Polak 2017). The structural view of nature in sciences aligns with Perzanowski's ontology in terms of the elements of what is and how they form/constitute complexes or structures of entities and relations (J.154.7; R.48.109; R.46.97; R.46.98; R.46.75; R.42.78). Thus, structures perceived in sciences are reflections of the ontological structure of nature (i.e., information$_O$ would be identified with information$_P$).

6.9.3.3   *The foundational role of information$_O$*

Collier (1989) writes, "Physical things have properties that give them a definite structure and causal capabilities. If information is an intrinsic property of physical objects, then it seems likely that it is contained in their physical structure" (p. 6). Hidalgo (2015), meanwhile, states, "Information... understood broadly as a physical order" and goes on to say, "... information is not restricted to messages. It is inherent in all physical objects" (p. 6). Seife (2006) also claims that "... there is something about information that transcends the medium it is stored in. It is a physical entity, a property of objects akin to energy or work or mass" (p. 57). Stonier (1990) similarly writes that "... information exists ... information has physical reality and constitutes an intrinsic property of the universe" (p. 12). Dodig-Crnkovic (2012) states, "The universe is, from the metaphysical point of view, nothing but processes in structural patterns all the way down ... In understanding patterns as information, one may infer that information is a fundamental ontological category" (p. 228). The claims about the foundational nature of information coming from specific sciences align with the ontological view that as nature is structural (J.154.7; R.48.109; R.46.97; R.46.98; R.46.75; R.42.78) and structure from an ontological perspective is *information$_p$* or *information$_o$*, nature is in essence informational (J.21.10).

6.9.3.4   *Domain-specific information and information$_O$*

Many sciences (e.g., biology, chemistry, and physics) identify information with meaning focused on that specific domain

(D-information). For example, in biology, DNA is seen as biological information (Smith 2000, Godfery-Smith and Sterelny 2016), while in physics (Piccinni 2017), it is physical information. Other similar examples can be found in cognitive sciences and particularly in communication, computing, and other information-based sciences. These domains all claim that they use information, and this D-information creates the impression that we deal with many types of information. The case of D-information closely resembles the ontological view of the world in Perzanowski's ontology. Each domain has its own ontology (called D-ontology) (J.31.5; R.109.5; J.63.39), but all these D-ontologies are reflections of the fundamental ontological structures (J.154.7; R.48.109; R.46.97; R.46.98; R.46.75; R.42.78) that constitute the totality of what is seen through the methodological prisms of particular domains. Thus, they all reflect the framework of being (J.154.7; R.48.109; R.46.97; R.46.98; R.46.75; R.42.78) and *information$_P$* (J.21.10). They are, in essence, partial descriptions of *information$_O$* (and *information$_P$*) (R.19.1; R.19.3; R.19.4). The structures seen in specific sciences are attempts to define them through the lenses of their own frameworks. That is why we have several definitions for what structure is and what information is (because information is "encoded" in structure). In ontological language, we have several D-structures and one O-structure (meaning ontologically basic) (J.31.5; R.109.5; J.63.39). Likewise, we have several cases of D-information and one O-information. It seems that by interpreting specific structures as reflections of the ontological structure, we can provide a clear view of what structures are, because in the ontological view, structures and their elements are information.

6.9.4 *Final observations*

There are many definitions for information, and the different understandings of what information is have proliferated in most modern sciences, but they can be subsumed, explained, and understood using the conceptual schema of Perzanowski's ontology of being. In this schema, the being, or what is, is composed of structures/complexes of elements and relations in embedded layers. At a certain level of complexity, they create the physical world as we know it. The complexes of structures are denoted as *information$_O$* which has both static and causal properties. What exists came from what is possible to exist in the *universum* of being, the entirety of what is possible. Specific scientific (D-) domains give us D-domain-specific views of the fundamental ontology, and as such, they provide us with numerous definitions, because they are all interpretations. In the ontological view, information (seen as *information$_P$*) is a basic property (a forming) of the ontological *universum* and the elements within it. D-information, meanwhile, is the same information seen through the methodological prism of a given domain D. It seems that using the ontological conceptual net, we can subsume all of the concepts for information (or most of them) and explain why there are so many of them and why information is interpreted in a fundamental way.

We could call this ontological reduction, with reduction referring to the use of one conceptual system to explain a multitude of interpretations. It therefore seems that most of the concepts of information used in D-information definitions—such as information as a constraint, information as structure, information as invariants or mathematical models, information as a forming element, information as an order or organization, information as the fabric of the universe, and information as a fundamental element of the universe—can be explained through ontological concepts (as *information$_P$*) and presented in a single, unified view.

Chapter 7

Final Comments—What Next?

7.1 What Is This Work About?

This book presents the properties that can be attributed to the concept of ontological information. Ontological information is a physical phenomenon, and it does not have any inherent meaning or value. In other words, it is information that is meaningless and epistemically neutral, and its existence and properties are not dependent on any communication process or part thereof. Instead, it is perceived through the structure, organization, or form of natural and artificial (artifacts) objects.

In two chapters, we searched for the properties of ontological information by reviewing brief claims about concepts bearing the characteristics of ontological information, as put forward in the works of Edmund Kowalczyk (1970), Keith Devlin (1991), John Polkinghorne (2000), Charles Seife (2006), Frank Wilczek (2015), Sean Carroll (2016), Carlo Rovelli (2016), John Barrow (2017), Paul Davies (2019), and Richard Sole and Santiago Elena (2019). Most of this research had been published in the first two decades of the 21st century, so it is as current as could reasonably be expected. Further, we reviewed the more detailed studies of information that were carried out by Carl von Weizsäcker (1970), Krzysztof Turek (1978), Stefan Mynarski (1981), Michał Heller (1987, 2014), John Collier (1989), Tom Stonier (1990), Jacek Jadacki and Anna Brożek (2005), Gordana Dodig Crnkovic (2012), Thomas Nagel (2012), and

Cesary Hidalgo (2015). These studies provide a vast range of perspectives on the idea of information, with the authors coming from diverse fields like computer science, philosophy, physics, biology, and cosmology. Despite this, they all see information as something of nature with the properties that we would attribute to ontological information. Each author's work is presented through direct quotations that are then thoroughly analyzed. Finally, we have formulated a minimalist list of properties that could be attributed to ontological information. We therefore collected the main observations about information from previous chapters in an effort to reduce the number of properties of ontological information to just the most essential subset. In the last chapter, we discussed how ontological information may change our perception of several concepts related to information. These included, among other discussed issues, the concept of information itself, the concept of epistemic information, the relation between ontological information and data, the problem of the existence of information, the role of the quantified models of information, and the relevance of Popper's three worlds.

7.2 What was This Study Able to Establish?

The concepts of information emerging from the works of Kowalczyk, Devlin, Wilczek, Barrow, Carroll, Sole and Elena, Rovelli, Seife, Polkinghorne, and Davies can be summarized through eight observations: (1) Information is a natural phenomenon, without meaning and related more to the properties of the universe (i.e., nature) than knowledge. (2) In several studies, we see a tension between the abstract (mental) concept of information and information as a concrete, physical thing. (3) In any discussion about information as a natural phenomenon, entropy (thermodynamics) plays a prominent role. (4) The term "information" is usually not clearly defined but rather described through its properties. (5) Despite diverse views, there are several commonalities among the descriptions of information in nature. (6) Information is closely related to the organization of nature or its structure. (7) Information in nature can be quantified.

(8) Information in nature is often conceptualized within a complex of matter, energy, and information.

The concept of information that emerges from the writings of Heller, von Weizsäcker, Turek, Stonier, Collier, Nagel, Mynarski, Jadacki and Brożek, Dodig Crnkovic, and Cesary Hidalgo can be summarized as eleven conjectures: (1) The notion of information associated with knowledge does not exhaust the concept of information. (2) Information is a physical/natural phenomenon. (3) Information as a physical/natural phenomenon has no meaning. (4) The meaning of information is derived by the mind of a cognitive agent, and meaning is not intrinsic to information as a physical/natural phenomenon. (5) The role of information in nature may be conceptualized within the matter–energy–information complex. (6) Information as a physical/natural phenomenon is fundamental to nature, so whatever exists physically contains information. (7) Information as a physical/natural phenomenon is expressed through the structure/form and organization of things. (8) Information as a physical/natural phenomenon cannot be reduced to what we conceptualize as structures. (9) Information as a physical/natural phenomenon is responsible for the internal organization of nature's objects and artifacts. (10) Natural processes are information processes that we may denote as computing. (11) Quantifications of information provide measures of sensible structures that reflect the presence of information, but these quantifications are not information itself.

We therefore concluded the following: Ontological information has no meaning, with this being defined as representing some value for a cognitive agent. In other words, an agent obtains from ontological information something that has some significance for its existence, so this creates or derives meaning. The same ontological information may have a different meaning for a different agent, though, or it may have no meaning at all. Ontological information is not abstract in the way that mathematical objects or thoughts and feelings are abstract. Ontological information exists like other physical phenomena, so it is real, observable, and measurable. Whatever exists contains information, and there are no physical phenomena without information in the same way that there are no physical phenomena without energy.

Ontological Information is an essential constituent of nature, because it is a factor responsible for the organization of the physical world. Organization is a fairly broad concept, but in this study, it is interpreted as the structure, order, form, shape, or (in some sense) rationality when perceived by a cognitive entity.

Finally, we attributed three properties and two corollaries to ontological information:

- (EN) Information has no meaning; meaning is derived from information by a cognitive agent.
- (PE) Information is a physical phenomenon.[1]
- (FN) Information is responsible for the organization of the physical world.

The two corollaries are as follows:

- (C1) Information is quantifiable.
- (C2) Changes in the organization of physical objects can be denoted as computation or information processing.

We also concluded that these three properties and two corollaries represent the most minimalistic description of the properties of ontological information, at least in terms of what we were able to identify across the studies works. We are aware, however, that future research may change how we see and conceptualize ontological information.

We also looked at some of the consequences of recognizing the existence of ontological information. We observed that holding onto a semantics-based concept of information—or as we call it, epistemic information—would ignore information conceived as an element of nature. In other words, this epistemic information would fail to account for a significant aspect of reality, one that is essential to our concept of information. We also observed that the border between epistemic and ontological information is based on whatever definitions are used for cognitive function, meaning, and cognitive agents. With these definitions in flux, a precise boundary between epistemic

---

[1]By being physical, we mean being an integral part of physical objects and being disclosed in physical phenomena.

and ontological information may be hard to establish. We also posited that epistemic information may be conceptualized as being partially derived from, and therefore dependent on, ontological information. We also discussed quantified models of information, pointing out that while these models offer significant operational gains, they do not explain the nature of information. This point is frequently missed by scholars. We also discussed the concept of data, which is usually positioned as some precursor to epistemic information. We pointed out that in reality, a collection of data is already epistemic information or interpreted ontological information, with the division into data and information generally being done for operational reasons rather than any inherent difference between data and epistemic information. We also discussed infons, which have been used in some studies as the ontological basis of information or a primary unit of information. We demonstrate that the concept of the infon is poorly defined and lacks any ontological, metaphysical, or scientific basis. The infon acts as an operational concept standing in for something unknown, and it may play a role in pointing out our ignorance, but it cannot be taken as representing something ontologically fundamental. Next, we discussed the abstract–concrete dichotomy of information. We pointed out how the problem with this apparent dichotomy stems from the misuse of the verb "to exist" and the lack of a sound concept for ontological information. Once we accept that we have two types of information, one abstract and one concrete, and recognize their dependence, we see that these two concepts do not refer to the same idea but rather two complementary ones. Indeed, these concepts refer to how different modes of information can be conceptualized: one that is concrete in space–time and one that is abstract outside space–time. When viewing it from this perspective, we think the conflict resolves itself.

In the final section, we discussed Popper's three worlds. Popper's ideas were pursued somewhat in response to critique that in this study, we deny the existence of the whole realm of culture and human thought. However, we cannot deny that the products of human thought exist, and we call them epistemic information, while for Popper, they comprise his world three. We also do not deny that the products of human thought can be represented or embedded in physical things. Likewise, we cannot deny that the world of concrete things exists, and this is where ontological information persists. We also have to agree that the world of human products needs an agent, because without an agent who "understands" the content of world three, it would be meaningless. Indeed, we humans are defined by our ideas, so we need to recognize the fragility of our world. The objects of the Popperian world three do not exist without a knowledgeable agent, just like a lost scripture is merely a series of meaningless symbols without an agent who knows how to read it. Indeed, the fate of lost civilizations and their cultural heritage sadly confirms the fragility of our world three.

7.3 Selected Criticisms of Ontological Information

Thus far, we have presented research that recognizes the existence of physical or ontological information (some denote also as concrete information or information$_C$), but some authors deny that such information exists. We look at some of these studies and weigh their arguments.[2]

Dinneen and Brauner (2018) talk about "information-as-a-thing", which for them is information as a physical phenomenon, as being unable to account for the "typical views of information". These problems are avoided, they say, if information is seen as an abstract entity. The only example of "information-as-a-thing" (i.e., physical information) they provide in their 2018 study is a book, which is a physical object. We could delve deeper into Dinneen and Brauner's argument, but this is not necessary, because it seems that they set up their definition of physical information to fail. Indeed, according to their own definition, the book cannot be information because anything physical cannot have meaning, so information is not physical. This is rather obvious, though. This book (a physical object) in their example is meaningless by definition. Dinneen and Brauner's claim is somewhat justified, however, because the book is meaningless in itself, just like

---

[2]This section was published in 2020 in a paper by Krzanowski (2020).

all physical objects are. However, their argument against the existence of information as a physical phenomenon, based on the example of the book, is incorrect because they are looking for meaning where there is none to be found. Dinneen and Brauner's attempt was therefore destined to fail because they looked for meaningful physical information rather than just physical information. For Dinneen and Brauner, the "typical views of information" reflect what we refer to in this study as information$_A$, but there is nothing typical about it, even though it may be the most prevalent view of information. In science, though, the truth of a proposition is not determined according to a majority vote, and the minority opinion often turns out to be the correct one. Dinneen and Brauner, it seems, missed the nature of information$_C$, namely, that it is not the physical object itself but rather its organization, at least in the sense discussed in this study.

In their earlier paper, Dinneen and Brauner (2015) formulate three arguments for why a physical thing cannot be information or, more precisely, why what they call "information-as-a-thing" cannot exist. First, "the value of the physical representation is first and foremost its content, and not the physical embodiment of it". Thus, putting forward information-as-a-thing as information clearly ignores the content of a physical thing, but we are concerned with this content. Second, talking about physical objects as information is not accurate, because when talking about physical information, we are less interested in the physical objects (e.g., DVDs, CDs, USB sticks) themselves, and more interested in what they contain. Thus, their definition of information as a physical object is misleading, as is their conclusion for the first argument. Third, the same physical object may contain different information depending on the time and place: For example, a book's content may be interpreted differently. This creates, according to Dinneen and Brauner, a metaphysical problem of identity. If information is a physical thing, it must be the same in all circumstances; otherwise, we would have two or more things being the same physical object. We partially addressed these three arguments in Chapter 5. In the above discussion, Dinneen and Brauner do not distinguish between physical or ontological information (information$_C$) and epistemic information (information$_A$), so when they talk about information, they are actually talking about information$_A$. In a way, they are trying to attribute information$_A$ to a physical presence, but as we have pointed out many times in this study, information$_A$ is not physical, and a physical object is not information$_A$. It may "contain" information$_A$ for one or more agents, at least in the sense of the word "contain" as explained above, but a physical object is never information$_A$. In a rather stretched analogy, we could say that energy is not work, nor does it contain work, but it is certainly related to work. The analogy stops here, however. By defining information (information$_A$) as a physical object or information-as-a-thing, we would be obviously making a mistake by conflating the abstract with the concrete, which will clearly never work. As we said before, physical information is not a physical object in the sense of a specific object—such as a book, a DVD, and so on—but rather the organization of these objects, as explained in the previous sections. What Dinneen and Brauner faced is the concrete–abstract dichotomy indicated by Davies (2019) and Rovelli (2016),[3] but while Rovelli and Davies managed to comprehend and overcome it, Dinneen and Brauner did not.

Bates (2015), following Edwin Parker (quoted by Bates), identifies information in nature as a pattern of, or within, physical things. However, Bates' information is not physical, because this pattern is an abstract concept realized through a physical medium and recognized by a cognitive agent. This interpretation is seen in Bates' claim that while information as a pattern is everywhere in the universe, total entropy is pattern-free,[4] so it has no information. Therefore, according to Bates, total entropy cannot be interpreted as a pattern, so Bates' notion of "information as a pattern of physical

---

[3]The problem is stated as follows: "How can information be physical and abstract at the same time?"

[4]We do not go into detail about what "total entropy" is or whether information as a pattern would appear if entropy was less than total (whatever that means for Bates) (i.e., would information as a pattern disappear at one point, or would it appear or disappear gradually).

things" is added to some physical phenomena but not to others.[5] In short, we may say that, in Bates' view, information is not a physical entity, even when it is associated with physical objects. Instead, it is a perceived pattern of physical objects. In her own example, some physical phenomena are information-free, so it therefore seems that Bates' information has nothing to do with information$_C$, and it is more akin to the concept of natural information in Millikan's work (2017), which is also not information$_C$. To recall the discussion from Millikan's very definition, natural information comprises infosigns carried by natural phenomena that "initiate perception" (*ibid.*, 2017). In this definition, natural information appears to be simply information$_C$ plus some meaning or interpretation for a physical carrier. Recall that information$_C$ does not need to initiate perception to exist. A similar definition for natural information is given by Piccinini and Scarantino (2011).

The conviction that information must have meaning has prevented many researchers from recognizing the existence of physical information. This "epistemic turn"[6] is characteristic of modern philosophy, and it began with Descartes. For example, von Weizsäcker and others later on claimed that information must be also physical in some way, yet he could not recognize information without meaning.

Some of the arguments against the concept of information$_C$ have been generated by identifying information$_C$ with Plato's Forms. One such argument, namely, a modified (for our context) version of the Third Man argument, asks the following: "If information$_C$ is in every physical object, is information$_C$ in information$_C$?" Another argument questions how the same information$_C$ may exist in different physical objects at the same time (i.e., how can one physical thing [information$_C$] exist in many different places at the same time).

---

[5]The claim that "total entropy is pattern-free" is incorrect, because every physical phenomenon has some organization or pattern, although it may be beyond our understanding in some cases. Bates repeats the common misconception of equating entropy (assumedly thermodynamic entropy) with the popular notion of chaos (of sorts).

[6]The "epistemic turn" denotes the reorientation of modern philosophy from ontology to epistemology as the main philosophical perspective on nature.

These problems apply to Plato's Forms in his metaphysical view, but as we said from the start, information$_C$ is not one of Plato's Forms, because such objects exist outside space and time and would, in this sense, be abstract objects. While Plato's Forms are in some way physical (in Plato's view), the nature of their existence outside space and time and their relation to reality are exactly what make them controversial. Information$_C$ as a physical phenomenon does not suffer from these shortcomings, just as physical objects do not suffer from them. For example, we do not question whether energy is within energy or whether matter is within matter, even though these phenomena are everywhere. Information$_C$ is more akin to the Aristotelian concept of *eidos*, but as we pointed out earlier, such analogies with the ancient ideas are very precarious and should be drawn with great restraint. This is why we do not discuss them further in this study, nor do we propose them as renditions of information$_C$.

Looking at the bigger picture, any researcher who claims that the concept of information is inherently and exclusively associated with meaning and knowledge is implicitly denying the existence of information as a physical phenomenon for the obvious reason that information cannot be both abstract and concrete in the same way and at the same time. Surprisingly, such claims are made with full knowledge that human agents are physical information-processing systems (e.g., Maturana 2011, Maturana and Valera 1980, Hintikka 2007, Kaplan 1989, Bajic 2005), and as computers, our main data-processing component is a purely physical, mindless, and meaningless device. We need to take us (or the mind) out of this picture in a kind of Copernican move to see information$_O$.[7]

As a reminder, the existence of information as a physical entity is supported by the studies in which information (the concept of information) has been found to have properties that are attributable to physical objects, the studies that have found information useful for explaining certain physical processes, and the studies that have found information as a unifying factor in explaining a range of natural

---

[7]By "a Copernican move", we refer to taking a position where humanity is no longer the vantage point for looking at nature.

phenomena. (See the authors quoted in the earlier sections of this study.)

7.4 Work to be Done and Future Research

The study leaves several questions open about the nature of onto-logical information. Some of them are listed below. These questions are speculative, but they appear in the research on information$_O$, so they are related to this work. Of course, the true list of unresolved questions about the nature of physical information is likely to be much longer than the one presented below. In the questions below, the term "information" refers to information$_O$.

Question 1: Do laws for the conservation of information exist, and if they do, what do they claim? Is the total amount of information in the universe therefore constant? This question probes the problem of "the conservation of information". If information is fundamental to whatever exists in the physical world, does it follow laws for its preservation, much like energy (suggested by the writings of Carroll, for example)?

Question 2: Can we claim that whatever exists must contain information$_C$? Can we defend the paninformatism claim that infor-mation is everything that exists? What is more, is paninformatism related to panpsychism? This question probes the claim that infor-mation is in everything that exists. Can such a claim be justified? And, does such a claim amount to some kind of paninformatism or panpsychism? If so, what precisely would this entail? Would such a claim trivialize the concept of information (suggested by the writings of Stonier, Turek, and Carroll, for example)?

Question 3: Can we interpret information$_C$ as a causal factor, and how could such a claim be verified? This question probes the alleged causal role of information in the physical world. It amounts to the question of whether information is a passive or active element in nature and what the nature of this activity would be (suggested by the writings of Carroll and von Weizsäcker, for example).

Question 4: Information$_C$ is foundational to the physical universe, but in what sense can this statement be made? This question probes the claim that information is fundamental to nature, but what exactly would this mean? Should such a claim be interpreted along the lines of the proposed information–matter–energy complex? Or, should it be interpreted more metaphysically like the Logos of The Bible or the Tao of Tao-Te-Ching as an all-pervading and primordial element of existence (suggested by the writings of Heller, Dodig Crnkovic, and Stonier, for example)?

Question 5: Can we say that highly complex and chaotic (i.e., nonlinear, dynamic) systems have no information$_C$? This concerns the problems of chaos and nonlinear, dynamic systems. Does information play a role in such systems? Quite often, chaos is associated with a lack of information, which seems to be a questionable interpretation of a physical phenomenon. (This issue was indicated by Bates.)

Question 6: Does information$_C$ imply some form of modern hylemorphism? This question seeks to identify the similarities between information and hylemorphism in its modern interpretations. The problem of the nature of information and matter and energy has resurfaced in the works of many authors (see the references in this paper), and they all seem to echo Aristotelian metaphysics (suggested by the writings of Polkinghorne, Turek, Krzanowski, and Carroll, for example).

Question 7: Does the fact that information is physical change the meaning of computation from one of symbolic processing to processing physical information? We associate computation with symbolic processing, but computation in computers is, in fact, a highly structured, pure physical process (e.g., as Searle said, "computation is in the eye of the beholder"). Could we extend the concept of computation to any physical process involving changes in physical organization without trivializing the concept of computing? Do we even care? (suggested by the writings of Seife, Dodig Crnkovic, and Dodig Crnkovic and Mueller, for example)?

Question 8: Can information be equated to some kind of structure, and what would this mean for the concept of structure? This question proposes explaining the concept of information$_C$ through the concepts of structure and structural realism (suggested by the writings of Heller and Schroeder, for example).

Question 9: Can we propose some kind of definition for ontological information? The truth is that some physical phenomena avoid clear definitions and are characterized by their properties. Energy is one example of this. Energy has many definitions, and some are clearly too simplistic, while some are too narrow. For example, see the works of Richard Feynman (1963, p. 4-2), Mario Iona (1973), Robert Lehrman (1973), Nancy Hicks (1983), Art Hobson (2004), Ricardo Coelho (2009), and Eugene Hecht (2007). One possible definition of energy states that it is a conserved scalar measure of the ability of a system to produce change (Hecht 2007), or in a more watered down version, energy is the ability to produce change. We have different measures for different forms of energy depending on the phenomenon we observe. Information, specifically understood as information$_O$, is related to the organization of a system. Depending on the system and the level of organization, we may therefore have different measures of information$_O$. The fact that information is a scalar measure just means that information$_O$ may be quantified, but it does not determine a unique quantification. Can such conjuncture be justified?

Bibliography

Internet Resources

"A world of fantasy we enter in our dreams", 2019. *The Entry "Never never land" in The Urban Dictionary*. Available at https://www.urbandictionary.com/define.php?term=NeverNever%20Land. [Accessed 1 October 2019].

"Anna Brozek", 2021. Anna Brozek. Biographical entry at Copernicus Center Press Web Site. Available at https://www.ccpress.pl/contributors/97. [Accessed 1 October 2019].

"Arecibo Message", 2019. The entry "Arecibo Message" in the SETI Website. Available at https://www.seti.org/seti-institute/project/details/arecibo-message. [Accessed 2 March 2019].

Barrow, J. D. 2019. Available at https://www.edge.org/memberbio/john_d_barrow. [Accessed 2 August 2019].

"Before it is", 2019. *The Website*. Available at http://beforeitsnews.com/health/2011/03/the-human-hearing-range-464937.html. [Accessed 12 July 2019].

"Bugatti", 2018. *The Website Bugatti*. Available at https://en.wikipedia.org/wiki/Bugatti. [Accessed 29 September 2018].

Candy, R. 2010. The article in Wikipedia by R. Z. Sheppard (1971-04-12), "Rock Candy", *Time Magazine*. Available at https://en.wikipedia.org/wiki/ Infosphere. [Accessed 5 May 2018].

Carroll, S. M. 2019. Sean M. Carroll. Wikipedia. Available at https://en.wikipedia.org/wiki/Sean_M._Carroll. [Accessed 12 December 2019].

Collier, J. 2018. John Collier CV. Available at https://bitrumagora.wordpress.com/about/john-collier/. [Accessed 8 December 2018].

"Cybernetics", 2019. The entry in the online *Encyclopedia Britannica*. Available at https://www.britannica.com/science/control-theory-mathematics/Control-of-large-systems. [Accessed 12 December 2019].

"Data vs. Information", 2019. The Web Site Diffen.com. Available at https://www.diffen.com/difference/Data_vs_Information. [Accessed 10 September 2019].

Davies, P. 2019. Paul Davies CV at Arizona State University Web site. Available at https://physics.asu.edu/content/paul-davies. [Accessed 12 December 2019].

Dodig-Crnkovic, G. 2018. Gordana Dodig-Crnkovic CV at The Chalmers University of Technology. Available at https://www.chalmers.se/en/staff/Pages/gordana-dodig-crnkovic.aspx. [Accessed 20 August 2018].

Elena, S. 2019. An entry in the Sanfa Fe Institute WEB page. Available at https://www.santafe.edu/people/profile/santiago-f-elena. [Accessed 12 December 2019].

"Fisher information", 2018. The Web site Math StockExchange. Available at https://math.stackexchange.com/questions/1314090/intuition-behind-fisher-information-and-expected-value?rq=1. [Accessed 12 August 2018].

Heller, M. 2018. Michał Heller in Wikipedia. Available at https://en.wikipedia.org/wiki/Micha%C5%82_Heller. [Accessed 7 April 2018].

Hidalgo, C. 2015. The bibliographical note on the book cover of *"Why Information Grows. The evolution of order, from Atoms to Economics"*. Cambridge: The MIT Press.

"History of earth in 24 hours", 2019. The Blog. Available at https://flowingdata.com/2012/10/09/history-of-earth-in-24-hour-clock/. [Accessed 12 June 2019].

"Informare", 2019. Informare. The Online Etymology Dictionary. Available at https://www.etymonline.com/word/inform. [Accessed 12 December 2019].

"Information—CED", 2019. The entry in the CED. Available at https://dictionary.cambridge.org/dictionary/english/information. [Accessed 9 September 2019].

"Information—Collins ED", 2019. The entry in the Collins English Dictionary. Available at https://www.collinsdictionary.com/dictionary/english/information. [Accessed 9 September 2019].

"Information—Macmillan", 2019. The entry in the Macmillan Dictionary. Available at https://www.macmillandictionary.com/dictionary/british/information. [Accessed 9 September 2019].

"Information—Merriam-Webster", 2019. The entry in the Merriam-Bester Dictionary. Available at https://www.merriam-webster.com/dictionary/information. [Accessed 9 September 2019].

"Information—OED", 2019. The entry in the OED. Available at https://en.oxforddictionaries.com/definition/information. [Accessed 9 September 2019].

"Information", 2018. The entry in Wikipedia. Available at https://en. wikipedia.org/wiki/Information. [Accessed 1 December 2018].

"Intuitive explanation...", 2004. *Intuitive Explanation of a Definition of Fisher Information.* Available at https://math.stackexchange.com/ questions/265917/intuitive-explanation-of-a-definition-of-the-fisher-in formation. [Accessed 12 August 2018].

"Jadacki". 2021. Jacek Juliusz Jadacki. Biographical WEB Page. Available at http://www.jadacki.eu/biogram/. [Accessed 8 December 2020].

"Junkyard Argument", 2019. The Wikipedia entry at Religious Wiki. Available at https://religions.wiki/index.php/747_Junkyard_ argument. [Accessed 10 September 2019].

"Keith Devlin at Stanford University", 2019. Available at https://web. stanford.edu/~kdevlin/. [Accessed 10 December 2019].

"Kilogram", 2021. Kilogram. Unit of Measurement. *Encyclopedia Britannica* Online. Available at https://www.britannica.com/science/ kilogram. [Accessed 3 April 2021].

"List of Natural Phenomena", 2018. The Wikipedia online. Available at https://en.wikipedia.org/wiki/List_of_natural_phenomena. [Accessed 2 September 2018].

"Mass", 2019. The entry in Wikipedia. Available at https://en.wikipedia. org/wiki/Mass. [Accessed 5 April 2019].

"Mathematisation", 2020. The entry in Collins Dictionary on line. Available at https://www.collinsdictionary.com/dictionary/english/ mathematisation. [Accessed 12 April 2019].

"Musica_universalis", 2019. *Musica_Universalis'.* The entry in the Wikipedia. Available at https://en.wikipedia.org/wiki/Musica_ universalis. [Accessed 12 August 2019].

Mynarski, S. 2013. Prof. Stefan Mynarski, C. V. Available at http://pntm. pl/biogramy/. [Accessed 12 December 2019].

Nagel, T. 2018. Wikipedia. Available at https://en.wikipedia.org/wiki/ Thomas_Nagel. [Accessed 10 November 2018].

"Phenomenon", 2018. Phenomenon. The online Encyclopedia Britannica. Phenomenon. Available at https://www.britannica.com/topic/ phenomenon-philosophy. [Accessed 2 August 2018].

"Physical", 2018a. Cambridge English Dictionary online. Available at https://dictionary.cambridge.org/dictionary/english/physical. [Accessed 12 September 2018].

"Physical", 2018b. Merriam-Webster English Dictionary online. Available at https://www.merriam-webster.com/dictionary/physical. [Accessed 12 September 2018].

Polkinghorne, J. 2019. John Polkinghorne CV at Socrates in the city WEB site. Available at https://socratesinthecity.com/guests/ sir-john-polkinghorne/. [Accessed 12 December 2019].

Rovelli, C. 2019. Carlo Rovelli's personal Web page. Available at http://www.cpt.univ-mrs.fr/~rovelli/. [Accessed 12 December 2019].

Seife, C. 2019. About the author. The WEB page on Penguin Random House Publishers. Available at https://www.penguinrandomhouse.com/authors/230132/charles-seife. [Accessed 12 December 2019].

Sole, R. 2019. Ricard Sole"s Web page. Available at http://complex.upf.es/~ricard/Main/RicardSole.html. [Accessed 12 December 2019].

Stonier, T. 2019. Tom Stonier entry in Wikipedia. Available at https://en.wikipedia.org/wiki/Tom_Stonier. [Accessed 12 December 2018].

"System", 2019. *System*. The entry in Cambridge Dictionary of English Language. Available at https://dictionary.cambridge.org/dictionary/english/system. [Accessed 10 December 2019].

Turek, K. 2019. WWW.ReserachGate.com, Biographical entry. Available at https://www.researchgate.net/profile/Krzysztof-Turek. [Accessed 3 April 2019].

von Weizsäcker, C. F. 2019. Wikipedia Entry. Available at https://en.wikipedia.org/wiki/Carl_Friedrich_von_Weizs%C3%A4cker. [Accessed 12 December 2018].

"What is inforg?", 2019. The entry in Internet WEB site, Findwords. Available at https://findwords.info/term/inforg. [Accessed 12 September 2019].

"White paper on M2M communication", 2019. Telecommunication Engineering Center, Ministry of Communications, Department of Telecommunications, Government of India. Available at http://tec.gov.in/pdf/Studypaper/White%20Paper%20on%20Machine-to-Machine%20(M2M)Communication.pdf. [Accessed 1 December 2019].

Wiener, P. P. (ed.) 1968. "Anthropomorphism in science". *Dictionary of the History of Ideas: Studies of Selected Pivotal Ideas*, pp. 87–91. NY: Scribner. Available at https://m.tau.ac.il/~agass/joseph-papers/anthro.pdf. [Accessed 1 August 2020].

Wilczek, F. 2018. The MIT Department of Physics. Available at https://web.mit.edu/physics/people/faculty/wilczek_frank.html. [Accessed 1 December 2019].

Published Sources

Acin, A., and Masanes, L. 2016. Certified randomness in quantum physics. *Nature*, 540, pp. 213–219.

Ackoff, R. L. 1989. From data to wisdom. *Journal of Applied System Analysis*, 16, pp. 3–9.

Adleman, L. A. 1998. Computing with DNA. *Scientific American*, pp. 34–41.

Adriaans, P., and van Benthem, J. 2008. *Information: Information is what Information does*. Available at https://eprints.illc.uva.nl/674/1/X-2008-10.text.pdf. [Accessed 8 September 2018]. Also in Adriaans, P., and van Benthan, J. (eds.) 2008. *Handbook of Philosophy of Information*. Amsterdam: Elsevier.

Adriaans, P. 2019. Information. In Zalta, E. N. (ed.), *The Stanford Encyclopedia of Philosophy* (Spring 2019 Edition). Metaphysics Research Lab, Stanford University. Available at https://plato.stanford.edu/archives/spr2019/entries/information/. [Accessed 31 March 2020].

Akerkar, R. A., and Sajjaa, P. S. 2010. *Knowledge-Based Systems*. Sudbury: Jones and Bartlett Publishers.

Albinus, L. 2013. Can science cope with more than one world? A Crossreading of Habermas, Popper, and Searle. *Journal of General Philosophy of Science*. Doi: 10.1007/s10838-013-9221-9.

Allo, P. 2016. The Logic of Information. In Floridi, L. (ed.), *The Routledge Handbook of Philosophy of Information*. Oxon: Routledge.

Alzohairy, A. 2009. Darwin's theory of evolution, April 2009. *Conference: Darwin's Anniversary, at Faculty of Agriculture* (Vol 1). Zagazig University, Egypt.

Aristotle, 2001. *The Basic Works of Aristotle*, McKeon, R. (ed.). Chapel Hill: University of North Carolina Press.

Armstrong, K. 2006. *A Short History of Myth*. Canongate: First Trade Paper.

Atkins, P. 2010. *The Laws of Thermodynamics*. Oxford: Oxford University Press.

Audi, R. 1999. *The Cambridge Dictionary of Philosophy*. Cambridge: Cambridge University Press.

Augusto, L. M. 1984. Unconscious knowledge: A survey. *Advances in Cognitive Psychology*, 6, pp. 116–141. Doi: 10.2478/v10053-008-0081-5.

Austin, C. J. 2017. *A Biologically Informed Hylomorphism*, William, M. R. Simpson, Koons, R. C., and Nicholas J. (eds.), *Neo-Aristotelian Perspectives on Contemporary Science*. Routledge, pp. 185–210, Chapter 8. Doi: 10.4324/9781315211626-9. Available at https://www.researchgate.net/publication/320840268_A_Biologically_Informed_Hylomorphism. [Accessed 2 November 2019].

Avery, J. 1993. *Information Theory and Evolution*. London: World Scientific.

Baeyer von, H. C. 2005. *Information. The New Language of science*. Cambridge: Harvard University Press.

Bailey, A. and Wilkins, S. M. 2018. *Contemporary Hylomorphism.* Doi: 10.1093/OBO/9780195396577-036. Available at http://www. andrewmbailey.com/ContemporaryHylomorphism.pdf. [Accessed 18 October 2018].

Bajić, V. B. and Wee, T. T. 2005. *Information Processing in Living Systems.* London: Imperial College Press.

Baker, B. 2021. Natural information, factivity and nomicity. *Biology & Philosophy*, 36(26). Available at https://doi.org/10.1007/s10539-021-09784-4. [Accessed 2 November 2021].

Balaguer, M. 2016. Platonism in Metaphysics. In Zalta, E. N. (ed.), *The Stanford Encyclopedia of Philosophy* (Spring 2016 Edition). Metaphysics Research Lab, Stanford University. Available at https://plato.stanford.edu/archives/spr2016/entries/platonism/. [Accessed 31 March 2020].

Baldwin, R. 2005. *Algorithmic Information Theory* (Chaitin, Solomonoff & Kolmogorov). Available at http://www.talkorigins.org/faqs/information/infotheory.html. [Accessed 12 August 2018].

Ball, P. 2016. The problems of biological information. *Philosophical Transactions of the Royal Society A*, 374(2063), pp. 2–9.

Barbieri, M. 2016. What is information? *Philosophical Transactions of the Royal Society A*, 374(2063), pp. 2–9.

Bar-Hillel, Y., and Carnap, R. 1953. Semantic information. *The British Journal of Philosophy of Science*, 4(14), pp. 147–157.

Barker, S., and Jago, M. 2011. Being positive about negative facts. *Philosophy and Phenomenological Research*, 85(1). Doi: 10.1111/j.1933-1592.2010.00479.x.

Barwise, J., and Etchemendy, J. 2000. *Computers, Visualization, and the Nature of reasoning*, Bynum, T., and Moor, J. (eds). Oxford: The Digital Phoenix. Blackwell Publishing Inc.,

Barrow, J. D. *The Artful Universe.* Boston: Back Bay Books, Little, Brown, and Company.

Barrow, J. D. 2007. *New Theories of Everything.* Oxford: Oxford University Press.

Batenson, G. 1979. *Mind and Nature.* New York: E. P. Dutton.

Bates, M. J. 2015. Information, and knowledge: An evolutionary framework for information science. *Information and Research*, 10.

Bennett, C. H. 2003. Notes on Landauer's principle, reversible computation and Maxwell's demon. *Studies in History and Philosophy of Modern Physics*, 34(3), pp. 501–510.

Benson, T. 2015. *Second Law of Thermodynamics.* The blog at Glenn Research Center, NASA. Available at https://www.grc.nasa.gov/www/k-12/VirtualAero/BottleRocket/airplane/thermo2.html. [Accessed 2 August 2019].

Beynon-Davies, P. 2009. *Business Information Systems*. London: Palgrave Macmillan.

Bharadwaj, S. Y. V. and Sastry, V. N. 2014. Analysis on sensors in a smart phone-survey. *International Journal of Innovative Research in Advanced Engineering* (IJIRAE), 1(9), pp. 2349–2163. Available at http://www.ijirae.com/volumes/vol1/issue9/OCCS10086.13. pdf. [Accessed 2 April 2018].

Bilat, A. 2018. *Metaontologia. O nature pojec i teorii ontologicznych*. Krakow: Copernicus Center Press.

Bird, A. 2002. *Philosophy of Science*. London: Routledge.

Bishop, R. 2017. Chaos. In Zalta, E. N. (ed.), *The Stanford Encyclopedia of Philosophy* (Spring 2017 Edition). Metaphysics Research Lab, Stanford University. Available at https://plato.stanford.edu/ archives/spr2017/entries/chaos/. [Accessed 12 September 2019].

Boehm, D. 1980. *Wholeness and the Implicate Order*. London: Routledge.

Bollack, J. 2016. *The Art of Reading: From Homer to Paul Celan*. Trans. C. Porter and Tarrow S., and King, B. In Koenig, C., Muellner, L., Nagy, G., and Pollock, S. (eds.), *Hellenic Studies Series 73*. Washington, DC: Center for Hellenic Studies. Available at http://nrs.harvard.edu/urn-3:hul.ebook:CHS_BollackJ.The_ Art_of_Reading.2016. [Accessed 12 December 2019].

Brading, K., and Landry, E. 2006. Scientific structuralism: Presentation and representation. *Philosophy of Science*, 73, pp. 571–581.

Brillouin, L. 2013. *Science and Information Theory* (2nd edn.). New York: Dover.

Brockman, J. 2019. *Possible Minds. 25 Ways of Looking at AI*. New York: Penguin Books.

Brooks, B. 1980. The foundations of information science. Part I. Philosophical Aspects. *Journal of Information Science*, 2, pp. 125–133.

Brock, S., and Mares, E. 2010. *Realism and Anti-realism*. Durham: Acument Publishing Limited.

Buckland, M. K. 1991. Information as thing. *Journal of the American Society for Information Science*, 42(5).

Burgin, M. 2003. Information: Problems, paradoxes, solutions. *TripleC*, 1(1), pp. 53–70. Available at http://tripleC.uti.at/. [Accessed 2 November 2017].

Burgin, M. 2004. Data, information, and knowledge. *Information*, 7(1), pp. 47–57.

Burgin, M. 2005. *Is Information Some Kind of Data?* Available at http:// www.mdpi.org/fis2005. [Accessed 2 November 2017].

Burgin, M. 2010. *Theory of Information*. San Francisco: World Scientific Publishing.

Burgin, M. 2011. Information in the structure of the world. *Information: Theories & Applications*, 18(1), pp. 16–32.

Burgin, M. 2011a. Information: Concept clarification and theoretical representation. *TripleC*, 9(2), pp. 347–357. Available at http://triplec. uti.at. [Accessed 2 November 2019].

Burgin, M. 2011b. Epistemic information in stratified M-Spaces. *Information*, 2(2), pp. 697–726.

Burgin, M. 2012. *Structural Reality*. New York: Nova Science Publishers.

Burgin, M. 2014. Weighted E-Spaces and epistemic information operators. *Information*, 5(3), pp. 357–388.

Burgin, M. 2017. Ideas of Plato in the context of contemporary science and mathematics. *Athens Journal of Humanities and Arts*, 4(3), pp. 161–182.

Burgin, M. 2017a. The General Theory of Information as a Unifying Factor for Information Studies: The Noble Eight-Fold Path. *Proceedings*, 1(3), 164, 6. Doi: 10.3390/IS4SI-2017-04044.

Capurro, R. 2009. Past, Present, and Future of the concept of information. *TripleC*, 7(2), pp. 125–141.

Capurro, R., Fleissner, P., and Hofkirchner, W. 1999. Is a unified theory of information feasible? In *The Quest for a Unified Theory of Information. Proceedings of the 2nd International Conference on the Foundations of Information Science*, pp. 9–30.

Carr, B. 1977. Popper's third world. *The Philosophical Quarterly*, 27(108), pp. 214–226.

Carroll, S. 2017. *The Big Picture on the Origins or Life, Meaning and the Universe Itself*. London: OneWord.

Cartwright, J. H. S., Giannerini, S., and González, D. L. 2016. DNA as information: At the crossroads between biology, mathematics, physics and chemistry. *Philosophical Transactions of the Royal Society A*, 374(2063), pp. 2–9.

Casagrande, D. 1999. Information as verb: Re conceptualizing information for cognitive and ecological models. *Georgia Journal of Ecological Anthropology*, 3, pp. 4–13.

Casti, J. L. 1990. *Paradigms Lost*. New York: Avon Books.

Chaitin, G. 2004. *Algorithmic Information Theory*. Cambridge: Cambridge University Press (1987 edition).

Chaitin. G. 1997. *Information, Randomness and Incompleteness*. Papers on Algorithmic information theory. IBM Research, Yorktown Heights.

Chakravartty, A. 2007. *A Metaphysics for Scientific Realism* (p. 233). Cambridge: Cambridge University Press.

Chakravartty, A. 2017. Scientific Realism. In Zalta, E. N. (ed.), *The Stanford Encyclopedia of Philosophy* (Summer 2017 Edition). Metaphysics

Research Lab, Stanford University. Available at https://plato.stanford.edu/archives/sum2017/entries/scientific-realism/. [Accessed 31 March 2020].

Chalmers, A. F. 1994. *What is this Thing Called Science?* Cambridge: Hackett Publishing Company.

Chan, A. 2018. Laozi. In Zalta, E. N. (ed.), *The Stanford Encyclopedia of Philosophy* (Winter 2018 Edition). Metaphysics Research Lab, Stanford University. Available at https://plato.stanford.edu/archives/win2018/entries/laozi/. [Accessed 31 March 2020].

Chater, N. 2019. *The Mind is Flat.* London: Penguin Books.

Cherry, C. 1978. *On Human Communication.* Cambridge: The MIT Press.

Chischolm, M. 2011. Blog. *What is an Empty Concept?* Available at http://definitionsinsemantics.blogspot.com/2012/03/what-is-empty-concept.html. [Accessed 12 December 2019].

Cho, A. 2002. A fresh take on disorder, or disorderly science? *Science*, 297(5585), pp. 1268–1269.

Chomsky, N. 2012. Interpretation and Understanding: Language and Beyond. Chomsky lecture to Le College de France. Lecture on line. Available at https://www.youtube.com/watch?v=86RY40TvRgE. [Accesses 12 December 2020].

Chomsky, N. 2013. *On Mind and Language.* Lecture on line. Available at https://www.youtube.com/watch?v=3DBDUlDA3t0. [Accessed 12 December 2019].

Chomsky, N. 2014. *The Concept of Language.* Lecture on line. Available at https://www.youtube.com/watch?v=hdUbIlwHRkY. [Accessed 12 December 2020].

Chomsky, N. 2016. *Language, Creativity, and the Limits of Understanding.* Lecture on line. Available at https://www.youtube.com/watch?v=XNSxj0TVeJs. [Accessed 12 December 2019].

Clarke, D. S. 2017. *Panpsychism.* New York: State University of New York.

Coelho, R. L. 2009. On the concept of energy: History and philosophy for science teaching. *Procedia Social and Behavioral Sciences*, 1, pp. 2648–2652.

Cole, D. 2015. The Chinese room argument. In Zalta, E. N. (ed.), *The Stanford Encyclopedia of Philosophy* (Winter 2015 Edition). Metaphysics Research Lab, Stanford University. Available at https://plato.stanford.edu/archives/win2015/entries/chinese-room/. [Accessed 31 March 2020].

Collier, J. 1989. Intrinsic Information. In Hanson, P. P. (ed.), *Information, Language and Cognition: Vancouver Studies in Cognitive Science* (Vol. 1) originally University of British Columbia Press, now Oxford University Press, 1990, pp. 390–409.

Coon, D., and Mitterer, J. O. 2015. *Introduction to Psychology: Gateways to Mind and Behavior* (14th edn.). Cengage Learning.

Copeland, B. J. 2017. The Church-Turing Thesis. In Zalta, E. N. (ed.), *The Stanford Encyclopedia of Philosophy* (Winter 2017 Edition). Metaphysics Research Lab, Stanford University. Available at https://plato.stanford.edu/archives/win2017/entries/church-turing/. [Accessed 31 March 2020].

Cover, T., and Joy, A. T. 2006. *Elements of Information Theory.* New York: John Wiley & Sons.

Da Silva, S., and Rathie, P. 2008. Shannon, Lévy, and Tsallis: A note. *Applied Mathematical Sciences,* 2(8), pp. 1359–1363.

Damasio, A. 2003. *Descartes' Error. Emotion, Reason, and the Human Brain.* London: Penguin Books.

Damasio, A. 2018. *Strange Order of Things. Life, Feelings and the Making of Culture.* The page numbers refer to the Polish edition of the book published the same year by REBIS Publishing House Ltd, Poznan.

Danila, E., Dumitru, D., and Dumitru, L. D. 2016. *Efficient Lighting System for Greenhouses.* Doi: 10.1109/ICEPE.2016.7781379.

Dasgupta, S. 2016. *Computer Science. A very short introduction.* Oxford: Oxford University Press.

Davenport, T. H. 1997. *Information Ecology.* Oxford: Oxford University Press.

Davies, P. 2019. *The Demon in the Machine.* New York: Allen Lane.

De Castro, L. 2007. Fundamentals of natural computing: An overview. *Physics of Life Review,* 4, pp. 1–36.

Dennett, D. 2017. *From Bacteria to Bach and Back: The Evolution of Minds.* New York: W. W. Norton & Company.

Deutsch, D. 1998. *Fabric of Reality: The Science of Parallel Universes—and Its Implications.* London: Penguin Books.

Devlin, K. 1991. *Logic and Information.* Cambridge: Cambridge University Press.

Dinneen, J. D., and Brauner, C. 2018. Information-not-thing: Further problems with and alternatives to the belief that information is physical. In *Proceedings of the Proceedings of the Annual Conference of CAIS/Actes du Congrès Annuel de l'ACSI.* University of Alberta Libraries, Edmonton, Canada.

Dinneen, J. D., and Brauner, C. 2015. Practical and philosophical considerations for defining information as well-formed, meaningful data in the information sciences. *Library Trends,* 63, pp. 378–400. Doi: 10.1353/lib.2015.0012.

Dodig Crnkovic, G., and Mueller, V. 2009. A Dialogue Concerning Two World Systems: Info-Computational vs. Mechanistic. In Dodig-Crnkovic, G., and Burgin, M. (eds.), *Information and Computation.*

Singapore: World Scientific Pub Co Inc. Available at http://arxiv.org/abs/0910.5001.

Dodig Crnkovic, G. 2006. *Investigations into Information Semantics and Ethics of Computing.* Mälardalen University, Department of Computer Science and Electronics. Available at https://pdfs.semanticscholar.org/b6bb/f280d9daacb78b692254c30e577b00764fbd.pdf. [Accessed 20 December 2019].

Dodig Crnkovic, G. 2008. Semantics of Information as Interactive Computation. In Moeller, M., Neuser, W., and Roth-Berghofer, T. (eds.), *Fifth International Workshop on Philosophy and Informatics.* Kaiserslautern 2008. Available at http://ceur-ws.org/Vol-332/paper4.pdf. [Accessed 12 August 2018].

Dodig Crnkovic, G. 2011. Significance of models of computation from turing model to natural computation. *Minds and Machines,* 21(2), pp. 301–322.

Dodig Crnkovic, G. 2012. *Alan Turing's Legacy: Info-computational Philosophy of Nature.* Available at http://arxiv.org/ftp/arxiv/papers/1207/1207.1033.pdf. [Accessed 7 October 2015].

Dodig Crnkovic, G. 2013a. The info-computational nature of morphological computing. In Müller, V. (ed.), *Philosophy and Theory of Artificial Intelligence. Studies in Applied Philosophy, Epistemology and Rational Ethics* (Vol. 5). Berlin, Heidelberg: Springer.

Dodig Crnkovic, G. 2013b. Information, computation, cognition. Agency-based hierarchies of levels presented at PT-AI 2013. *Philosophy and Theory of Artificial Intelligence St Antony's College,* Oxford, UK. Available at http://www.pt-ai.org/2013/programme.

Dretske, F. 1999. *Knowledge and the Flow of Information.* Cambridge: CSLI Publications.

Drogan, J. 2009. *Data, Information, and Knowledge—Relevance And Understanding.* Available on line at http://static1.1.sqspcdn.com/static/f/23196/12369003/1306255277903/Data+Information+and+Knowledge+-+Relevance+and+Understanding.pdf?token=qXSZz6nhIKiwutGvrXNIeIQjm6M%3D. [Accessed 2 April 2019].

Drucker, P. 2001. *Management Challenges for the 21st Century.* New York: Harper Business Press.

Edwards, L. E. 2015. What is the anthropocene? *Eos.,* 96.

Effingham, N. 2003. *An Introduction to Ontology.* London: Polity.

Feldman, R. 1998. Charity, Principle of. In *The Routledge Encyclopedia of Philosophy.* Taylor and Francis. Retrieved 16 May 2019, from https://www.rep.routledge.com/articles/thematic/charity-principle-of/v-1. Doi:10.4324/9780415249126-P006-1.

Ferreira, A., Isabel, M., and Miguel, G. C. 2013. Modelling artificial cognition in biosemiotic terms. *Biosemiotics*, 6(245). Doi: 10.1007/s12304-012-9159-z.

Feynman, R. 1988. *QED*. Princeton: Princeton University Press.

Feynman, R. 1963. *The Feynman Lectures on Physics* (Vol. I). Chapter 4. Conservation of Energy. Cambridge: Addison-Wesley.

Feynman, R. 1995. *The Character of Physical Law*. Cambridge: The MIT Press.

Finkelstein, L. 2005. *Introduction to Measurement Theory and Philosophy. Handbook of Measuring System Design*. Oxford: Oxford University Press.

Firn, R. 2004. Plant intelligence: an alternative point of view. *Annals of Botany*, 93, pp. 345–351. Available online at www.aob.oupjournals. org. [Accessed 2 May 2018]. doi: 10.1093/aob/mch058.

Fiske, J. 1990. *Introduction to Communication Studies* (2nd edn.). London: Rutledge.

Floridi, L. 2004. Open problems in the philosophy of information. *Metaphilosophy*, 35, pp. 554–582.

Floridi, L. 1999. *Philosophy and Computing. An Introduction*. London: Routledge.

Floridi, L. 2010. *Information: A Very Short Introduction*. Oxford: Oxford University Press.

Floridi, L. 2013. *The Philosophy of Information*. Oxford: Oxford University Press.

Floridi, L. (ed.) 2016. *The Routledge Handbook of Philosophy of Information*. Oxon: Routledge.

Fong, M. 2019. *The Surveillance Economy has set its Sights on Smartphone Sensors*. Available at https://www.helpnetsecurity.com/2019/04/12/smartphone-sensors-surveillance/. [Accessed 12 July 2019].

Forrest, P. 2016. The identity of indiscernibles. In Zalta, E. N. (ed.), *The Stanford Encyclopedia of Philosophy* (Winter 2016 Edition). Metaphysics Research Lab, Stanford University. Available at https://plato. stanford.edu/archives/win2016/entries/identity-indiscernible/. [Accessed 31 March 2020].

Frantzen, S. 2007. *Anyone Who Considers Arithmetical Methods of Producing Random Digits is, of course, in a State of Sin*. The Blog SANS ISC InfoSec Forums. Available at https://isc.sans.edu/forums/diary/ Anyone+who+considers+arithmetical+methods+of+producing+random+digits+is+of+course+in+a+state+of+sin/3657/. [Accessed 10 May 2017].

Fredkin, E. 1991. Digital mechanics: An informational process based on reversible universal automata. In Gutowitz, H. (ed.), *Cellular*

Automata; Theory and Experiment. Cambridge: Mass., The MIT Press.

French, S. 1998. On the withering away of physical objects. In Castellani, E. (ed.), *Interpreting Bodies: Classical and Quantum Objects in Modern Physics.* Princeton: Princeton University Press, pp. 93–113.

Friden, R. 1998. *Physics from Fisher Information.* Cambridge: Cambridge University Press.

Frigg, R., and Votsis, I. 2011. Everything you always wanted to know about structural realism but were afraid to ask. *European Journal for Philosophy of Science,* 1(2), pp. 227–276.

Furber, S. 2016. Large-scale neuromorphic computing systems. *Journal of Neural Engineering,* 13. Doi: 10.1088/1741-2560/13/5/051001.

Galetić, V., Bojić, I., Kušek, M., Zežić, G., Dešić, S., and Huljen, D. 2019. Basic principles of machine-to-machine communication and its impact on telecommunications industry. Available at http://citeseerx.ist.psu.edu/viewdoc/download?doi=10.1.1.454.2596&rep=rep1&type=pdf. [Accessed 10 January 2019].

Geller, U., and Jablonka, E. (eds.) 2008. *Mathematisation and Demathematisation.* Sense Publishers.

Gillies, D. 2000. *Philosophical Theories of Probability.* New York: Rutledge.

Gillet, C., and Loewer, B. (eds.) 2001. *Physicalism and its Discontent.* Cambridge: Cambridge University Press.

Gilroy, J. D. 1985. A critique of Carl Popper's Word 3 Theory. *The Modern Schoolman,* XLII, pp. 185–200.

Gonzalez, D. L., Giannerini, S., and Rosa, R. 2016. The non-power model of the genetic code: A paradigm for interpreting genomic information. *Philosophical Transactions of the Royal Society A,* 374(2063), pp. 2–9.

Goodfrey-Smith, P., and Sterelny, K. 2016. Biological Information. In Zalta, E. N. (ed.), *The Stanford Encyclopedia of Philosophy* (Summer 2016 Edition). Metaphysics Research Lab, Stanford University. Available at https://plato.stanford.edu/archives/sum2016/entries/information-biological/. [Accessed 31 March 2020].

Green, B. 2004. *The Fabric of the Cosmos: Space, Time, and the Texture of Reality.* New York: Random House.

Guarino, N. 1998. Formal Ontology in Information Systems. *Proceedings of FOIS'98, Trento, Italy, 6–8 June 1998.* Amsterdam: IOS Press, pp. 3–15.

Guggenheim, E. A. 1985. *Thermodynamics. An Advanced Treatment for Chemists and Physicists* (7th edn.). Amsterdam: North Holland.

Guicciardini, N. 2018. *Isaac Newton and Natural Philosophy.* London: Reaction Books.

Hacking, I. 1982. Experimentation and scientific realism. *Philosophical Topics. Realism* (Spring 1982), 13(1), pp. 71–87.

Hájek, A. 2010. Interpretations of probability. In Zalta, E. N. (ed.), *The Stanford Encyclopedia of Philosophy* (Winter 2012 Edition). Metaphysics Research Lab, Stanford University. Available at https://plato. stanford.edu/archives/win2012/entries/probability-interpret/. [Accessed 31 March 2020].

Hartley, R. V. L. 1928. Transmission of information. *Bell System Technical Journal*, 7(3), pp. 535–563.

Hasher, L., and Zacks, R. T. 1984. Automatic processing of fundamental information: The case of frequency of occurrence. *American Psychologist*, 39(12), pp. 1372–1388. Doi: 10.1037/0003-066X.39.12.1372.

Hauser, L. 2018. *Chinese Room Argument*. The Internet Encyclopedia of Philosophy. Available at https://www.iep.utm.edu/chineser/#H7 [Accessed 12 September 2018].

Hayot, E., and Pao, L. 2018. Introduction. In Janich, P. (ed.), *What is information?* Minneapolis: University of Minnesota Press.

Hecht, E. 2006. There is no really good definition of mass. *The Physics Teacher*, 44.

Hecht, E. 2007. Energy and change. *The Physics Teacher*, 45, 88.

Heller, M. 1995. *Nauka i wyobraźnia*. Kraków: Znak.

Heller, M. 1987. Ewolucja Pojęcia Masy. In Heller, M., Michalik, A., and Mączka, J. (eds.), *Filozofować w kontekście nauki*. Krakow: PTT, pp. 152–169.

Heller, M. 2009. *Filozofia Nauki. Wprowadzenie*. Kraków: Petrus.

Heller, M. 2014. *Elementy Mechaniki kwantowej dla filozofow*. Krakow: Copernicus Center Press.

Hicks, N. 1983. Energy is the capacity to do work or is it? *The Physics Teacher*, 21.

Hidalgo, C. 2015. *Why Information Grows?* London: Penguin Books.

Hintikka, J. 1984. Some varieties of information, *Inf. Process. Management*, 20(1–2), pp. 175–181.

Hintikka, J. 2007. *Socratic Epistemology. Explorations of Knowledge— Seeking by Questioning*. Cambridge: Cambridge University Press.

Hobson, A. 2004. Energy and work. *Phys. Teach.* 42, 260.

Holmes, D. 2005. *Communication Theory*. London: Sage Publications.

Honderich, T. 1995. *The Oxford Companion to Philosophy*. Oxford: Oxford University Press.

Hong, J., Lambson, B., Dhuey, S., and Bokor, J. 2016. Experimental test of Landauer's principle in single-bit operations on nanomagnetic memory bits. *Science Advances*, 2(3).

Hylton, T. 2018. *Introduction to Neuromorphic Computing.* Available at https://rebootingcomputing.ieee.org/images/files/pdf/4-rcs2-hylton_ -_intro_to_neuromorphic_computing.pdf. [Accessed 2 April 2019].

Ichikawa, J., Jenkins, J., and Steup, M. 2018. The analysis of knowledge. In Zalta, E. N. (ed.), *The Stanford Encyclopedia of Philosophy* (Summer 2018 Edition). Metaphysics Research Lab, Stanford University. Available at https://plato.stanford.edu/archives/sum2018/ entries/knowledge-analysis/ [Accessed 2 December 2019].

Ingarden, R. 1964. *Controversy over the Existence of the World* (Vols. I and II), translated by Arthur Szylewicz, Bern: Peter Lang, 2013/2016. Translation of *Der Streit um die Existenz der Welt*, Bd. I, II/I, II/2. Tübingen: Max Niemeyer.

Jacquette, D. 2002. *Ontology.* Chesham: Acument Publishing Limited.

Jadacki, J., and Brozek, A. 2005. Na czym polega rozumienie w ogóle- a rozumienie informacji w szczególności. In Heller, M., and Mączka, J. (eds.), *Informacja a rozumienie.* Tarnow: Biblos, pp. 141–155.

Jammer M. 2000. *Concept of Mass.* Princeton: Princeton University Press.

Janich, P. 2006. *What is Information?* London: University of Minnesota Press.

Jaworski, W. 2018. *Hylemorphic Structure, Emergence and Supervenience.* University of Oxford Podcasts—Audio and Video Lectures. Available at https://podcasts.ox.ac.uk/hylomorphic-structure-emergence-and-supervenience. [Accessed 1 August 2019].

Johnson, G. 1999. How is the universe build? *New York Times.* The Web Page The Washington State University. Available at https://faculty.washington.edu/smcohen/320/GrainySpace.html. [Accesses 10 December 2019].

Kalat, J. 2007. *Biological Psychology* (13th edn.). London: Cengage Learning.

Kandel, E. R. 2006. *In Search of Memory.* London: Norton.

Kandel, E. R., Schwartz, J. H., and Jessell, T. M. 2013. *Principles of Neural Science* (3rd edn.). Norwalk: Appleton & Lange.

Kaplan, S. 1989. *The Experience of nature.* Cambridge: Cambridge University Press.

Kim, J. 1993. *Supervenience and Mind: Selected Philosophical Essays.* Cambridge: Cambridge University Press.

Klir, G., and Folger, T. 1988. *Fuzzy sets, Uncertainty, and Information.* Delhi: PHI Learning Private Limited.

Kolmogorov, A. N. 1965. Three approached to the quantitative definition of information. *Problemy Pieredachi Informatsii*, 3(1), pp. 3–11.

Kołakowski, L. 2008. *Why There is Something Rather than Nothing?* London: Penguin Books.

Koonin, E. V. 2016. The meaning of biological information. *Philosophical Transactions of the Royal Society A*, 374(2063), pp. 2–9.

Kowalczyk, E. 1974. *Czlowiek w swiecie informacji.* Warszawa: Ksiazka i Wiedza.

Kozliak, E., and Lambert, L. 2008. Residual entropy, the third law and latent heat. *Entropy*, 10(3), pp. 274–84. Doi: 10.3390/e10030274.

Krzanowski, R. 2016a. Towards a Formal Ontology of Information. Selected Ideas of K. Turek. *Zagadnienia Filozofii w Nauce*, no. 61.

Krzanowski, R. 2016b. Shannon's Information Revisited or Shannon's Redux. Presentation at XII Zlot Filozoficzny, Białystok, 4-6 VII 2016.

Krzanowski, R. 2017a. *Minimal Information Structural Realism.* The paper presented at NNPS2017, Copenhagen, 22 April 2017.

Krzanowski, R. 2017b. *Czym jest informacyjny realizm strukturalny?* Ontological Perspective on Information. The paper presented at Filozofia w Informatyce. III Ogolnopolska Konferencja naukowa. UAM Poznan.

Krzanowski, R. 2018. Did Heraclitus know about information? Or What did he know? The paper presented at *International Association for Presocratic Studies Sixth Biennial Conference*, Delphi, 24–28 June 2018.

Krzanowski, R. 2020a. What is physical information? *Philosophies*, 5(10). Doi: 10.3390/philosophies5020010

Krzanowski, R. 2020b. Ontological information. Investigation into the properties of ontological information, Ph.D. thesis, UPJP2. Available at http://bc.upjp2.edu.pl/dlibra/docmetadata?id=5024& from=&dirids=1&ver_id=&lp=2&QI=. [Accessed 2 February 2021].

Krzanowski, R. 2017c. Koncept informacji Stoniera i jego implikacje. Monografia. *Różne oblicza informacji.* Oficyna Wydawnicza Politechniki Warszawskiej. II połowa.

Kuhn, T. 1962. *The Structure of Scientific Revolution.* Chicago: University of Chicago Press.

Ladyman, J., Presnell, S., Short, A., and Groisman, B. 2007. The connection between logical and thermodynamic irreversibility. *Studies in History and Philosophy of Science Part B: Studies in History and Philosophy of Modern Physics*, 38(1), pp. 58–79.

Ladyman, J. 1998. What is structural realism?. *Studies in History and Philosophy of Science*, 29, pp. 409–424.

Ladyman, J. 2019. Structural realism. In Zalta, E. N. (ed.), *The Stanford Encyclopedia of Philosophy* (Fall 2019 Edition). Metaphysics Research Lab, Stanford University. Available at https://plato. stanford.edu/archives/fall2019/entries/structural-realism/. [Accessed 31 March 2020].

Lamża, Ł. 2017. *Przekroj przez wrzechświat* (3rd edn.). Krakow: Copernicus Center Press.

Landauer, R. 1996. The Physical nature of information. *Physical Letters*, A 217, pp. 188–193.

Laughlin, R. B. 2006. *A Different Universe*. New York: Basic Books.

Laughlin, R. B. 2008. *The Crime of Reason*. New York: Basic Books.

Lehrman, R. 1973. Energy is not the ability to do work. *Physics Teacher*, 11(15).

Lensky, W. 2010. Information: Conceptual Investigation. *Information. Open Access Journal*, pp. 74–118. Available at www.mdpi.com/journal/information. [Accessed 6 October 2015].

Lievesley, D. 2006. Data information knowledge chain. Health Informatics Now. *The British Computer Society*, 1(1), p. 14.

Liew, A. 2007. Understanding data, information, knowledge and their inter-relationships. *Journal of Knowledge Management Practice*, 7.

Linnebo, Ø. 2017. *Philosophy of Mathematics*. Princeton: Princeton University Press.

Linnebo, Ø. 2018. Platonism in the philosophy of mathematics. In Zalta, E. N. (ed.), *The Stanford Encyclopedia of Philosophy* (Spring 2018 Edition). Metaphysics Research Lab, Stanford University. Available at https://plato.stanford.edu/archives/spr2018/entries/platonism-mathematics/. [Accessed 31 March 2020].

Liston, M. 2019. *Scientific Realism and Antirealism*. The Internet Encyclopedia online. Available at https://www.iep.utm.edu/sci-real/. [Accessed 23 June 2019].

Littlejohn, W. S., Foss, K. A., and Oetzel, J. G. 2017. *Theories of Human Communication*. Long Grove: Waveland Press, Inc., Long Grove.

Loosee, R. M. 1998. A discipline independent definition of information. *Journal of the American Society for Information Science*, 48(3), pp. 254–269.

Łukasik, A. 2017. *Filozoficzne Zagadnienia mechaniki kwantowej*. Lublin: Wydawnictwo Uniwersytetu Marri Curie-Sklodowskiej.

Lutz, E. 2012. Experimental verification of Landauer's principle linking information and thermodynamics. *Nature*, 483(7388), pp. 187–190.

Ly, A., Marsman, M., Verhagen, J., Grasman, R., and Wagenmakers, E-J. 2017. *A Tutorial on Fisher Information* (Vol. X, pp. 1–59). Available at https://arxiv.org/abs/1705.01064. [Accessed 12 December 2019].

Machlub, F. 1983. Semantic quirks in studies of information. In Machlub, F., and Mansfield, U. (eds.), *The Study of Information: Interdisciplinary Message*. New York: John Wiley.

Maciuszek, J. 1996. *Obraz człowieka w dziele Kąpińskiego*. Wrocław: Wydawnictwo Monografie Fundacji na Rzecz Nauki Polskiej.

Madden, A. D. 2004. Evolution and information. *Journal of Documentation,* 60(1), pp. 9–23.

Majewski, L. 2020. *Ukryty język symboli.* Poznań: Rebis.

Mann, A. 2020. Schrödinger's cat: The favorite, misunderstood pet of quantum mechanics. Available at https://www.livescience.com/schrodingers-cat.html. [Accessed 2 September 2020].

Marmodoro, A. 2013. Aristotle's hylemorphism without reconditioning. *Philosophical Inquiry,* V.

Martinez, M., and Sequoiah-Grayson, S. 2016. Logic and information. In Zalta, E. N. (ed.), *The Stanford Encyclopedia of Philosophy* (Winter 2018 Edition). Metaphysics Research Lab, Stanford University. Available at https://plato.stanford.edu/archives/win2016/entries/logic-information/. [Accessed 1 April 2019].

Mashood, K. K. 2009. Historico-critical analysis of the concept of mass: From antiquity to Newton. *Proceedings of Conference EPISTEME,* 3, pp. 33–37.

Maturana, H. R. 1970. *Biology of Cognition.* Reprinted in Maturana and Valera (1980).

Maturana, H. R., and Varela, S. F. J. 1980. *Autopoiesis and Cognition: The Realization of the Living.* Dordrecht: Reidel.

McCormick, M. 2019. Emanuel Kant: Metaphysics. The entry in Internet *Encyclopedia of Philosophy.* Available at https://www.iep.utm.edu/kantmeta/#H3. [Accessed 10 September 2019].

McGonigle, A. J. S., Wilkes, T. C., Pering, T. D., Willmott, J. R., Cook, J. M., Mims, F. M., and Parisi, A. V. 2018. Smartphone spectrometers. *Sensors,* 18(1), p. 223. Available at https://www.mdpi.com/1424-8220/18/1/223/htm. [Accessed 21 July 2019].

Melik-Gaikazyan, I. V. 1997. *Information Processes and Reality.* Nauka, Moscow (in Russian, English summary).

Mercier, H., and Sperber, D. 2017. *The Enigma of Reason.* London: Penguin Books.

Millikan, R. 2013. Natural information, intentional signs and animal communication. In Stegmann, U. (ed.), *Animal Communication Theory: Information and Influence.* Cambridge: Cambridge University Press.

Millikan, R. 2017. *Beyond Concepts.* Oxford: Oxford University Press.

Mingers, J., and Standing, C. 2018. What is Information? Toward a Theory of Information as Objective and Veridical. *Journal of Information Technology,* 33(2), pp. 85–104. DOI: 10.1057/s41265-017-0038-6.

Moore, S. K. 2012. Landauer limit demonstrated. *IEEE Spectrum.* Available at https://spectrum.ieee.org/computing/hardware/landauer-limit-demonstrated. [Accessed 5 May 2015].

Mott-Smith, M. 1967. *The Concept of Energy.* New York: The Dover Publications, Inc. (originally published in 1934 under the title of The Story of Energy).

Mścisławski, L. 2014. *Wyzwania realizmu. Strukturalne i konceptualne zagadnienia teorii kwantów w świetle badań nad kwantową grawitacją Chrisa Ishama.* Krakow: Copernicus Center Press.

Muller, V. 2008. Pancomputationalism: Theory or metaphor? In Hagengruber, R., and Riss, U. (eds.), Philosophy, computing and information Science. *History and Philosophy of Technoscience*, 3. Chattoo, Pickering and Chattoo, pp. 231–221.

Muller, I. 2007. *A History of Thermodynamics.* Berlin: Springer.

Myers, D. 2003. *Psychology in Modules* (7th edn.) New York: Worth.

Mynarski, S. 1981. *Elementy Teorii Systemow i Cybernetyki.* Warszawa: Panstwowe Wydawnictwo Naukowe.

Nafria, J. 2010. What is information? A multidimensional concern. *TripleC*, 8(1), pp. 77–108. Available at http://www.triple-c.at. [Accessed 6 October 2015].

Nagano, K. 2019. *Classical Music. Expect the Unexpected.* Montreal: McGill-Queen's University Press.

Nagel, T. 2012. *Mind and Cosmos: Why the Materialist neo-Darwinian Conception of Nature is Almost Certainly False.* Oxford: Oxford University Press.

Nakajima, K., Hauser, H., Li, T., and Pfeifer, R. 2015. Information processing via physical soft body. *Scientific Reports*, 5(10487). Doi: 10.1038/srep10487. Available at http://www.nature.com/srep/2015/150527/srep10487/full/srep10487.html.

Nesteruk, A. 2013. A "Participatory Universe" of J. A. Wheeler as an Intentional correlate of embodied subjects and an example of purposiveness in physics. *Journal of Siberian Federal University, Humanities and Social Sciences*, 6(3), pp. 415–437. Available at https://arxiv.org/ftp/arxiv/papers/1304/1304.2277.pdf. [Accessed 3 April 2021].

Newton-Smith, W. H. 1996. *The Rationality of Science.* London: Routledge.

Ney, E. 2019. Reductionism. *The Internet Encyclopedia of Philosophy.* Available at https://www.iep.utm.edu/red-ism/. [Accessed 10 August 2019].

Nicolic, H. 2007. Quantum mechanics: Myths and facts. *Foundation of Physics*, 37, pp. 1563–1611. Accessible at https://xxx.lanl.gov/abs/quant-ph/0609163. [Accessed 28 August 2018].

Noy, N. F., and McGuinness, D. L. 2018. *Ontology Development 101: A Guide to Creating Your First Ontology.* Available at https://protege.stanford.edu/publications/ontology_development/ontology101-noy-mcguinness.html. [Accessed 2 September 2018].

O'Connell, C. 2016. What is energy. Cosmos. Available at https://cosmosmagazine.com/physics/what-is-energy. [Accessed 2 April 2017].

Okun, L. 1989. The concept of mass. *Physics Today*, 42(6), p. 31.

Oldstone-Moore, J. 2011. *Understanding Taoism*. London: Watkins Publishing.

Pandey, N. 2016. *M2M Communication Concept*. White paper on M2M communication. Available at http://tec.gov.in/pdf/Studypaper/White%20Paper%20on%20Machine-to-Machine%20(M2M)Communication.pdf. [Accessed 1 December 2019].

Papineau, D. 2020. Naturalism. In Zalta, E. N. (ed.), *The Stanford Encyclopedia of Philosophy*. Metaphysics Research Lab, Stanford University. Available at https://plato.stanford.edu/archives/sum2020/entries/naturalism/. [Accessed 2 July 2020].

Pasnau, R. 2010. *Form and Matter*. Available at http://spot.colorado.edu/~pasnau/inprint/pasnau.formmatter.pdf. [Accessed 10 June 2015].

Passer, M. W., and Smith, R. E. 2007. *Psychology. The Science of mind and brain*. New York: McGraw Hill.

Pawan, K., Verna, R. V., Prakash, A., Agrawal, A., Kshirasagar, N., Rajeev, T., Maazen, A., Tarek, K., Tamer, A., and Abdulhakim, A. 2016. Machine-to-Machine (M2M) communications: A survey. *Journal of Network and Computer Applications*, 66, pp. 83–105.

Penrose, R. 1989. *The Emperor's New Mind: Concerning Computers, Minds and The Laws of Physics*. Oxford: Oxford University Press.

Perzanowski, J. 2015. *Ontological Disputes and other essays*. Torun: Wydawnictwo Adam Marszalek.

Perzanowski, J. 2016. Is or the treatise about the philosophy of being (in Polish). Wydawnictwo Adam Marszalek: Torun.

Piccinini, G. 2017. Computation in physical systems. In Zalta, E. N. (ed.), *The Stanford Encyclopedia of Philosophy* (Summer 2017 Edition). Metaphysics Research Lab, Stanford University. Available at https://plato.stanford.edu/archives/sum2017/entries/computation-physicalsystems/. [Accessed 31 March 2020].

Piccinini, G., and Scarantino, A. 2011. Information processing, computation, and cognition. *Journal of Biological Physics*, 37, pp. 1–38.

Pierce, J. R. 1961. *Symbols, Signals and Noise*. New York: Harper Torch Books.

Piglucci, M. 2010. *Nonsense on Stilts*. Chicago: The University of Chicago Press.

Polak, P. 2017a. Does everything compute? Philosophical implications of pancompuationalism interpretation of natural computing (in Polish). To be published in *Studia Metodologiczne*, Poznan: Adam Mickiewicz University.

Polak, P. 2017b. Current perspectives on the development of philosophy of informatics: The case of Polish philosophy (in Poland). (Accepted for publication).

Polkinghorne, J. 2000. *Faith, Science & Understanding.* New Haven: Yale University Press.

Polkinghorne, J., and Beale, N. 2009. *Questions of Truth.* Louisville: Westminster John Knox Press.

Poole, D. L., and Mackworth, A. K. 2019. *Artificial Intelligence, Foundations of Computer Agents* (4th edn.). Cambridge: Cambridge University Press.

Popper, C. 1978. *Three Worlds.* The Tanner Lecture on Human Values. Delivered at The University of Michigan April 7, 1978. Available at https://tannerlectures.utah.edu/_documents/a-to-z/p/popper80.pdf. [Accessed 2 April 2019].

Prömel, H. J. 2005. Complete Disorder is Impossible: The Mathematical Work of Walter Deuber. *Combinatorics, Probability and Computing* (Vol. 14, pp. 3–16). Cambridge University Press. Doi:10.1017/S0963548304006674.

Psillos, S. 2001. Is structural realism possible? *Philosophy of Science*, 68 (Supplementary Volume), pp. 13–24.

Ratzan, L. 2004. *Understanding Information Systems.* Chicago: American Library Association.

Rea, M. 2014. *Metaphysics: A Basics.* London: Rutledge.

Reeve, C. D. C. 2000. *Substantial Knowledge. Aristotle's Metaphysics.* Cambridge: Hacket Publishing Company.

Reeve, C. D. C. 1995. *Practices of Reason. Aristotle's Nicomachean Ethics.* London: Clarendon Press.

Rényi, A. 1961. On measures of information and entropy. *Proceedings of the fourth Berkeley Symposium on Mathematics, Statistics and Probability*, 1960, pp. 547–561.

Rescorla, M. 2017. The Computational Theory of Mind. In Zalta, E. N. (ed.), *The Stanford Encyclopedia of Philosophy* (Sprint 2017 Edition). Metaphysics Research Lab, Stanford University. Available at https://plato.stanford.edu/archives/spr2017/entries/computational-mind/. [Accessed 31 March 2020].

Robinson, H. 2017. Dualism. In Zalta, E. N. (ed.), *The Stanford Encyclopedia of Philosophy* (Fall 2017 Edition). Metaphysics Research Lab, Stanford University. Available at https://plato.stanford.edu/archives/fall2017/entries/dualism. [Accessed 2 August 2018].

Rock, I. 1984. *Perception.* New York: Scientific American Books.

Roederer, J. G. 2016. Pragmatic information in biology and physics. *Philosophical Transactions of the Royal Society A*, 374(2063), pp. 2–9.

Rosen, G. 2020. Abstract Objects. In Zalta, E. N. (ed.), *The Stanford Ency-clopedia of Philosophy* (Spring 2020 Edition). Metaphysics Research Lab, Stanford University. Available at https://plato.stanford. edu/archives/spr2020/entries/abstract-objects/. [Accessed 31 March 2020].

Rosenberg, A. 2005. *Philosophy of Science, A Contemporary Introduction* (2nd edn.). New York: Routledge.

Rovelli, C. 2016. *Reality is Not What it Seems.* New York: Allen Lane.

Rowley, J. 2007. The wisdom hierarchy: Representations of the DIKW hier-archy. *Journal of Information and Communication Science*, 33(2), pp. 163–180.

Rucker, R. 2013. *Mind Tools.* Minneola: Dover Publications, Inc. (first pub-lished in 1987).

Rudnianski, J. 1981. *Homo Cogitans.* Warszawa: Wiedza Powszechna.

Russell, B. 1959. *The Problems of Philosophy* (1912). Oxford: Oxford Uni-versity Press.

Sacks, O. 1996. *An Anthropologist on Mars.* New York: Vintage Books.

Saint-Onge, H. 2002. *Linking Knowledge to Strategy.* Presentation at the *Strategic Planning for KM Conference.* Toronto, May, pp. 28–29.

Schacter, D. L., Gilbert, D. T., and Wegner, D. M. 2009. *Psychology.* New York: Worth Publishers.

Schrödinger, E. 2004. *What is Life? & Mind and Matter.* Cambridge: Cambridge University Press (1st edn., 1974).

Schroeder, M. 2005. *Philosophical Foundations for the Concept of Informa-tion: Selective and Structural Information.* Available at www.mdpi/ fis2005. [Accessed 1 December 2019].

Schroeder, M. 2014. Ontological study of information: Identity and state. *Kybernetics*, 43(6), pp. 882–894.

Schroeder, M. 2017a. Spor o pojecie informacji. In *Studia Metodologiczne.* Poznan: Adam Mickiewicz University. nr. 35, pp. 11–37. Available at http://studiametodologiczne.amu.edu.pl/vol-34/. [Accessed 2 April 2018].

Schroeder, M. 2017b. *Structural Reality, Structural Information, and Gen-eral Concept of Structure.* The paper presented at FIS 2017, IS4IS Summit, Gothenburg, June 12–16, 2017. Available at www.mdpi.com/ journal/proceedings. [Accessed 1 December 2019].

Searle, J. 1983. *Intentionality: An Essay in the Philosophy of Mind.* Cambridge: Cambridge University Press.

Searle, J. 1996. *Intentionality.* Cambridge: CUP.

Searle, J. 1998. *Mind, Language and Society.* New York: Basic Books.

Searle, J. 2002. Why i am not a property dualist. *Journal of Consciousness Studies*, 9.

Searle, J. 2013a. *Philosophy of Mind.* Lecture 9 in the series of 27 lectures. Available at https://www.youtube.com/watch?v=9st8gGz0rOI. [Accessed 1 March 2019].

Searle, J. 2013b. *Philosophy of Mind.* Lectures 15–18 in the series of 27 lectures. Available at https://www.youtube.com/watch?v=zi7Va_4ekko. [Accessed 22 September 2018].

Searle, J. 2015a. *John Searle: Consciousness as a Problem in Philosophy and Neurobiology.* A public lecture as part of the CRASSH Mellon CDI Visiting Professor programme. Available at https://www.youtube.com/watch?v=6nTQnvGxEXw. [Accessed 1 December 2019].

Searle, J. 2015b. *Consciousness in Artificial Intelligence.* Talks at Google. Available at https://www.youtube.com/watch?v=rHKwIYsPXLg. [Accessed 1 December 2019].

Searle, J. 2015c. *John Searle on Perception & Philosophy of Mind.* Available at https://www.youtube.com/watch?v=Oh2NylJZRHs. [Accessed 1 December 2019].

Seife, C. 2006. *Decoding the Universe.* London: Viking.

Shah, I. 1974. *The Elephant in the Dark: Christianity, Islam and the Sufis.* London: Octagon Press.

Shanahan, M. 2015. *The Technological Singularity.* Cambridge: The MIT Press.

Shannon, C., and Weaver, W. 1964. *The Mathematical Theory of Communication.* Urbana: The University of Illinois Press.

Shannon, C. E. 1948. A mathematical theory of communication. *The Bell System Technical Journal*, 27, pp. 379–423.

Shannon, C. E. 1956. The Bandwagon. *IRE Transactions—Information Theory*, 2(1), p. 3. Doi: 10.1109/TIT.1956.1056774.

Shapiro, S. 2000. *Thinking about Mathematics.* Oxford: The Oxford University Press.

Silverton, D. U. 2007. *Human Physiology.* San Francisco: Pearson Education, Inc.

Smith J. M. 2000. The concept of information in biology. *Philosophy of science*, 67(2), pp. 177–194.

Smith, B. 2003. Ontology. In Luciano Floridi (ed.), *The Blackwell Guide to the Philosophy of Computing and Information.* London: Blackwell Publishing, pp. 155–167.

Smith, E. E., Bem, D. J., Nolen-Hoeksema, S., Fredrickson, B. L., Loftus, G. R., and Wagenaar, W. A. 2009. *Atkinson & Hilgard's Introduction to Psychology.* New York: Wadsworth Pub Co.

Snowden, E. 2019. *Permanent Record.* London: Macmillan.

Sole, R., and Elena, S. 2019. *Viruses as Complex Adaptive Systems.* Princeton: Princeton University Press.

Solomonoff, R. 1997. The Discovery of Algorithmic Probability. *Journal of Computer and System Sciences*, 55(1), pp. 73–88.

Sommaruga, G. 1998. One or Many concepts of information. In Sommaruga, G. (ed.), *Formal Theories of Information*. Berlin: Springer-Verlag, pp. 253–267.

Speaks, M. 2017. Theories of meaning. In Zalta, E. N. (ed.), *The Stanford Encyclopedia of Philosophy* (Fall 2017 Edition). Metaphysics Research Lab, Stanford University. Available at https://plato.stanford.edu/archives/fall2017/entries/meaning/. [Accessed 31 March 2020].

Squire, L. R., and Butters, N. (eds.) 1992. *Neuropsychology of Memory*. London: Guilford Press.

Steward, I., and Cohen, J. 1997. *Figments of Reality*. Cambridge: Cambridge University Press.

Stoljar, D. 2017. Physicalism. In Zalta, E. N. (ed.), *The Stanford Encyclopedia of Philosophy* (Winter 2017 Edition). Metaphysics Research Lab, Stanford University. Available at https://plato.stanford.edu/archives/win2017/entries/physicalism/. [Accessed 31 March 2020].

Stone, J. 2015. *Information Theory*. Sheffield: Sebtel Press.

Stonier, T. 1990. *Information and the Internal Structure of the Universe*. New York: Springer-Verlag.

Strawson, P. P. 1992. *Analysis and Metaphysics*. Oxford: Oxford University Press.

Surbhi, S. 2016. *Difference between Data and Information*. Available at http://www.differencebetween.info/difference-between-data-and-information. [Accessed 1 May 2019].

Sutherland, D., and Koltko-Rivera, M. 2009. *Cracking Codes and Cryptograms For Dummies*. London: John Wiley.

Sveiby, K.-E. 1998. *What is Information?* Available at http://www.sveiby.com/articles/ information.html. [Accessed 20 April 2016].

Sweller, J. 2006. Natural information processing systems. *Evolutionary Psychology*, 4, pp. 434–458. Available at Human-nature.com/ep.

Terra, J. L., and Angeloni, T. 2010. Understanding the difference between Information Management and Knowledge Management. Available at http://citeseerx.ist.psu.edu/viewdoc/download? Doi: 10.1.1.549.9911&rep=rep1&type=pdf. [Accessed 2 April 2019].

Thaggard, P. 2000. *Computation and Philosophy of Science*, Bynum, T., and Moor, J. (eds.). New York: The Digital Phoenix, Blackwell Publishing Inc, pp. 48–61.

Trewavas, A. 2016. Plant intelligence: An overview. *BioScience*, 66(7).

Trewavas, A. 2017. The foundations of plant intelligence. *Interface Focus*. Doi: 7. 20160098. 10.1098/rsfs.2016.0098.

Tsallis, C. 1988. Possible generalization of Boltzmann-Gibbs statistics. *Journal of Statistical Physics*, 52, pp. 479–487.

Turek, K. 1978. Filozoficzne aspekty pojęcia informacji. *Zagadnienia Filozoficzne w Nauce*, I, pp. 32–41.

Turek, K. 1981. Rozważania o pojęciu structury. *Zagadnienia Filozoficzne w Nauce*, III, pp. 73–95.

Van Loon, L. C. 2016. The Intelligent Behavior of Plants. *Trends in Plant Science*, 21(4), pp. 286–294. Doi: 10.1016/j.tplants.2015.11.009.

Van Riel, R., and Van Gulick, R. 2019. Scientific reduction. In Zalta, E. N. (ed.), *The Stanford Encyclopedia of Philosophy* (Spring 2019 Edition). Metaphysics Research Lab, Stanford University. Available at https://plato.stanford.edu/archives/spr2019/entries/scientific-reduction/. [Accessed 31 March 2020].

Vernon, D. G. 2014. *Artificial Cognitive Systems. A Primer*. Cambridge: The MIT Press.

Vincente, A. 2006. On the causal completeness of physics. *International Studies in the Philosophy of Science*, 20(2), pp. 149–171.

von Neumann, J. 1945. *First Draft of a Report on the EDVAC*, archived from the original (PDF). [Accessed 14 March 2013].

Xavier, R. S., and de Castro, S. N. 2013. *Natural Information and Computation: A Proposal Based on Interaction and Decision Making*. AAAI Technical Report FS-13-02. Natural Computing Laboratory—LCoN. Mackenzie Presbyterian University. Sao Paulo, Brazil.

Walker, S. I., Kim, H., and Davies, P. C. W. 2016. The informational architecture of the cell. *Philosophical Transactions of the Royal Society A*, 374(2063), pp. 2–9.

Waters, C. N., Summerhays, C. P., Zalasiewicz, J., and Barnowsky, A. D. 2016. The Anthropocene is functionally and stratigraphically distinct from the Holocene. *Science*, 351(6269), Available at https://www.researchgate.net/publication/289670932_The_Anthropocene_Is_Functionally_and_Stratigraphically_Distinct_from_the_Holocene/link/59d74521458515db19cb6dd4/download. [Accessed 12 December 2019].

Weber, B. 2018. Life. In Zalta, E. N. (ed.), *The Stanford Encyclopedia of Philosophy* (Summer 2018 Edition). Metaphysics Research Lab, Stanford University. Available at https://plato.stanford.edu/archives/sum2018/entries/life/. [Accessed 2 April 2019].

Weizsäcker von, C. 1971. *Die Einheit der Natur*. Munchen: Verlag, Berlin. Polish edition, 1978, PIW, Warszawa.

Wersig, G., and Neveling, U. 1975. The phenomena of interest to Information Sciences. *Information Scientist*, 9(4), pp. 127–140.

Weyl, H. 1949. *The Philosophy of Mathematics and Natural Science.* Princeton: Princeton University Press.

Wheeler, J. A. 1989. Information, physics, quantum: The search for links. *Proc. 3rd Int. Symp. Foundations of Quantum Mechanics.* Tokyo, pp. 354–368.

Whitehead, A. N. 1911. *An Introduction to Mathematics.* Oxford: Oxford University Press.

Whitehead, A. N. 2015. *The Concept of Nature.* Cambridge: Cambridge University Press (1st published 1920).

Wiener, N. 1948. *Cybernetics: Or Control and Communication in the Animal and the Machine.* Paris: Hermann & Co.

Wilczek, F. 2015. *A Beautiful Question.* London: Penguin Books.

Wills, P. R. 2016. DNA as information. *Philosophical Transactions of the Royal Society A*, 374(2063), pp. 2–9.

Wójcicki, R. 1974. *Metodologia formalna nauk empirycznych*, Wrocław: PIW.

Wolpertand, D. H., and Kolchinsky, A. 2016. Observers as systems that acquire information to stay out of equilibrium. In *"The Physics of the Observer"* Conference. Banff, 17–22 August 2016. Available at https://www.youtube.com/watch?v=zVpSAjAe-tE. [Accessed 1 April 2020].

Woodhouse, M. B. 1994. *A Preface to Philosophy* (5th edn.). Belmont: Wadsworth Publishing Company.

Worrall, J. 1982. Scientific realism and scientific change. *The Philosophical Quarterly*, 32(128). Special Issue: Scientific Realism (July1982), pp. 201–223.

Worrall, J. 1989. Structural realism: The best of both worlds? *Dialectica*, 43, pp. 99–124.

Yockey, H. 1999. *Information Theory and Molecular Biology.* Cambridge: Cambridge University Press.

Zanini. R. 2017. *Internet of Things—M2M Communication.* Available at http://www.ic.unicamp.br/~edmundo/MC822/mc822/MO655/Semi n%C3%A1rio%20MO655%20-%20IoT%20&%20M2M.pdf. [Accessed 2 December 2019].

Zeleny, M. 2005. *Human Systems Management: Integrating Knowledge, Management and Systems.* London: World Scientific Publishing Co.

Zeki, S. 1999. *Inner Vision: An Exploration of Art and the Brain.* Oxford: OUP.

Zeki, S. 2009. *Splendors and Miseries of the Brain.* New York: Wiley-Blackwell.

Ziman, J. 1991. *Reliable Knowledge.* Cambridge: Canto edition.

Zins, C. 2007. Conceptual approaches for defining data, information, and knowledge. *Journal of the American Society for Information Science and Technology*, 58(4), pp. 479–493.

Zuse, K. 1970. *Calculating Space*. MIT Technical Translation AZT-70-164-GEMIT. Cambridge: Massachusetts Institute of Technology (Project MAC).

Index

A

abstract information, 15, 23, 36, 58, 87, 124, 154, 183, 185
abstract–concrete dichotomy, 154, 186, 190, 223
Anthropomorphic information, 52, 65, 80–81
anthroponcene, 36
Aristotle, 13

B

Burgin, M., 69, 87, 127, 154, 166, 204, 206–209

C

cognition, 42, 50, 63, 80, 87, 94, 108–110, 122, 127, 143, 145–147, 180, 186, 190, 214
cognitive system, 6, 41, 48, 54, 63–64, 108–110, 124, 127–131, 147–149, 171, 174, 176, 190
combinatorial ontology, 112, 154, 177, 204
communication process, 6, 52, 81, 100, 129, 156, 163, 179, 189, 193, 219
concrete information, 34, 39, 48, 154, 224
cybernetics, 9, 22–23, 25, 42, 45, 58, 93, 205

D

data, 4, 52, 107, 124, 128, 131–132, 144, 148–149, 153, 166, 168–175, 193, 196–198, 205, 209–210, 212, 220, 223, 228
DNA, 31, 52, 55, 78, 128, 132, 144–145, 158, 207, 217

E

eidos, 6, 30, 32, 34–35, 38, 41, 48, 50, 53, 77, 91, 108, 110, 115, 120, 122, 228
Embodiment Principle, 207
energy–information, 9, 34, 37, 41, 61, 86, 90, 98, 100, 102–103, 110, 221
entropy, 4, 22, 25, 27–28, 37, 39, 62, 78–79, 98, 100, 128, 133, 157–161, 163–166, 187–188, 194, 220, 226–227
epistemic information, 5, 15, 33, 59, 63, 66, 78–80, 84, 87, 107–109, 117, 123–127, 129–135, 137–138, 140–141, 143–144, 148–151, 153–154, 160, 166, 168, 171–174, 177–180, 182–185, 196, 198–199, 202, 204, 207, 209, 220, 222–223, 225
epistemic incompleteness, 196
epistemic neutrality, 101, 105
evolution, 23, 31, 37, 46, 82–85, 89, 106, 132, 139, 167, 187, 189, 195

G

general definition of information, 2,
25, 36, 124, 176, 193–194, 196
general theory of information, 154,
204, 208
general transformation principle, 204

H

hylemorphism, 7–8, 34, 41, 54, 56, 67,
91, 97, 100, 105, 109, 230

I

infon, 3, 124, 148–149, 153, 175–177,
193, 196–197, 223
informare, 35, 48, 53–54, 60, 84–85,
92, 97, 115, 210
information entropy, 26, 28, 33, 39,
79, 128, 159–161, 163–164,
187–188
information structural realism, 191,
193, 195, 197–198
infosign, 178–179
Isomorphism of mathematical models
of nature, 195

K

knowledge, 2, 4–6, 10–12, 18, 20, 25,
29, 36–38, 48, 73, 75, 82, 84, 86, 88,
97–98, 100, 108, 110–111, 124–129,
131, 133–135, 137–138, 141–142,
146–147, 160, 166, 168, 170–172,
175–176, 180–182, 185–186, 191,
193, 198, 201–202, 205, 207, 209,
220–221, 228

M

matter–information, 16, 61, 77
minimum information structural
realism
    MISR, 191–193, 195, 197–198
Morphe, 38, 41, 67, 69, 91
morphological computing, 75–76,
181

N

natural computation, 46, 75
natural information, 40, 46, 154,
178–181, 227
negative entropy, 39

O

ontological information, 1, 5–13, 15,
18–19, 21–22, 32, 36, 45, 53, 90, 99,
101–105, 107, 109–110, 112,
114–115, 117–126, 133–135,
140–144, 148–151, 153–155, 162,
164, 167–168, 172, 174–175,
177–182, 184, 198, 202, 204,
206–208, 211, 219, 221–222,
224–225, 229, 231
ontological principle, 204–207

P

pancomputationalism, 1, 33, 68,
75–76, 79, 113, 126, 192
paninformatism, 8, 17, 147, 229
physical information, 3, 15, 40, 45,
65–66, 90, 109, 187, 189–191, 198,
217, 224–225, 227–230
Plato's form, 18, 30, 32, 38, 41, 45,
48, 53–54, 58, 77, 91, 115, 122,
213

Q

quantified models of information, 123,
153, 155, 166, 220, 223

R

Representability Principle, 207

S

semantic information, 3, 15, 63, 117,
124, 145, 171, 173, 176, 180
Shannon's theory of communication,
2–3, 24, 186–191
structural realism, 9, 30, 53, 74, 115,
192, 210, 215, 231

T

Tao-Te-Ching, 6, 38, 121–122, 230

the identity of indiscernibles, 150–151

turing machine, 118–119

U

universal turing machine, 74, 79, 124, 128, 164

W

wisdom, 170

Printed in the United States
by Baker & Taylor Publisher Services

Printed in the United States
by Baker & Taylor Publisher Services